To Barbara Riggins,
with warmest regards,

Merrill Ashley

D1195133

Dancing For BALANCHINE

Dancing For BALANCHINE

MERRILL ASHLEY

WITH THE ASSISTANCE OF
LARRY KAPLAN

AND WITH A FOREWORD BY
CLEMENT CRISP

Special photography by Jack Vartoogian

E. P. DUTTON, INC.   NEW YORK

Frontispiece:
Balanchine and Merrill in conversation
before Act II of *The Nutcracker.*
(© Steven Caras)

Copyright © 1984 by Merrill Ashley and Kibbe Fitzpatrick
Special Photography © by Jack Vartoogian 1984
All rights reserved. Printed in the U.S.A.

No part of this publication may be reproduced or
transmitted in any form or by any means, electronic
or mechanical, including photocopy, recording, or any
information storage and retrieval system now known
or to be invented, without permission in writing from
the publisher, except by a reviewer who wishes to
quote brief passages in connection with a review written for inclusion in a magazine, newspaper, or broadcast.

Published in the United States by E.P. Dutton, Inc.
2 Park Avenue, New York, N.Y. 10016

Library of Congress Cataloging in Publication Data

Ashley, Merrill.
Dancing for Balanchine.

1. Ashley, Merrill.   2. Ballet dancers—United
States—Biography.   3. Balanchine, George.   I. Title.
GV1785.A78A34 1984   792.8'2'0922 [B]   84-8057

ISBN: 0-525-24280-5

Published simultaneously in Canada by
Fitzhenry & Whiteside Limited, Toronto

DESIGNED BY EARL TIDWELL

10 9 8 7 6 5 4 3 2 1
First Edition

This book is dedicated to my mother and father
with love and everlasting gratitude
for their foresight and selflessness.

ACKNOWLEDGMENTS

THROUGHOUT this project, I received assistance from many different sources in many different ways. I am indebted to everyone who became involved, but I would specifically like to thank the following people:

Jack Vartoogian and his assistants Don Penny, Ted Kappler, Michael Peters, and Geoff Spear for spending long tedious hours under difficult conditions, with a temperamental camera, while still maintaining their good humor.

Shawn Stevens and Darla Hoover for standing in for me during test shots, and special thanks to Susan Hendl who had the knowledge and the eye to make sure I actually executed what I was trying to show.

My thanks to everyone in the New York City Ballet press department for their cooperation and assistance.

For their interest in this project and their many helpful comments, my thanks go to: Violette Verdy, Stanley Williams, Antonia Tumkovsky, Suki Schorer, Lourdes Lopez, Stacy Caddell, Miriam Mahdaviani, Catherine Morris, and especially Renée Estopinal.

Special thanks to Richard Boehm for his role in making this book possible.

Heartfelt thanks to Lynn Visson for her constant aid. Her sharp eye for detail led to countless improvements in the text.

viii

It was a pleasure working with everyone at E. P. Dutton. Elizabeth Saft was particularly helpful in innumerable ways.

An infinite debt of gratitude is due Bill Whitehead, my editor, for his insight, invaluable guidance, and unfailing patience in dealing with the extraordinary problems associated with this project.

I deeply appreciate my family's reading of the manuscript and their constructive criticism.

There are no words to tell my husband, Kibbe, what I owe him. I couldn't and wouldn't have written this book without his help. He acted as a catalyst throughout: he helped clarify my thinking, served as a sensitive sounding board, and was my harshest but most sympathetic critic. In addition, he devoted endless hours to typing the many drafts this manuscript went through. Also, the sequence photographs were his idea, one he had many years ago when I had been chosen to demonstrate the Balanchine technique in a photographic book that has not yet been published. I am pleased to see his marvelous idea finally realized.

FOREWORD

As a child I was fascinated by a piece of crystal, a large domed prism having hundreds of facets, which lay on a windowsill in my home. The sunlight, striking it, was intensified into a bright central fire which then broke into a rainbow of colors spilling over the white paint of the sill. The image is indelible still, and it came vividly to mind as I watched Merrill Ashley dancing in *Ballo della Regina* and *Square Dance* for the first time. Here again was the imprisoned, eye-dazzling light, the varied technical hues refracted from the dance, the glitter and sharp-cut precision from a brilliantly faceted surface that I remembered with the crystal.

The performances were in Copenhagen in 1978 when the New York City Ballet was appearing on the less than generous confines of the Concert Hall in Tivoli. Though I had missed the earlier part of Merrill Ashley's career, whose careful progress toward leading roles she recounts in this book, I came to know her dancing as her artistry flowered. Whatever regrets I have as a London critic who did not watch the early tendrils and shoots of her talent—and every self-respecting balletgoer rejoices in seeing how dancers' gifts bud and burgeon from first ballet school graduation shows—I count myself lucky to have seen the grand expansion of this exceptional, exhilarating talent.

The New York City Ballet's performances in Copenhagen dazzled by their assurance, especially to eyes more accustomed to the decorum and sometimes fatal politeness, or the unbridled emotionalism, of many European troupes. In *Square Dance,* it was Merrill Ashley's radiance, a sunlit ease in the final prestissimo, that seemed to epitomize the company's style at its most astounding and virtuosic. Where European dancers might have gabbled the steps, fudged and faked and flaunted a personality as a last desperate resort against technical disintegration, Miss Ashley fitted in prodigies of speed with transcendental assurance. As with Josef Hofmann, or Rachmaninoff or Horowitz, when one marvels at what fingers may achieve in terms of bravura pianism, so Ashley cut each step clearly, placed it, linked it to the next, and revealed this parure of diamonds as something unflawed. Her style was devoid of affectation or virtuoso smugness, the dance honored and lovingly served to the peak of her ability. Here was a performance whose honesty, whose purposeful and generous energy, allowed one the rare joy of seeing dancer and dance as one. It was technique in excelsis.

"Technique," observed Stravinsky, "is the whole man.* We learn to use it but we cannot acquire it in the first place; or perhaps I should say that we are born with the ability to acquire it. At present it has come to mean the opposite of 'heart,' though of course 'heart' is technique too." It is in no way to undervalue Ashley as an artist to speak first of her technical accomplishment. Technique is what dancers strive for every day of their careers, and in the best sense of the word, *technique* is not just a mechanical ability but the means of releasing and enhancing the body's natural voice. Mastery of the intractable, constantly challenging and constantly betraying physical frame is the obsession of dancers. Everything is dictated by this conflict with their own frailty.

Technique is not an end in itself, people say, yet it essentially is an end, a goal. Balanchine called it "the ability to have agility and the mechanics to express it." It is certainly freedom to dance, and to respond to the demands of a choreographer, especially one so acutely aware of technique's implications as Balanchine. He observed that people might one day remember him as a teacher, and he wrote that "a choreographer must also be a teacher." He must, as we learn from the present identity of the New York City Ballet and the School of American Ballet, be acknowledged as a great and innovative dance pedagogue, like Carlo Blasis, Auguste Vestris, Bournonville. Or Petipa.

It is from Petipa that Balanchine inherited a language, that of the Imperial Russian academy, which he developed in form and utterance, refining and extending it into a way of speaking—his dancers' way of appearing and being—for our century, just as Petipa's language had spoken for the nineteenth-century ballet. The innovations and enlargements of vocabulary in this language are the history of the School of American Ballet and the New York City Ballet. It is also an American language and it is not least this national inflection that delights me as a European observer, who finds in it something of the energy, the soaring aspiration implicit in the architecture of New York.

* And, of course, the whole woman.

Balanchine's willingness to accept Lincoln Kirstein's invitation to come to the United States meant for him an escape from the exhausted balletic tastes of Europe. His own *Ballets 1933,* determinedly innovative, had proved no match for the Diaghilev nostalgia propounded by the revived Ballets Russes of the same era, and he had even worked for some months after Diaghilev's death in staging such spectral delights as *Scheherazade* and *The Legend of Joseph* in Copenhagen.* In America he was to find different and more unfettered material from which to shape dancers in whom he could instill the traditional virtues of the classic academic dance; indeed, that dance was itself to become a revival and reassessment of his own Petipa-rooted academism. The history of the Balanchine-Kirstein enterprise is, as we know, just that: the creation of a school to prepare dancers in whom Balanchine's *pur sang* classicism, shorn of any dubious nostalgia and soulfulness, would become an aspect of American character, energy, speed, and the establishment of a company in which these qualities might be shaped.

The result has been a school and a company that are the truest repository of twentieth-century classic dance. This has been achieved at no sacrifice of essentials—save that essential for certain audiences: the stellar paraphernalia of the "great" dancer. We love stars; they stimulate us, excite us. But Balanchine, as teacher and choreographer, retained for himself the dominant role in the realization of an ensemble greater than the sum of its parts (even its starriest parts), wherein the identity of the troupe came from choreographic wealth rather than temperament or narrative device. Yet it is not without significance that there have resulted several generations of leading New York City Ballet dancers—I hesitate to call them ballerine and premiers danseurs—whose performances have been quite as starry, quite as thrilling in their effects, as any of the most incandescent of public favorites.

Their luster has sprung from a source very different from that of temperament, or that personality cult which seems to say "Look at me dancing." The New York City Ballet's artists propose, simply, cleanly: "Look at this dance." At its purest, as we see in the performances by Merrill Ashley, this style can be both rigorous in respecting the canons of Balanchinian manner, yet still thrill by its exaltation and by a selfless bravura. (In this it can sustain a comparison with some of the finest Kirov dancers—Irina Kolpakova, Yury Solovyov—whose identity was sublimely what they danced.) And in exposing what have come to be appreciated as New York City Ballet qualities—an alert

* He had also presented his "Sixteen Delightful Balanchine Girls" in a music-hall program at the London Coliseum, then managed by Sir Oswald Stoll. That theatre's orchestra was conducted by Sir Oswald's son, Dennis Stoll. My dear, late friend Betty Scorer Frank, one of the sixteen girls, recounted with joy the classic exchange after a first and disastrous orchestral rehearsal when the pit band failed signally to cope with one of the modern scores Balanchine used for his dances. Balanchine advanced to the footlights and called into the darkened auditorium: "Sir Stoll! What tunes does your little boy know?" The band offered some such gem as Rubinstein's Melody in F and Balanchine swiftly and happily adjusted the girls' choreography to this new tune.

physique; an electric energy that the visitor finds in the atmosphere of New York it-self—Ashley offers a key image. In an age of speed, she dances faster than her predecessors; in a century when music has traveled further and more adventurously than ever before, and one in which Balanchine demanded a musical acuity that reflected his own catholic and professionally trained perceptions, Ashley and her peers offer an admirable responsiveness that is the grain running through their dancing.

Yet at a time when many old attitudes and sanctions have been eroded by war and upheaval (and it is surely significant that Balanchine came of age during a time of profound revolutionary change, and came to maturity in an organization whose only technical roots were in pre-Revolutionary traditionalism), the choreographer asserted laws and absolutes of physical and moral stance (*la danse est une question morale*) that are the ground-bases of ballet. He proved thereby that, whatever the extravagances and experiments of iconoclasts and idiosyncratic toilers in the field of dance, discipline and technique, a proper comprehension of academic laws, are still important, still potent in revealing truths about the human body, still capable of urging a more beautiful capability upon the dancer's frame.

The basis for this was Balanchine's concern for mechanical ability, for shaping dancers as malleable tools for his work. In urging his dancers toward technical freedom, he freed their best qualities, and his ballets become highly revealing portraits of his interpreters at their best. He also freed himself. The trust that dancers like Ashley gave him was what he needed for his work. With such material, tremendous things—and how tremendous the catalogue of his ballets tells us—were possible. The ideal Balanchine dancer became the clear vessel through which his creative prodigality was poured for public delectation.

The sustaining note through Ashley's narrative is that of her dedication to the dancing which she sensed was possible under Balanchine's guidance and through Balanchine's teaching, both practically in class and inferentially in the ballets he assigned her. Her reward has been the roles she created and those many others that she has assumed and so grandly enhanced. Like other members of the company, she appreciated Balanchine's own quest for a "beyond" of power and brilliance, a defiance of physical constraint to discover something that might eventually lie more closely within the reach of the dancer's skills. It suggested how we may perceive something of the divine in man through harmoniously organized movement by superlatively trained and responsive artists. (It offers, in an odd fashion, parallels with the Renaissance belief that something of celestial harmony could be comprehended through the union of skilled dance patterns and music.) The moral rectitude, the "spirituality" of which ballet might be capable, has never seemed more clear to me than in performances by the New York City Ballet of *Divertimento No. 15,* or in the exhilaration of *Symphony in C* or in the power of *Four Temperaments.* In these, as in so many other ballets, Ashley has given performances so cleanly etched in outline that they imprint themselves on the retina, and the memory retains them like photographs of the dance action. And in photographs, actual photographs, Merrill Ashley presents just the same exact, linearly bold image.

Few dancers of today in my experience appear so uncompromisingly themselves, or more truly themselves as servants of what they are dancing, as Ashley. She has been caught on the wing, in flight, in arabesque, and the quality of the role seems to radiate from the clear, taut frame with its vivid harmony of limbs, its clear center, its vibrant actuality. There, certainly, is the classic dance, burnished and lustrous, and the bright actuality of performance. The image seems triumphant, the placement of the torso is pure (the rigors of academic training ever respected), and the life of the dance seems to run through limbs and trunk, imprisoned in the amber of time, but still warmly alive.

In May 1980 the cover of the New York City Ballet's daily program bore a photograph of Ashley wearing one of those anonymous pink City Ballet dresses, poised in arabesque. Her line was generous, open; the stretch of the torso was full, easy; there was an eager, onward-darting lightness and energy about the pose, as well as beautiful placement of the body. She looked glorious, but more glorious still in action in *Allegro Brillante* whence pose and pink dress came. For the central ballerina in *Allegro,* Balanchine conceived dances of glittering power, as he did again in *Piano Concerto No. 2,* to match the cascading rush of Tchaikovskian pianism. Merrill Ashley provided all the speed—none speedier—and the clear-cut, dynamically varied and effortless bravura that the choreography demands. Nothing seemed beyond her, yet since her performances in the previous season it was as if she had gained in imaginative dimension, found some fresh source of feeling in her dance. It meant in *Allegro Brillante* that her attack was still marvelously clear but that she now dared allow herself to play slightly with the movement. She appeared so wholly identified with the music and the choreography that she could find time—when plainly no time existed—to let a pose open out to its fullest extension and then linger there, blossoming. In the piano cadenza, which is set as a solo for the ballerina, she produced rubato, which allowed her trunk and arms to ease gently into positions while still maintaining the truly brilliant allegro of music and dance. It was dancing taken to a point beyond interpretation; choreography and music united in Ashley's body and impelled it serenely, joyously onward.

Dancers' memoirs can be disappointing if one seeks revelations about the "professional secret." Tamara Karsavina's *Theatre Street,* one of the most enchanting and stylish books ever written about ballet, is uncommunicative if you turn to it merely for information about a role or a choreographer. Readers of Ashley's text will, however, soon be aware of a fine analytical intelligence, which can probe and expose the minutiae of technical matters and which can be uncompromising in assessing the dancer's task. How rare it is to find a dancer equally sure in enunciating the matter of her art on stage.

The beautiful speaking of poetry, which is the ballerina's task, demands purity of tone as of diction. *Le style, c'est l'homme*—and in this case *la femme*—and there is in Ashley's dancing an exactness, a will toward clarity that implies a spiritual rigor quite as exceptional as the required physical stamina and skill. Ashley's clarity in articulation might, early on, have made her dancing seem a collection of brilliant stones rather than the jewel that could ultimately be made of them. Balanchine was wont to refer to himself in craftsman terms as a cook or a carpenter. With Merrill Ashley's gifts he assumed the role of jeweler—*bijoutier du roi* as he was also *ébéniste du roi* in ballet-making—and set the gemstones to their most glittering and lovely advantage, which is the story of *Ballo della Regina* and *Ballade.*

I recall in *Ballo* how the marvels of speed proposed by Miss Ashley were matched by her entire simplicity of manner, so that her fleetness in allegro, when the eye could barely comprehend her quickness of muscular reflex or the sophistication with which she shaped a phrase, was allied to an easy nobility in adagio. Fast or slow, the dance looked serene. In *Ballo* the choreography nods at, even mocks, the marmoreal conventions of the genre (those preposterous evolutions in the statutory ballet scene of a nineteenth-century grand opera) and then, freed, sails splendidly on. In Merrill Ashley's role, the movement has a joyous impulse, and she seems to pounce upon the most fiendish difficulties, rejoice in them, and then flash by to the next technical death trap with a smiling eagerness, and not a step missed or misstated. It is like the flawless coloratura known with the greatest operatic divas of the golden age; she is a Galli-Curci, a Tetrazzini of the dance, and like them she is capable of lyric feeling as well as of roulades and fioriture having a birdlike ease and freshness.

This lyricism is what gives *Ballade* its special potency. This ballet might appear small in scale, but it is not small in the horizon of its dances, or in its impetus. Like its music, it says a great deal without rodomontade. There is in Fauré's score, as in all his piano writing, an exactness of form and a textural clarity that make for an understated strength beneath the melodic grace and sweetly purling cascades of its writing.

Balanchine's sympathy with Fauré's music had been earlier seen in *Emeralds,* and his casting of Ashley in its leading role some time before *Ballade,* which might have appeared against the grain of her then crystalline stage *persona,* was a significant move in his wish to guide her artistry. His choreography in *Ballade* showed off, yet again, her arrowy limbs, the aerodynamic economy of her dancing, and her ability to preserve the integrity of a step, no matter what its accelerando execution. But it also conveyed something capricious in her temperament, a different kind of womanliness from that we knew in her previous roles as a fleet-footed Atalanta, an all-conquering virtuoso. The emotional coloring of the dances, like the music, suggested potent feeling despite the control of formal discipline. There is a moment when Miss Ashley spins vertiginously toward her partner, Ib Andersen, and falls impetuously forward into his arms: it is the equivalent of a sudden declaration of passion, made all the more telling by the contrast with the lyric freshness of the dancing that has gone before. Ashley's technical identity is not diminished in

Ballade; rather did Balanchine find for it a freer, more sensuous vein. She floats, drifts, the lines of her dancing threading over the stage and holding her cavalier in its web as if to establish an atmosphere of emotion, light but pervasive, in which the two dancers will meet and part. *Ballade* is a fugitive piece in its understated manner, but at no moment does Miss Ashley's dancing seem tenuous or thin in timbre: there is a new kind of physical shading, a coloration of tone to enhance her customary delight in the dance itself.

Some choreography designed for virtuoso dancers can become as superficial as the tricks that are being displayed. Many of the circus and competition performances we see of the *Don Quixote* pas de deux are no more than dancers rattling as fast as they can with as much vivacity as they can muster through the equivalent of the alphabet, and sometimes without the full complement of letters. Because Merrill Ashley set her prodigious gifts at the service of a master choreographer, there is a resonance, a depth to the radiance of her performance, like the fire in the heart of a jewel rather than the flash from *Don Quixote*'s sequins. It passes beyond more obvious forms of display, or more exactly, springs from different aesthetic and technical attitudes.

Merrill Ashley's performances in London in 1983 in *Piano Concerto No. 2* had a presence drawn from her identification with both music and choreography. Tchaikovsky and Balanchine seem united in the bravest pianism, the boldest display. Ashley offered an aristocratic assurance, nothing mean in dynamics or phrasing, and a mysterious union with the aesthetic energies of the piece so that she incarnated both its nostalgic romanticism and the glitter and roar of its prestissimos: the dance was tossed sparkling into the air for our delight, in the glorious onward progress of Miss Ashley's dancing.

In two other Tchaikovsky roles, *Diamonds* and *Swan Lake,* whose links are sometimes subliminal and sometimes overt, Ashley provides interpretations of ringing authority. Her Swan Queen is not one of those emotionally wrought bird women whose movements seem the voice of Tchaikovskian despair, but a mysterious figure from unguessed lands whom Siegfried tries to hold, a heroine from Gautier's *Symphonie en blanc majeur* caught in the *grande bataille blanche,* whose "whiteness" is not, as in certain dancers, an absence of color, but itself positively an emotional coloration. In *Diamonds* she seems the incarnation of the Maryinsky ballerina as doomed heroine; in this, as in the *Theme and Variations* from *Suite No. 3,* she has that dignity, that command of a role which gives bloom to the choreography, and she is glorious to watch. As she is in so many other ballets: in *Who Cares?,* where "My One and Only" is like very good champagne; in *Divertimento No. 15,* where her dancing has truly Mozartian elegance; in *Symphony in C,* that sunniest of masterpieces, where she draws the dance in sunlight.

Her dancing is richly varied, because her roles are varied, but it is never selfish. The denial of self as a way to a better self that comes from humility in the face of a choreographer's greatness, trust in his judgment, belief in his vision not just of the dancer but of the dance, are the underpinnings of Ashley's artistry, as they are of all of New York City

Ballet's dancers worth their salt. In his "Notes on How to Enjoy Ballet" in *Complete Stories of the Great Ballets,* Balanchine observed in 1968: "Great technical ability is only part of being a great dancer. At first we might find ourselves applauding a feat that seems astonishing, and six months later when we've seen dozens of dancers do the same thing with an equal amount of facility, we might applaud less. We have to see to know better. We have to compare. But what we will all like at the beginning, and what will make us want to go again soon, is a dancer who interests us in an extremely simple way: we will remember afterward what her dance looked like. We will remember the girl, but only because of the dance she showed us. No doubt she was attractive, but she didn't play on that and didn't make us think of it. No doubt she did some steps that seemed incredibly hard, but she didn't stress this and she didn't try to hit us between the eyes with her skill as if to say 'Look! *This* is good.' Instead, the big moments of the dance came with the same lack of effort and stress as the small ones. She will quietly and effortlessly seem to conquer the stage space in which she moves to the time of the music."

Even before *Ballo della Regina* and *Ballade,* Balanchine had drawn a portrait of Merrill Ashley.

CLEMENT CRISP

London
May 1984

PREFACE

I HAD sixteen wonderful years dancing for Balanchine. Just to be in his presence was a privilege, but the opportunity to learn from him, and to pursue his ideals, was the greatest adventure of my life. At first I was bewildered by his corrections and daunted by his high standards, but, as I began to experience the thrill of deciphering his instructions and understanding his principles, I became a true disciple. Understanding, however, was merely the first step. Ten years of intense and disciplined practice were required before I mastered what Balanchine taught.

What followed was a brief but glorious period when Balanchine, still at the peak of his powers, created two ballets for me—my most cherished memories of our work together. Then came the sad years of his physical decline when, as he gradually gave up teaching and choreography, I came to appreciate him even more as the great man he was—the man who had made so many of us in the New York City Ballet transcend the limits of what we thought was possible.

When Balanchine died, I found my greatest solace dancing in his ballets. The music, his choreography, and my memories of him were all so closely intertwined that, as I danced, I felt his presence, as if he were in the wings watching. During the long days and many evenings when I was not dancing, I found myself endlessly reliving my experiences with him, hearing his words and responding to them as if he were still alive. Later I began to write down my random thoughts and memories with no clear purpose in mind, knowing only that from going back over the past I was drawing strength and a sense of purpose as I faced an uncertain future.

Increasingly, as the months passed, it struck me as unjust that Balanchine should have entered history only as a creator of great ballets. To me, he had been equally great as a teacher, a creator of dancers. The one-dimensional picture of him was not surprising, however, for millions had admired his ballets and appreciated his choreographic genius, but only relatively few dancers had known him as a teacher. A second dimension could be added only if his dancers tried to convey this special point of view to a wider public.

With that thought in mind, I decided to organize my notes and ideas and write a book about what dancing for Balanchine and learning from him was like for me. I wanted to share this great learning adventure with those who had never worked with him. I hoped, too, that my story would be a small contribution to a fuller understanding of Balanchine's place in dance history.

The project began as a conventional biography of my life, both in the New York City Ballet and outside it. Being unsure of what would be most interesting to outsiders and wanting to present not only my own view of working with Balanchine, but an objective view as well, I asked Larry Kaplan to assist me in writing the book. Soon, however, the conception of the book changed and it became clear that a firsthand account of dancing for Balanchine would bring readers closest to the events I was describing. I was grateful for the initial impetus but thought it best to take over the writing myself, in hopes that my own words and phrases would best tell my story. However, I would have hesitated to undertake this monumental task, and certainly never would have been able to see it through to the end without the constant encouragement and much-needed support of my husband, Kibbe Fitzpatrick, who I could always count on to help me face the formidable challenge of a blank page when I was completely overwhelmed.

This, then, is an account of my life as a dancer, starting with my audition at the School of American Ballet, ending with the roles I am dancing as of this writing, and highlighting everything that mattered to me along the way. I have tried to give an accurate impression of what it was like for a sixteen-year-old with little knowledge, and less experience, to join the New York City Ballet and go on to work for the greatest genius in ballet history.

In portraying the various stages of my progression, I have described only what pertained directly to my life as a dancer, hoping thereby to bring the reader as close as possible to events as I experienced them. I have avoided discussion of other dancers—even the excellent partners I have had—except insofar as they have directly affected my career, for, in order to be fair to each one, I would have had to make detailed comments unrelated to my story.

In the pages that follow, I enter the classroom and rehearsal hall with Balanchine and relate the long, difficult process of understanding, learning, and finally doing what he wanted. I hope to convey what working with—and dancing for—Balanchine was like, how the experience changed at the various stages of my career, and how the results of my efforts culminated in those memorable hours when he choreographed *Ballo della Regina* and *Ballade* for me.

The sequence photos, with captions highlighting aspects of technique that were important and in many cases unique to Balanchine, are intended to illuminate the text and to provide a hint of the encyclopedic knowledge that Balanchine made available to those who wanted and were able to absorb it. I have kept in mind, however, that many readers may not be familiar with ballet terms and have therefore tried either to explain them or to ensure that my story can be understood without a knowledge of these terms.

Since my story is not a complete autobiography, I asked Larry Kaplan to write a short biographical sketch of me and to include comments by other dancers and some of my earlier teachers in an effort to provide a more well-rounded and objective portrait.

While the writing of this book has been a difficult and emotional process, it has also been a valuable journey of rediscovery. Time and again I have been struck by how temperamentally well-suited I was to work for Balanchine. His relentless insistence on "more, more" always appealed to me, and his form of precise high-energy dancing brought out the best in me. No matter how great the difficulty he posed, no matter how mystified I was—and I was often confused in my early years—I always felt I was in the right place, and never for a moment did I consider giving up. We had something marvelous in common that I have never been able to put into words; perhaps readers of this book will sense it in the dance story that follows.

MERRILL ASHLEY

New York
March 1984

BIOGRAPHICAL INTRODUCTION

IT IS commonly believed that Merrill Ashley is the last of the New York City Ballet ballerinas to have been entirely trained and developed under George Balanchine's active tutelage. Opinions aside, it is a fact that Ashley's dancing embodies Balanchine's vision and, in effect, defines his style. A virtuoso ballerina, Ashley epitomizes in performance the qualities that characterize the New York City Ballet itself; in fact, the language invoked by writers and commentators to praise her is invariably identical with that which they use to describe the company. Reviewers speak of Ashley's "energy," "speed and attack," "pristine clarity," and "intense musicality," traits that Balanchine tried to cultivate in all of his dancers. Ashley's career also demonstrates the principles Balanchine stood for all his life: the techniques of traditional academic classic dance, the emphasis on movement itself, and the importance of music as the heart of ballet. In the purity of Ashley's approach to Balanchine's aesthetics, she comes close in performance to realizing his ideal. In Ashley's dancing there are no extremes of style or personality, no easy-to-catch mannerisms or quirks that detract from the choreography, and this sets her apart from all other Balanchine ballerinas.

Having observed the New York City Ballet during the years in which Merrill Ashley emerged as one of its leading dancers, I published an article on her in *Ballet Review*.

But being able to watch her work in class and backstage in the course of preparing this book, I soon came to see even more precisely the qualities that make her the dancer she is, the connection between Ashley the person and Ashley the ballerina. In some respects she fits the conventional image of a Balanchine ballerina. She is tall (five feet seven inches), lithe, with beautifully shaped legs. But despite her powerful presence and her speed (especially astonishing in a "tall" dancer), offstage Ashley appears delicately built, almost frail. She is, in fact, neither so tall nor strong as some of the other dancers in the company. Yet as on stage, in class she immediately stands out because of her unusual concentration and involvement in all her movements. This is the same whenever she works. Watching her warm up for a performance, for example, I was struck by the rigorous barre she took, one that reminded me of those she described Balanchine giving in class. But hard work and commitment are only two of her characteristic traits. Her dancing is also enhanced by her human qualities, her modesty, intelligence, and humor, the sensitive awareness she displays of the world around her.

Ashley's physical characteristics, of course, play an essential role in the way we see her on stage. Lincoln Kirstein has written that Balanchine imaginatively identified with America even before leaving Russia. To him, Kirstein wrote, "America was a vast continent . . . its girls were not sylphides. They were basketball champions, queens of the tennis courts. The drum majorettes, the cheerleaders of the high school football team of the Thirties filled his eye." Ashley's allure is related to these "imagined" images of Balanchine's youth rather than to the exotic, Old World ballerinas of the nineteenth and twentieth centuries. Beautiful in an open, frank, all-American way, with large hazel eyes, Ashley has a vibrant, fresh-faced appeal that makes her one of the most "American" of Balanchine's ballerinas, a pure example of the new kind of selfless dancer he bred to express the complexities of his style and to meet the physical demands of his classicism.

Merrill Ashley's roots are in the Midwest. Her father, Harvie Merrill, was born in Detroit and raised in Kenosha, Wisconsin. Mardelle Edwards, Ashley's mother, was born and brought up in and around Indianapolis, Indiana. Harvie and Mardelle met as students at Purdue University and, after their marriage, Harvie served in the U.S. Army Air Corps, stationed in New Haven, Connecticut. At the end of World War II, the Merrills returned to the Midwest where Harvie was hired as a junior executive with the Minnesota Mining and Manufacturing Company in St. Paul, Minnesota. The couple's children were born there, first Susan and about three years later Ashley, who was born Linda Merrill on December 2, 1950.

Linda's first exposure to ballet occurred in St. Paul where she watched her sister take ballet class. The lesson was informal and consisted mostly of students pretending to be leaves jumping over a pile of coats in the middle of the room. But Harvie recalls that his wife told him, "Linda showed a tremendous alertness at the studio. She could hardly restrain herself from joining in. She just wanted to be part of the other children jumping and leaping about."

Unfortunately, at five she was too young to enroll. A year later, however, Harvie's company transferred him to the East and the family moved to Rutland, Vermont, where Linda began taking ballet classes conducted in makeshift studios.

As a child, Linda showed an affinity for activities that required speed and physical coordination. Naturally athletic, she was an avid swimmer and diver. She also skied, rode horseback, and skated—and played tennis, golf, and even baseball. But the freedom and sense of controlling space she derived (and adored) from these sports she found even more exhilarating when she studied ballet. Above all, she loved to move to music.

Linda's involvement with music dates from her earliest years. The Merrills were a musical family. Harvie played the violin, and Mardelle the piano, and both children studied musical instruments—Susan the harp and Linda the piano. Linda was accomplished enough to give a local solo piano recital when she was still a young girl, and, accompanying her sister, she also participated in musicales in the homes of their parents' friends as well as in their own house. But despite all her youthful interests and activities, Linda's overriding passion was ballet.

Mardelle says, "She could never get enough of it. From the age of five or six if you asked her what she wanted to be she'd answer, 'a ballerina.' Of course, which five- or six-year-old doesn't say that? But at the time it sounded very convincing to me."

Throughout her elementary school years, Linda studied with Sybil de Neergaard in Rutland, and at the age of ten took classes five days a week in the summer with Marina Svetlova at the Manchester Arts Center in Vermont. During her first summer at the Center she had a walk-on part in Svetlova's production of *Giselle* and the following year danced the role of one of the heroine's friends in *La Fille Mal Gardée*. In addition to these lessons and performances, Linda often visited New York City for weekends of balletgoing with her family, and some of the works she first saw at the New York City Ballet were *Liebeslieder Walzer, Interplay,* and *Filling Station.* She also went to the full-length classics staged by the Royal Ballet and American Ballet Theatre, and saw Plisetskaya perform the Dying Swan with the Bolshoi Ballet.

During these weekend excursions, Linda often took class with Vera Nemtchinova, a Russian ballerina who had danced with Diaghilev's Ballets Russes, and also studied with another Russian, Igor Youskevitch. These teachers were extremely impressed with her natural ability (Nemtchinova said she was exceptionally talented), but they stressed the need for proper training if she were serious about ballet. Encouraged by Linda's intense desire to dance and by the favorable comments from her teachers, Mardelle made inquiries about the best professional training for her, and when Linda was twelve Mardelle arranged for an audition at Balanchine's School of American Ballet. The audition was conducted by Antonina Tumkovsky who remembers it vividly.

"I looked at her feet," she says with a Russian accent. "I had her do few steps, battement tendu, assemblé. I thought, Nice figure, perfect proportions. I want her!

"She had everything for dancing. She was always good student, very, very serious.

Merrill at the piano, age four.

Merrill in costume for her first recital in 1958. She had black toe shoes even then!

She was very intelligent child. She listened hard. She never talked too much, never spent the hour for nothing. She wanted to work."

Stanley Williams, another eminent SAB instructor, was also aware of Linda's potential in those days.

"She caught my eye just from the way she worked. She was a very consistent worker, even as a child," Williams points out. "She had that keen concentration that is inborn. It's a fantastic thing, really. And there was something else in addition to concentration. It's hard to explain but it's there in all important dancers. It's that they want to accomplish something with themselves. They have a drive to accomplish something and you respond to it. And so even then I was interested in her and I gave her a lot of attention."

When the Merrills moved from Rutland to Schenectady in 1964, Linda studied there with a local teacher, Phyllis Marmein. Returning to SAB at the end of the year for a six-week summer course, she was awarded a scholarship to the School, as part of its Ford Foundation Scholarship Program, for the coming winter course. She appeared with the New York City Ballet as a Candy Cane in *The Nutcracker* during her first full year at SAB, and as a student later danced leading roles in two SAB workshop performances staged by Alexandra Danilova. Despite her athletic ability, when she was a student Linda was quite thin and frail. She appeared vulnerable, somewhat fragile, and hadn't yet developed the strength and power that were necessary to succeed as a Balanchine dancer. Nevertheless she appeared to be making progress toward a career, but her parents did not have a clear picture of what the future might actually hold for her, so Mardelle made an appointment to see Eugenie Ouroussow, the administrative director of the School, to discuss Linda's prospects.

"My question was whether she thought Lyn was an average dancer, a really fine dancer or whatever. And as I sat down in her office, Mme. Ouroussow looked me straight in the eye and said, 'I'm very sorry to have to tell you, Mrs. Merrill, but your daughter shows the potential of being an extraordinarily fine dancer. These things can change, of course, as you know, because we can't predict the future. But there it is.' And I knew exactly what she meant when she said she was sorry to have to tell me the news," Mardelle recalls.

Linda's potential, of course, had not escaped Balanchine's notice, and, at the start of her fourth year at the School, he invited her to join the New York City Ballet. Because there was another dancer in the company who had taken the name Linda Merrill, Linda changed hers to Merrill Ashley. At sixteen, the Company's youngest member, she made her debut on tour in Chicago in *A Midsummer Night's Dream* in October 1967 and later that year danced in New York in the corps of *Swan Lake, Firebird, Diamonds, Western Symphony, Stars and Stripes,* and many other ballets.

Plunged into the often chaotic and fiercely competitive routine of company life, it wasn't long before Ashley understood the necessity of committing herself wholeheartedly to Balanchine's methods. She devoted herself to his daily class and began the long, arduous process of developing her technique and her style under Balanchine's watchful eye, but because he revealed so little of what he was thinking she had no way of knowing the kind of impression she was making on him. During her second year in the Company, however, he cast her in her first solo in *Divertimento No. 15,* and soon after in another, the "harp" solo in *Raymonda Variations.* At this time she also began appearing as part of a troupe of dancers Jacques d'Amboise assembled to perform with him in concerts and lecture demonstrations in various cities across the United States between the regular New York City Ballet seasons. This experience gave her the chance to dance other important solos.

Two years after Ashley joined the Company, her parents moved to San Francisco, where they live today, and where her father is President and Chairman of the Board of the Hexcel Corporation, an international manufacturing concern.

In 1970, Balanchine used Ashley as Karin von Aroldingen's understudy in *Who Cares?,* his new work to music of Gershwin, and though she occasionally danced this role, it was in 1972, in the role created for Marnee Morris, that she first made a strong impression in the ballet, on the company tour of the USSR. As she danced to "Embraceable You" and "My One and Only," it soon became clear that she was an exceptionally talented dancer who was developing an original allegro style. It was the brightness of her dancing that attracted attention in *Who Cares?* She was able to present each moment, almost carve it out in space without distorting the choreography; performed in this manner, the classicism in the choreography was revealed as particularly sharp and satisfying in contrast to the more romantic material in the ballet. Over the years as she became even more of a technical wonder, frankly powerful and secure, performing daring feats of technical wizardry, she continued to project a becoming modesty.

In 1973, aware of her ever-increasing strengths, Balanchine choreographed a variation for Ashley in *Cortège Hongrois,* and the following year in the production of *Coppélia* he staged with Danilova, he created the Dawn variation for her. This dance featured "big" jumps and à la seconde turns (that foreshadowed the breathtaking combinations he would create for her in *Ballo della Regina* and *Ballade*). Writing in *The New Yorker* about Ashley's peformance in *Coppélia,* Arlene Croce called it "electrifying."

By the time *Coppélia* premiered in New York City, Ashley had already appeared in a number of important roles, including Jerome Robbins's *Requiem Canticles* and the Girl in Mauve in his *Dances at a Gathering* as well as in d'Amboise's *Tchaikovsky Suite No. 2, Irish Fantasy,* and *Saltarelli,* originating her role in the latter. She also danced in *Symphony in C* (first, second, and third movements), the soloist role in *Tchaikovsky Piano Concerto, Brahms-Schoenberg Quartet* ("Rondo alla Zingarese" movement), *Diamonds,* and *Symphony in Three Movements.* In 1974 she assumed the leading role in *Tchaikovsky Piano Concerto* and also made her debut in the ballerina role in *Theme and Variations* in *Tchaikovsky Suite*

This picture was taken just before Merrill went to New York in 1964.

The Merrill family in Paris, 1983 (left to right): Her father, Harvie; Merrill; her sister, Susan; and her mother, Mardelle. (© *Kibbe Fitzpatrick*)

No. 3—another ballet, like the *Piano Concerto,* that has since figured prominently in her career. By the end of the year she was named a soloist.

Nineteen seventy-four was significant for her in another respect. On a rainy day in May, as Merrill was hurrying along Third Avenue to her sister's apartment, a tall young man eating an ice cream cone recognized her: "You're Merrill Ashley, aren't you?" he said. Merrill was a bit startled but the stranger seemed friendly and genuinely interested in dance. A week later he called her and soon they were seeing each other with increasing regularity. Within a year they knew they were right for each other.

The new man in her life, Kibbe Fitzpatrick, was a simultaneous interpreter at the United Nations. A former captain of the Yale University cross-country running team and a competitive tennis player who had earned a national ranking, Fitzpatrick brought a fresh, unjaundiced eye to the world of ballet. He had a keen appreciation for matters of style and took an active interest in Ashley's career, offering her constructive criticism on matters of general aesthetics as well as emotional support. The progress she had been making in her career accelerated sharply, and the result was a dramatic breakthrough the following year when she was cast as Sanguinic in the important revival of *The Four Temperaments.*

The mode of movement Balanchine had invented for this ballet perfectly suited Ashley's technique. Arlene Croce described Sanguinic as a role for an allegro technician who is a virtuoso ballerina, and Ashley had a huge success in this part. The ballet liberated her true dance personality; in it she radiated new confidence. It was easier to appreciate her dancing now—the extravagant technique that enabled her to present Balanchine's choreography in all its dimensions and embellish it with whatever dynamic or flourish she deemed necessary. Her musicality, the clarity and diamond-sharp precision of each step she took, the way she projected joy and intelligence—no one had danced quite like this before. In particular, her musicality stood out as one of her most pleasing virtues. The ability to execute steps well while maintaining the beat and rhythm of the music was a trait she had consciously cultivated. Though many dancers find it necessary to sacrifice their musicality in order to perform bravura steps, there is never an instance when Ashley dances in which she displays her technique at the expense of the music.

In 1976, Balanchine decided to revive his ballet *Square Dance,* with Ashley in the leading role. Prior to the start of rehearsals, however, even before she was aware of Balanchine's plans, Ashley slipped and fell in company class doing a fast combination, badly injuring herself. She tore all the ligaments in the upper part of her right ankle. The injury took a long time to heal, and during the first days of recovery she had to use crutches to walk. In 1973 and 1974, Ashley's progress had been checked by various injuries, and now she was forced to sit on the sidelines again, this time while *Square Dance* was being prepared. Six months passed before she was able to dance, and she returned to the stage at first in ballets that made no great technical demands on her. It wasn't until early 1977 that Ashley finally appeared in *Square Dance,* a performance, as Croce wrote in

The New Yorker, "the ballet had been waiting for." Ashley's impact in the ballet was tremendous. Her technique seemed to have transcended itself, to have been enriched by a new depth of expression, and this ballet and her performance in it became another stunning example of the City Ballet's powerful profile in the late 1970s: By now she was one of the company's brightest stars.

In February 1977, just after the settlement of a protracted labor dispute between the company and the New York City Ballet orchestra, Ashley created a role in the *La Ventana* pas de trois in a new ballet, *Bournonville Divertissements,* staged by Stanley Williams. The company had a new hit. In the ensuing months attention focused on Ashley in the press as some writers and interviewers speculated about a promotion for her: It appeared overdue. Ashley herself wondered when she would be made a principal. Dancing principal roles exclusively now, and continually growing as an artist, she anticipated a promotion, especially since the partner with whom she danced so many ballets had been recently elevated. But throughout most of the year she heard nothing about it. Then, with no fanfare, at the start of the rehearsal period for the fall 1977 season, she found out that she had finally been named a principal dancer and, furthermore, that Balanchine was going to choreograph a new ballet for her—in effect, fulfilling two of her most cherished dreams. The ballet, to music by Verdi, was *Ballo della Regina.*

Officially premiered in January 1978, *Ballo della Regina* explores the range of allegro dancing that Balanchine couldn't have attempted without a dancer of Ashley's capabilities. The ballet is a summation of her gifts at that point in her artistic evolution, a portrait of her, at her most glittering and dynamic, as the completely accomplished virtuoso—a classical ballerina. The choreography for Ashley runs the gamut in the ballet from small steps that show off the precision of her footwork to sweeping, bold jumps and turns that attest to her easy virtuosity. A critical and popular success, *Ballo della Regina* immediately established itself in the City Ballet repertory.

Nineteen seventy-seven was also important as the year that ushered in a period that remains, even to the present, the most active of her career. For approximately three and a half years, until she was injured in 1980, there were seasons in which she performed as many as twelve ballets a week. Beyond dancing the roles already mentioned, her repertory included *Valse-Fantaisie, Stars and Stripes, Donizetti Variations, The Nutcracker* (Sugar Plum Fairy and Dew Drop), *Agon* (second pas de trois), and *Dances at a Gathering* (Girl in Green), and she also appeared in a succession of important new roles, among them, *Divertimento No. 15* (sixth variation), *Tchaikovsky Pas de Deux, Allegro Brillante, Emeralds, A Midsummer Night's Dream* (Act II divertissement), *Raymonda Variations* (ballerina), *La Source, Cortège Hongrois* (ballerina), *Union Jack, Vienna Waltzes, Chaconne,* and Robbins's *The Goldberg Variations, In the Night, In G Major,* and *The Four Seasons.*

In 1978, she created the leading role in Jean Pierre Bonnefous's "Pas Dégas," the middle section of the three-movement *Tricolore,* and she also danced at the White House for President and Mrs. Carter and their guests from NATO. In 1978 and 1979, she was seen on television in many of her roles on PBS's *Dance in America* series.

Her versatility enabled her to appear in a wide range of ballets of different styles and moods, and she made a strong impression in everything she danced. Some roles, like *Tchaikovsky Piano Concerto,* seemed created for her. She danced this ballet as if charged by the music, meeting its daunting technical demands without omitting or modifying any of the steps and combinations that Balanchine originally choreographed into it. In reviews she was hailed for giving the definitive performance of the ballet.

After so many years of watching her and working with her, Balanchine was aware of the singularity of Ashley's accomplishments and of her technical abilities. But he knew there was more to her than just powerhouse technique. There was, for example, a lyric dimension, the expression in her dancing of feeling and emotion that went beyond the traditional lyricism of such ballets as *La Sylphide, Giselle,* and *Les Sylphides.* But in order to reveal it in all its facets, he had to make another ballet for her, and it was in this work, *Ballade,* to dreamy, delicate music by Gabriel Fauré, that the poetical, the lyrical impulse in her dancing was displayed to its fullest extent.

Once again Balanchine took Ashley's ability to perform the most demanding steps as a starting point, but he went on to use her technique to make, as he put it, "a beautiful ballet." Despite its propulsive pace, *Ballade* is decidedly romantic. A series of both simple and bravura steps and combinations succeed one another in a rapid, seamless flow, and, because few of these steps recur, the viewer is left with a feeling that the ballet is elusive. This sense of elusiveness, and the feelings of longing and of love recalled in the dancing, accounts for the Proustian aura that pervades the ballet. But as in so many of Balanchine's creations, this ballet also takes for its subject the specific nature of the dancing of the ballerina for whom it was choreographed, and *Ballade* exists as another portrait of Ashley.

Ballade was well received, and Balanchine himself was delighted with it, but a shadow marred Ashley's triumph. After the premiere, a hip pain that had flared up during the preparation of the ballet grew progressively worse. She danced with this pain as the season wore on but was eventually forced to take time off, and she missed the 1980 New York City Ballet European tour. Instead, for rest and recuperation, she traveled to Hawaii for an extended vacation, and there she and Kibbe were married in an outdoor ceremony conducted in Hawaiian and English in the tiny village of Hana, overlooking the Pacific, on the island of Maui. During this period Ashley was able to indulge some of her outside interests. An avid reader and still athletically inclined, she enthusiastically follows as a spectator such sports as tennis and skiing, which she can't participate in because of her career.

At the end of 1980, stronger but still not fully recovered, Ashley nevertheless felt ready to dance again and appeared as the Dew Drop in a performance of *The Nutcracker.* Though she danced sporadically during the concluding weeks of the winter 1981 season, the problem with her hip persisted. On a trip to London, the difficulty was diagnosed as a problem with a nerve and some scar tissue in her hip; the nerve was "released" surgically in a successful operation. Within six weeks Ashley was dancing again. She was not yet strong enough to play a major role in the company's Tchaikovsky Festival in June 1981 so her roles in *Tchaikovsky Piano Concerto* and *Tchaikovsky Suite No. 3* had to be assigned to others. But she did perform *Swan Lake* and, on the Festival's closing night, the *Diamonds* pas de deux.

In the summer of 1981 (and again in 1982), Ashley returned to Hawaii with a troupe of ten dancers she assembled to present an evening of ballets from the New York City Ballet repertory. She also danced that year in China with a group organized by Jerome Robbins, and she appeared in New York in three alternate years on NET's television special, "Gala of Stars." In 1982, for the New York City Ballet's Centennial Celebration of Stravinsky's birth, Robbins choreographed *Concertino* for Ashley, a ballet he presented with three other pieces under the collective title *Four Chamber Works.*

In 1983 and 1984, dancing more frequently than in the two preceding years in New York as well as on tour with the company in Europe, Ashley enlarged her repertory with significant new roles: *Concerto Barocco, Serenade,* and Helgi Tomasson's *Ballet d'Isoline.* In June 1984 she created one of the leading roles in the Jerome Robbins–Twyla Tharp collaboration, *Brahms/Handel.* Her dancing as of this writing, and, in fact, throughout the period from the premiere of *Ballade,* has been marked by an uncommon level of accomplishment even when measured against her own high standards. Her style, which had always been distinguished by her individual talents and her understanding of Balanchine's aesthetic, exhibited a new crucial element. She had introduced into her dancing a new sensuousness and an awareness of herself as a ballerina. These elements eventually asserted themselves in each of her performances and were duly noted in the press.

Writing in *The New York Times,* Jennifer Dunning said that Ashley's dancing "helps shape standards of greatness," while Tobi Tobias wrote a paean to her in *New York Magazine.* "What dancing she does! [It] grows more ravishing every season. The very essence of a step is apparent when she dances it, crisp and unadorned. . . . She's a superb technician, but by no means merely a technician. The purity of execution is not mechanical; there's a moral fervor to it."

Similar remarks have also been expressed by Ashley's colleagues. Dancers, in fact, have always been the first to appreciate the nature of her accomplishments. Former New York City Ballet ballerina Violette Verdy, who, after retirement from the company was the head of the Paris Opera Ballet and is now the director of the Boston Ballet, had described Ashley's dancing as "completely legal."

"By this I mean that everything she does is open and honest," Verdy says. "Nothing is held back, done at half-measure or compromised, and it is this honesty which is of such value. You know, her dancing is like a radio that plays free of interference or static: the broadcast of her dancing is so clear and pure it approaches a state of beauty.

"Her placement is perfection—especially of the hips, which means that she is perfectly centered—and she has a classical line, beautiful turnout, an ability to isolate energy and use it in performance to illuminate a point and, above all, a sublime harmony of movement and gesture."

Other dancers echo Verdy's praise from their own point of view. Lourdes Lopez, a City Ballet principal dancer, explains how she values Ashley's dancing not only on its own terms but for what it tells her about her own dancing: "I always admired Merrill from afar when I was a student," she says. "And when I joined the company I found it was easy to ask her for help. It was easy to talk to her—we spoke the same language. She seemed genuinely interested in helping people and she was able to explain what it was she was doing so that you could understand it and apply it to yourself.

"I learned from watching and working with her the basic principle that Balanchine was always trying to get across, that in order to make each step separate and individual, and to have in my dancing all the qualities that are necessary, like speed, for instance, I couldn't imitate any one dancer but that I had to retrace my steps to the barre, to begin at the beginning where you really learn how to dance."

An even younger generation of dancers is aware of what Ashley stands for in this respect. When Balanchine was choreographing *Ballade,* the corps consisted of many young apprentices who were not yet technically members of the Company and who had a minimum of experience working with Balanchine. Miriam Mahdaviani, now a member of the Company, was one of these girls. She remembers that whenever the young dancers were having difficulty and things slowed down, Balanchine would have Ashley demonstrate the step for everyone.

" 'Watch Merrill,' he would say," Mahdaviani recalls. It wasn't that he wanted everyone to slavishly imitate her, she points out, but rather to observe in her dancing, as Lopez had, the clear dissection of the step's mechanics she was always able to show. And "Watch Merrill" became a familiar phrase in company class.

"It was like a course," Mahdaviani says of the sessions in which *Ballade* was being choreographed, "and he used Merrill as an example. We learned by watching her. In class now I still watch her. I always go in the group she's not in so that I am able to see what she does. It's good for everyone when Merrill is in class. You feel you can't slouch. Merrill never does anything halfway. She gives everything—in class and on stage. When people think of Balanchine technique, they think of Merrill—the Balanchine dancer. She has this ideal in mind and she lives for that."

Another young NYCB dancer, Stacy Caddell, also in the original cast of *Ballade,* says, "It was exciting to see Mr. B and Merrill working together. He would give us steps and watch us do them. He'd say, 'No, dear, do like Merrill.' In particular there was one type of jeté. He wanted us to do it just like she did. Now, whenever I do the step I think of her and what Balanchine said. Dancers really appreciate Merrill because she sets a high standard. She sets it for teachers, too. And she helps you a lot in class. She has a keen eye.

When she tells you you've done something well, you feel really good. She's so critical about herself you know it means something when she says something about you."

Ashley often takes the time to help dancers in class and in rehearsal. It is of inestimable value for her to share her experience and knowledge with them in these situations and it is in her nature to want to do so—especially today.

On the closing night of the 1982 spring season, after dancing *Tchaikovsky Suite No. 3,* Ashley stood on stage alongside Balanchine with the rest of the cast. He had come out for his now customary, triumphant closing night bow, but this occasion was to be his final appearance on the stage and in front of the New York State Theater curtain. Soon after this, Balanchine's health deteriorated. He was hospitalized in the autumn of 1982 and died there on April 30, 1983.

Peter Martins and Jerome Robbins inherited the artistic directorship of the company. Yet, as the direct recipients of Balanchine's legacy, his dancers, too, are responsible for the protection of his heritage and the maintenance of his style. As one of his few senior ballerinas active in a truly wide and diverse repertory, Ashley's dancing is of particular significance in this regard. In being able to realize with such clarity not only what Balanchine wanted in his ballets but what has existed in the art of classical dance since its inception, she preserves it all in the moment of performance. This is her particular glory in the period we have now entered, the post-Balanchine era.

LARRY KAPLAN

Dancing For BALANCHINE

CHAPTER

1

As my mother and I drove from Vermont to the School of American Ballet in New York for my audition, visions of bright spacious studios lined with gleaming mirrors passed before my eyes. I had never danced in a real studio with barres, mirrors, and a proper wooden floor. The only classes I had ever taken were in a gymnasium, a church kindergarten classroom, the recreation area on the top floor of a firehouse, an old converted barn, a town meeting hall—even in the basement of my own house.

My illusions quickly disappeared when we finally reached our destination on Broadway and Eighty-second Street and found ourselves standing in front of a drab old two-story building. Could this be the right place? We went in and climbed two long, steep flights of stairs leading straight up to a huge metal door, where a sign read: SCHOOL OF AMERICAN BALLET. We walked in. Paint was peeling off the walls, the offices were crammed with filing cabinets, and the hallway looked as if it hadn't been swept in weeks.

Yet somehow I wasn't disappointed. The very untidiness of the place suggested a seriousness of purpose that was reflected on the faces of the students who were hurrying between dressing rooms and studios. The sound of a piano from a distant studio reached my ears, and I caught a glimpse of another studio through an open door. A smell of rosin mixed with perspiration filled the air. It was marvelous.

My mother and I were greeted by two directors of the School, Nathalie Gleboff and Natalia Molostwoff. Trying to appear calm, I went off to change into my black leotard, black tights, and black toe shoes. All black! That, I was convinced, was precisely the way the perfect ballet student dressed. When I went back to the hallway where my mother was sitting on a long wooden bench, smiling encouragingly at me, I was horrified when I realized that all the students passing by were wearing pink tights and pink shoes. My next shock came when I was asked to wear soft ballet slippers to the audition instead of my toe shoes. The only pair I had with me was pink. Pink shoes with black tights—what a way to dress for an audition!

I was led into the smallest of the School's three ballet studios by Gleboff and Antonina Tumkovsky, a teacher who had once been a soloist with the Kiev State Theater. Soon Gleboff was gone, leaving me alone with Tumkovsky. There wasn't even a pianist!

Tumkovsky seemed very stern and got right down to business. I was immediately intimidated by her no-nonsense manner and her heavy Russian accent, which I could barely understand. First, she looked me over carefully and asked me to point my feet and raise one leg to the side as high as I could. I did so. Without a word, she came over and took my foot in her hands and pointed it herself to test its strength and see if there was any more flexibility than I had shown her. Then she lifted my leg in all directions to see what range of mobility might be developed. Next she asked me to do one or two steps at the barre and a few turns and jumps in the center of the room. Suddenly, it was over. The whole thing had lasted all of about ten minutes. I had been asked to do so little that my muscles hadn't even had a chance to warm up, and I had been continually distracted by my image in the mirror. I had rarely done a step in front of a mirror before.

I went back to my mother in the hallway, and we both sat quietly but nervously awaiting the verdict. Soon she was called into one of the offices, and I remained alone. How could I be judged fairly in such a short time? I had done so few steps. Or maybe I wasn't good enough and it was obvious right away. Would that mean I would have to go back to my one class a week in Rutland?

When my mother emerged, I could see right away from the smile on her face that I had been accepted. We were thrilled, and terribly relieved. Years later I saw the card that had been put in my file that day. It read: "Good feet, rather nice." By SAB standards, that was a ringing endorsement!

My mother had chosen SAB not only because it was the best school but because it was a springboard into the New York City Ballet. She was familiar with the Company and its repertory, and, knowing that my interest in ballet had to do with movement and music, not with costumes or the chance to act out roles and show off my personality on a stage, she may have sensed that the NYCB would eventually be the right place for me.

All that mattered to me was that I could now enjoy the challenges and pleasures of ballet class every day. My favorite part of class was being asked constantly to move and to cover space while trying to make beautiful shapes with my body. It was much more fun to express my feelings with movement than with words or pictures.

As I moved, I felt I had special powers that others outside ballet class didn't have. When I jumped, I was practically airborne and could pretend I was defying gravity. When I moved my legs fast, the speed excited me. At times I felt as quick and strong as a racehorse.

I enjoyed classes so much that I wanted a class every day, but I had been placed in Children's IV Division at SAB, which had only four classes a week. Rather than letting me remain idle the other days, my mother arranged for me to take classes from Vera Nemtchinova, with whom I had already studied briefly on weekend trips to New York.

I was so excited at the prospect of beginning classes at SAB that I didn't mind leaving my family and school friends and going to live in New York City. I was excused from my seventh grade classes for the rest of the academic year—April, May, and June—by the principal of my school in Rutland on the understanding I would return to take the final exams. My grandparents, both retired schoolteachers, came to New York to live with me and give me the tutoring I needed to pass my tests.

My new life got off to an unpromising start. I arrived ten minutes late for my very first class at SAB and was mortified. I, who always wanted to respect the rules and show everyone that I knew what was what, couldn't get to that first class on time! Being late was serious, but the worst was yet to come. I could barely understand the teachers. It wasn't just the struggle to understand the Russian accents; I had never been taught the names of most of the steps and positions. I didn't know *croisé* from *effacé, en dehors* from *en dedans, dessus* from *dessous,* and much more. My former teachers had always demonstrated precisely what they wanted us to do. Now I heard: "Do first arabesque!" I didn't even know there was a first arabesque, let alone a second, or third, or fourth arabesque. Too embarrassed to speak up and ask for help from the teachers, or even from the other students, I just watched and followed along, hoping that somehow I would catch on. Slowly and painfully, with many mistakes along the way, I did.

I was in over my head, behind the others in nearly everything. I was thin and had delicate bones, but until then I hadn't realized how weak I really was. My limited ballet background could not match that of most of my classmates, many of whom had been at SAB since Children's I or II. They were used to the commands, drills, repetitive exercises, and technical explanations. It was all very intense: steps and combinations and then more steps and combinations. No dance history, no mime, no personal guidance or moral support. The focus was very narrow, just steps and combinations. It was not supposed to be fun, and for quite a few it wasn't. But for me it was sheer bliss. I soon came to realize, however, that all I had was energy and desire. Yet I was sure my lack of muscular strength and skill was due to insufficient training, which could be overcome with hard work.

Tumkovsky and Hélène Dudin, who like Tumkovsky had been trained at the State Choreographic School in Kiev, gave hour-and-a-half-long classes four times a week. They both paid the strictest attention to the way we pointed our feet and how well we straightened our knees, but they also made sure we used our arms and head properly. When they gave us combinations, they wanted all the details right.

They laid special stress on *turnout,* the most important element of ballet technique, and also the most difficult to achieve, since it is so unnatural. Luckily, I had developed my turnout years earlier. By chance a friend in Rutland who had studied ballet had shown me an exercise specifically to develop turnout and had impressed its importance on me. She had told me to sit on the floor with my back straight against the wall, put the soles of my feet together by bending my knees, and, without lifting my feet off the floor, draw them up close to my body. Then I had to lower my knees to the floor, pushing with my hands, if necessary. When I was eight, my knees didn't come close to touching the floor; but my hip joints cooperated and, by the time I was twelve, my knees could touch the floor with no help at all. When I stood up, I could turn each leg outward from the hip at the ideal ninety-degree angle. I had developed my turnout, although I didn't yet know how to use it. It was the School's job to teach me.

Those three spring months at SAB were a rude awakening in many ways, but the experience only served to whet my appetite. I loved taking class every day. For the first time, I was in class only with people my own age, with steps and combinations geared to what we could and should do. The teachers liked me and appreciated how hard I worked and how I tried to pick up everything they taught. I would have loved to go straight into SAB's summer school, but at that point I was too young. Thirteen was the minimum age, and I had six months to go before my thirteenth birthday.

Ballet classes were a dream world, one that was marvelously orderly and disciplined and far from the uncertainties of the rest of life. I thrived on the real difficulties of the steps and loved learning the rules that dictated how each movement should be performed. I liked knowing what was expected of me, and, although I couldn't always do what I was told, it was exciting just trying.

I liked to watch the Company and tried to understand what it would take to progress from the corps to principal status. I decided all the corps members were good dancers, but there were many things they couldn't do. The soloists could do almost anything—but the principals could do *everything. I* wanted to be able to do everything they could do, and more!

The most memorable moment of those three months at SAB was my first glimpse of Balanchine. I was sitting on the same long wooden bench where only weeks before I had waited for the results of my audition. The front door opened and Balanchine walked in. I had seen pictures of him and recognized him immediately. Awestruck, I couldn't take my eyes off him. An aura of mystery—or was it energy—seemed to surround him; even if he hadn't been who he was, I would have been drawn to him. His aquiline nose fascinated me, but my attention was quickly drawn to a huge bandage on his index finger. (I later learned he had lost the tip of that finger due to a gardening accident.) He spoke briefly with one of the directors of the School and was gone, but his image stayed in my mind. I was already under his spell.

When the course at SAB ended in June, I returned to my family, who had just moved to Schenectady. There my parents were fortunate to find a good ballet school where I could take three classes a week. When the fall came, I could have returned to SAB, but my parents preferred not to let me spend a full school year away from home, because I was still only twelve years old, and so I stayed with them in Schenectady.

The move from Rutland to Schenectady did not suit me at all. Skiing, skating, riding, swimming, and other sports were no longer readily available, and so ballet became my sole activity. It was probably for the best, since I was beginning to see that, if I was to pursue ballet seriously, I would have to give up sports to avoid injuring myself or developing the wrong muscles.

My Saturday afternoon class also interfered with my best opportunity to make new friends and socialize. Soon I was being made fun of for being so interested in ballet and for wearing my hair in a bun. The school newspaper featured a Miss Hospitality, a Miss Popularity, a Miss Congeniality, and others. I was Miss Bun! Though it bothered me, it didn't stop me.

The school year was coming to an end and plans for the summer had to be made. At thirteen, I was now eligible for the summer course at SAB, and because I had so much to learn I wanted to go back very badly. It was obvious to my parents that my growing love for ballet was leading me straight toward a professional career as a ballet dancer. Although they had never discouraged me, they could look further ahead than I could, and they saw many serious problems looming. What kind of career would it be? The odds against success were overwhelming, but, even if I were successful, could I make a good living? What about my education? And what about all the other experiences in life I would miss? These were not easy questions for concerned parents.

One weekend, when my whole family was in New York, my mother came across a newspaper article by Clive Barnes about the Ford Foundation Grant that had just been awarded to SAB. One of the many provisions of the grant was a scholarship fund for promising young students from around the country to study at the School. (The scholarships covered all classes at SAB, partial tuition for academic studies at the Professional Children's School, and some money for living expenses.) This news had a profound effect on my parents' thinking. They felt it confirmed the growing stature of dance in this country and gave ballet a newly acquired "seal of approval." They began to believe there was a better chance of my having a respectable career in ballet. As Barnes put it, "The ballet world will never be the same again." Finally my parents decided that, given my enthusiasm and potential, they would let me go to New York and take the SAB summer course.

My mother arranged to sublet an apartment in New York for six weeks, and off we went. Near the end of the six weeks, the news came that I had been offered a full Ford Foundation Scholarship for the coming winter course. I felt I had found the pot of gold at the end of the rainbow and was oblivious to all the problems accepting the scholarship raised. My parents didn't want to burden me with their doubts, though they saw the problems only too clearly. They had an agonizing decision to make. If they said no at this point, they might spoil my chances forever, for good training at an early age is crucial; if I waited a year or two, it might be too late. Finally they courageously decided it was an opportunity that could not be missed, and I shall be forever grateful.

Thus I became a full-time student in B class, an intermediate division; at the same time I enrolled in the Professional Children's School.

PCS made it a policy to schedule students' classes around their professional activities. My academic classes there were in the morning, and in the afternoon and early evening I went to my ballet classes at SAB. I was determined to do well at PCS, for I knew my parents wanted me to get a well-rounded education to enable me to fend for myself, come what may. And, I didn't want to give them any reason not to let me stay in New York.

I lived with three ballet students and one of their mothers in a small two-bedroom apartment near the School. The lady, who functioned as a housemother, served portions of food that never satisfied my hunger, and I resorted to drinking quarts of milk in an effort to fill myself up. I did have pocket money, but it was more important to me to spend it on pointe shoes than on food. My parents would have been horrified, but I didn't want to tell them because I was afraid it would jeopardize my staying in New York.

I had started out thin, but soon became scrawnier and scrawnier. From time to time Ricky Weiss (Robert Weiss, later a principal dancer for NYCB), who wasn't even in my class, took it upon himself to bring me a sandwich from home. It never occurred to me to complain to my housemother or to ask for more money from home. I must have started to look a little alarming, for one day Diana Adams, a former NYCB ballerina who was then head of the School, called me into her office.

"Are you trying to lose weight?" she asked.

"No," I answered truthfully.

"Well, you're thin enough. Please don't lose any more."

Things went from bad to worse. My housemother had found some reason to ask two of the other girls to leave and I worried I too might suddenly be without a place to live. Then something happened that picked up my spirits and made me forget my troubles.

It all started one day when I was sitting watching a class I couldn't take because of an inflamed tendon in my groin. Diana Adams came up to me. With her was Balanchine himself. Diana asked me to stand up. I jumped to my feet, my heart racing.

"Please take off your shoes," Adams asked.

I removed my two-inch heels and waited while Balanchine stood looking me over. "Thank you," he said, and they both left. I was bewildered, and a little frightened. A few days later, I was told to go to a Candy Cane rehearsal, for *The Nutcracker*. It hadn't occurred to me that Balanchine's interest in me was related to *The Nutcracker*. I was in a higher level than most of the girls they used, and, small though I was, had assumed I was too tall. I realized then that Balanchine had been looking me over to see if I was the right size to fit in with the younger girls.

At the first rehearsal, taken by Una Kai, a ballet mistress, we were lined up by height and taught the steps. Shortly afterward, I was put in the front of the line. It was important to have someone who could lead the others properly, and I was thrilled to have been chosen.

New costumes were being made for the Candy Canes, and I reported to Karinska's costume shop to have my measurements taken. Karinska, who never used her first name, Barbara, had designed and executed the costumes for most of Balanchine's ballets, and both she and Balanchine agreed that the finest satins and silks should always be used, and the tiniest details never overlooked.

Karinska herself appeared while I was being fitted for my costume. Though in her mid-seventies, she was still agile and full of energy, overseeing a dozen projects at the same time. She was dressed in navy blue from head to toe—even her hair was blue—and I later discovered she *always* wore blue, and her hair never changed color. Huge rings adorned her fingers and heavy necklaces dangled from her neck. Of all the Russians I had met, she was the most unusual.

Meeting Karinska and seeing all this up close for the first time was exciting, but having a costume made just for me was a thrill beyond words. I said to myself, "How lucky that they are making all new costumes this year. Candy Canes for years to come will be wearing my costume."

I marveled at the Sugar Plum Fairy's tutu hanging on a mannequin in the studio and was enthralled at how every layer of the skirt was edged in gold piping. How could people go to so much trouble for just one tutu? Would anyone even see it? It certainly would make the Sugar Plum Fairy feel beautiful.

At the dress rehearsal, our first time on the stage, Balanchine came up to me and took me by the hand and led me around, showing me where I was to make the first circle. The excitement of it: he touched me! He took my hand! It was the highlight of my years at SAB. I idolized him more than ever, and the respect that everyone so obviously paid him only reinforced my feelings. Dancers, teachers, musicians, stagehands, everyone always did his or her utmost to please him, and, whenever he spoke, it was as if his words came from on high. I remember, too, how kind and patient and gentle he was with all the children. He never lost his temper despite the inevitable provocations. This was particularly impressive, since I had heard that he was not especially fond of children.

The Nutcracker performances gave me a taste of what it was like to dance day after day in a professional atmosphere. It was very different from any of my previous performing experiences in Vermont or in Schenectady, where so much class time had been spent learning and perfecting steps that would be performed only once or twice. The excitement of *The Nutcracker* was enhanced rather than dulled by repetition. I loved the mere fact of being on the stage of the New York State Theater. I was also intrigued by how all the various props worked: how the snow fell, how the tree grew, how all the furniture was whisked off the stage, and how Marie's bed glided around.

The New York State Theater was, I believe, the first major theater to be built expressly with the dancer in mind. Its best feature is a floor with exactly the right amount of springiness. Of course, the theater today has its problems, especially now that the NYCB has grown so large. The building may be bursting at the seams, but it is still my favorite theater to perform in.

Just being backstage was fun. Since the Company was then much smaller (about 80 dancers, compared to about 105 today), the Candy Canes had the luxury of a large, empty dressing room, next to the corps girls' dressing room, all for themselves; all the other children dressed in the basement. As the Candy Canes were not in Act I, we were supposed to stay in our dressing room until we were called to appear on stage. Every evening, however, two of us were allowed to watch Act I from the great vantage point of the wings. Armed with a slightly inflated sense of our own knowledge, we were highly critical of the NYCB corps. We loved leafing through the souvenir booklet, picking out the dancers we thought were the least deserving, and we had no difficulty imagining ourselves replacing them in the very near future.

We pretended we were the Sugar Plum Fairy and Dew Drop, and couldn't resist practicing some of the trickiest steps from those roles. Most frequently we tried the precarious promenades at the end of the Sugar Plum Fairy's pas de deux. Of course, they never worked, but we never stopped trying.

This pleasant experience in *The Nutcracker* had its darker side. A classmate of mine, Colleen Neary, who was two years younger than I and also a Candy Cane, was cast to do the Girl Doll in Act I, a role ordinarily performed by a Company member. I was envious and couldn't get it out of my mind.

Colleen was the favorite of both teachers in Children's IV, but from the moment I entered that class some of the attention shifted to me. It was my first taste of the kind of competition that is so common in SAB and the NYCB.

Colleen's earlier training had been better than mine and she had developed far more skill than I had. She had exceptionally long legs, and everyone knew that Balanchine liked that. Because her older sister, Patricia, was a soloist with the Company, she was able to mingle with Company members and get to know Balanchine personally. Rumor even had it that Colleen had been told that at fourteen she would be taken into the Company.

Nutcracker rehearsals and performances often conflicted with classes at SAB, so when it was over I was happy to be back taking all my classes again, although I missed the excitement of performing—and the money. I had earned five dollars per performance, every cent of which was earmarked for pointe shoes. The money disappeared quickly, because the shoes cost ten dollars a pair.

As the winter went on, my woes returned. I caught a bad cold and, as I had no resistance, I started getting severe nosebleeds. One night, when I was alone in the apartment, blood started gushing from my nose. There was no stopping it, and I imagined myself bleeding to death. When my housemother finally returned, she took me to a doctor who cauterized an artery that had burst. My mother, of course, rushed to New York to see me. Shocked at my skeletal appearance, she took me back to Minneapolis, where my family had moved earlier in the fall. I didn't like having to miss class, but I was sure that after a few weeks on a healthy diet I would be strong again and able to go back to New York.

I recovered quickly but my parents were no longer willing to let anyone else take care of me. Again my mother came to the rescue and decided to go to New York to live with me, even though it meant being away from my father.

Fortunately my "sick leave" had not set me back, but I still was maddeningly unable to cope with certain basic steps, such as pirouettes. I simply could not turn with any degree of predictability. To make matters worse, my turns to the left were much more reliable than those to the right, and that was as much of a handicap as being left-handed in a right-handed world. It didn't help my confidence that, sprinkled throughout the School, were a number of "natural turners," including Colleen.

The instruction was intense and very varied. Dudin and Tumkovsky tried to cultivate stamina in us. They would have us do strenuous repetitive exercises at the barre, and have us hold each leg up for what seemed an interminable amount of time. There were long jumping combinations that gave us stitches in our sides. Unlike some, I had plenty of energy to get through these classes, but often I didn't have the necessary muscular strength or technical skill.

In addition to the regular classes, Tumkovsky and Dudin also gave pointe classes, which were so demanding that I would find them interesting even today. In those days, an hour and a half on pointe made my feet very sore, and to make matters worse I had to make my shoes last a whole week. By then, they were so worn out they provided practically no support at all. (Today, I use a minimum of one pair, and often two or three pairs, of pointe shoes in one pointe class, at thirty dollars a pair.)

Classes were also given regularly by a stimulating variety of other teachers: Muriel Stuart, Felia Doubrovska, Pierre Vladimiroff, and by Stanley Williams, who had just arrived at the School.

Born in England, Stuart had been trained entirely by Anna Pavlova. She had danced in Pavlova's company and joined SAB in 1935. She seemed obsessed with body placement, something most of us had never heard much about. Or perhaps our body placement at that point fell so far short of her ideal that what seemed to us an obsession was merely a much needed emphasis on a glaring weakness. Class after class she would go around grabbing our stomachs with one hand and placing her other hand on our buttocks and saying, "Now, dear, pull up and drop down." Sometimes, unable to get the point, we would just giggle behind her back, but I feel now that her insistence on this may have laid the groundwork for the breakthrough I made years later in the correct placement of my body.

Doubrovska had attended the St. Petersburg Imperial Theater Ballet School and had danced with the Maryinsky Theatre and the original Ballet Russe. Balanchine had also created roles for her. She had great style and carried herself beautifully, and she tried to impart those qualities to us. In her classes she always gave combinations that were similar to those in actual ballets, and she made learning things correctly fun rather than a chore.

Vladimiroff, who was married to Doubrovska and who had been on the staff of the School since its founding, was also an alumnus of the Imperial Theater Ballet School. He had been a partner of Tamara Karsavina and Anna Pavlova as well as a premier danseur of the Maryinsky Theatre and the original Ballet Russe. He was a kind and gentle man who wanted to be friendly with everyone. He didn't want to hurt anyone's feelings and sometimes seemed reluctant to give students corrections. He liked to see us work hard, but it was more important to him to see us enjoying ourselves in class. If he saw someone getting discouraged, he would go up and whisper "very good" or "excellent" to make the person feel better.

Stanley Williams was born in England and raised in Denmark, where he graduated from the Royal Danish Ballet School. He went on to be a soloist with the Royal Danish Ballet, and later became an influential teacher in Denmark and a renowned expert on the Bournonville style. He joined the faculty at SAB in the fall of 1964, the same time I became a full-time student there.

Stanley was a quiet, gentle man with a friendly smile, but he commanded immediate respect. He was more analytical than any other teacher I had ever had, for he not only talked about what we should aim for but he explained how to get there. No one else did that. I had never thought about using specific muscles, such as those of the inner thigh. I had never thought of concentrating on the supporting leg as much as on the working leg, and I hadn't realized that, even if all the elements of a step are correct, such as the movements of the head, arms, and legs, the step would not work unless everything was properly coordinated. Stanley opened up a whole new way of working and thinking for me, and thanks to him I was far better prepared to understand the subtleties of Balanchine's teaching.

At times, the fact that Stanley's approach was different from that of other teachers could cause trouble. For example, in the preparation for a pirouette from fourth position, he taught that both knees should be bent and that the weight should be evenly distributed between both feet. The others taught that the front leg should be bent and the back leg straight. (Stanley has since adopted this preparation.) Some of us used Stanley's method in the other classes because we liked him so much, and then the other teachers got mad. Differences of that magnitude were rare, but we quickly learned that each teacher had his or her own approach.

I wanted very much to please Stanley, because I felt he could be of great help to me. Any sign from him that he was unhappy meant, I feared, that I would stop being one of his favorites and, thus, would no longer benefit from his corrections. Sometimes, when correcting me, he would say: "Can't you remember what I tell you?" or "How many times do I have to tell you?" If I had in fact been concentrating on precisely the correction he had in mind, I felt torn apart emotionally and a flood of tears came to my eyes. Usually I would continue with the next step, with tears streaming down my face, but sometimes I'd stay in the back of the room and cry uncontrollably.

He never commented to me on my behavior, but one afternoon Diana Adams approached me. "I heard you had a *crise* this morning," she said. I didn't know that was the French word for "crisis" and so I stared at her blankly. "What were you so upset about?" She had made her point, but it was hard for me not to overreact. I wanted so badly to do well. I don't remember crying in anybody else's class, but that doesn't mean I never did.

It was an exciting bonus when Maria Tallchief turned up a couple of times as a guest teacher. She was then a principal dancer with the New York City Ballet and that made her the next best thing to Balanchine, as far as I was concerned. She was very demanding and always seemed a little cross with us. She worked intensely on a little in-between step, glissade—a gliding step—and I couldn't for the life of me figure out why she was paying so much attention to what I thought was an insignificant step. Years later when I was in Balanchine's class I understood. Balanchine wanted us to "dance" in-between steps, or preparations, and make them beautiful in their own right, rather than to do them haphazardly.

At the end of my year in B, I was notified I would be placed in C class the following year. I think the School was in a dilemma about what class I should be in. The teachers couldn't decide whether it was advisable to move me ahead into C. I was about five feet three inches and weighed only ninety pounds, giving me a very fragile appearance for a fourteen-year-old. On top of that, I was still not strong technically. They weren't sure—nor was I—I was ready to cope with the difficulties of the advanced class, but finally they decided it was worth a gamble because I was considered very serious and hardworking. And that I was. I may have had a small body, but I had a big desire to learn. Putting me into C class also made it possible for me to stay with my friends, which the teachers felt was important.

That summer I returned to Minneapolis to be with my parents. It was the only time our whole family could be together, since my mother had already decided to return to

New York with me in the fall. While in Minneapolis I took no ballet classes; I was afraid I would be "ruined" by any other school.

As a result, when I returned to SAB in the fall I was as weak as a kitten. The students who had already spent a year in C (it was usual to spend two years there) and who were a year or two older didn't fail to notice. When they stared at me, it was easy to read their minds: "Why did they let her in here? She's falling all over the place." I didn't blame them for giving me those looks. They saw that my weakness was bringing me more of the teachers' attention than I deserved. I was determined to catch up as quickly as I could.

In C, we had either two or three one-and-a-half-hour classes a day. I had two new teachers, André Eglevsky and Alexandra Danilova. Eglevsky, a premier danseur who had danced with the New York City Ballet when it was first founded, still appeared young and very strong and could demonstrate steps beautifully, particularly pirouettes and jumps. In pirouettes he wanted the hands carried below the waist—fine for a man, but we wondered what that would look like in a tutu. Since we didn't wear tutus in class, we were in no position to protest. In jumps he attempted to teach us the soft catlike take-offs and landings at which he excelled, but the timing involved was so subtle we couldn't unravel the mystery.

A new and special treat was the weekly variations class with Danilova. Like Balanchine, Danilova had been trained at the St. Petersburg Imperial Theater Ballet School and had been a leading ballerina with Diaghilev's Ballets Russes when Balanchine was ballet master. She had toured the United States with the Ballet Russe de Monte Carlo in the 1940s and 1950s, coming to teach at the School in 1963. Danilova was every inch a ballerina. With her proud carriage, pearl necklaces, careful makeup, and chiffon tie-on skirts (drawn aside in the front and tucked into her carefully coordinated leotard, showing off her legs), she brought glamour to SAB. And in class she always demonstrated all the steps full out for us, as if she were in performance.

She divided her classes into two groups and would not let the younger students try the more difficult variations. As the time approached to begin rehearsing for the year-end workshop, we each learned all the solos that would be performed in the workshop. Later, a few lucky ones would be chosen for these roles.

That year Danilova staged Act I of *Swan Lake,* choreographed by Petipa. Colleen Neary and I were cast in the pas de quatre with the Sackett brothers, Paul and Francis, as our partners. I think I would have enjoyed the performances much more if I hadn't been so wrapped up in trying to get the steps exactly right.

At the dress rehearsal, Danilova coached us on our stage presence: "Remember," she said, "you have to play to the balcony. Don't forget."

I didn't forget. I thought I knew what she meant, and danced the entire performance staring up at the balcony. In my mind, "playing to" meant "looking at," and I had followed her instructions to the letter. Several days later Diana Adams said to me, "You know, I never noticed it before, but you have this strange habit of holding your head really high when you dance, as though you're looking up at the ceiling."

I couldn't answer. I just wanted to crawl into a hole and disappear. I had only been trying to do the right thing. I got over that "habit" very quickly.

The workshop was, as always, the culmination of the year's efforts. I went on to take the summer course at SAB and then spent a second year in C. By then I had caught up with most of the others; in fact, I was one of the better second-year C students. I had grown to my present height, five feet seven inches. I was still well proportioned, though very thin, and had gained some strength, confidence, and technical facility. I was more secure in adagios: my ability to maintain my balance while standing on one leg had much improved. Pirouettes were still my nemesis, but I had greater extension, and more stamina for long jumping combinations. As the year progressed I began to feel that the New York City Ballet was definitely in my future.

When the time came to prepare for the workshop, I was cast with Colleen and Gelsey Kirkland to do the Precious Stones pas de trois from *The Sleeping Beauty,* staged by Danilova. Although I was happy to have this role, I couldn't understand why—as we were being groomed for the New York City Ballet—we weren't also doing some of Balanchine's ballets in the workshop. It was several more years before Balanchine ballets became a regular part of the workshop, correcting what I can only imagine was an oversight.

There was a room at the School for storing toe shoes that had been rejected by Company members. SAB students could buy them for less than half-price, three dollars instead of ten. One day about six months before the workshop, I rummaged around in the shoe room and found a pair that had been rejected by Allegra Kent, who had tiny narrow feet. I tried them on and not only were they a perfect fit but the shanks were hard, just the way I like them. In fact, they were right in every way and so I bought them and put them aside for the workshop.

Performance time was fast approaching. I was in costume and makeup, and my perfect new shoes were sewn (ribbons and elastic have to be sewn on each pair) and ready to wear. When I went to put them on, just a few minutes before going on stage, I found to my dismay that I couldn't get my feet into them. My feet had grown wider, or perhaps they were swollen from all the intense rehearsing. But I had no other shoes to wear so, in a frenzy, I crammed my feet into them, tied the ribbons, and danced. I wound up with huge blisters all over my feet. Clive Barnes's review in *The New York Times* the next day helped ease the pain: "And one dancer with promise was Linda Merrill." It was my one and only review as Linda Merrill, my given name, a name I was later forced to give up.

Blisters such as those I got in the workshop performance were usually an acceptable excuse not to wear toe, or pointe, shoes in class, but the general rule was, "No soft ballet slippers for any class." Old worn-out pointe shoes were acceptable, but "real" pointe shoes were ideal. That was a directive from Balanchine, who was given to popping into class unannounced. When he did so he was usually alone, but sometimes he was accompanied by Diana Adams, who stood by his side with a big yellow pad, taking notes. He would stand for a few moments on a platform high above the studio floor and, with his head still and slightly tilted back, quietly and impassively survey everything and everyone. If we had a chance, we might steal a glance in his direction to see if he was looking at anyone in particular, but he always seemed to be taking everything in, all at once. Then he was gone, having gotten what he wanted, and we were left with our anxieties.

We didn't want our names put down on the yellow pad for wearing ballet slippers, but most of us could afford only old toe shoes in our regular daily classes. We saved our good shoes for the weekly pointe, variations, and adagio classes. A few lucky students had friends in the Company who gave them old discarded shoes that were still serviceable. It was absolutely necessary that we start getting used to being in pointe shoes all the time. Steps done in ballet slippers gave a very different feeling.

There were two memorable occasions when bright new pointe shoes were very much in evidence for a regular class. Word came twice during my second year of C that Balanchine himself would be teaching class. When the first occasion came, everyone wore new pointe shoes and a few put on perfume, pinned flowers in their hair, or found some other way to look especially attractive. I don't remember what I did, but I'm sure I wanted to look as neat as possible and therefore probably chose my favorite leotard and took extra care fixing my hair.

Class with Balanchine! Class in the presence of this man who, like a god, embodied everything we admired and revered. Class given by this man whom we had to please above all others. It was terrifying. Everyone in the class seemed straighter, more alert, expectant. We all had mixed feelings about getting his attention. We wanted to be noticed, but we feared his corrections. What if we couldn't do what he wanted right just after he showed us?

Balanchine entered the studio in a very businesslike manner—no greetings, no idle words to create a friendly atmosphere. We were all at the barre, in preparation for the pliés that always started our classes at the School. Class began. We held the barre with our left hand, while our right arm was extended out to the side. Balanchine gave a quick glance around the room and spoke his first words: "Nobody knows how to stand."

We hadn't done anything, and we were wrong already!

"Stand like turkey," he said, thumping his chest.

"Chest out, shoulders back, head high. Look awake and alive."

After we had straightened up a little bit, he said, "And what about your hands?"

He took the hand of a girl standing near me, tried to round the palm and make it more concave. He separated her fingers, indicating the right position of each one. He

The "Precious Stones" pas de trois from Danilova's staging of *Sleeping Beauty* for the 1967 School of American Ballet workshop. (Left to right): Merrill, Gelsey Kirkland, and Colleen Neary. (© *1984 Martha Swope*)

still wasn't happy: "Dear, too soft; looks like dead chicken. Must be strong, like this. Feel mine!"

With that, the girl took his beautifully sculpted hand and squeezed it as hard as she could. Not a finger moved.

"Yours should be like that, dear."

To me it seemed like magic. Where did the strength come from? I tried to imitate him, but my hand simply looked like a claw.

Balanchine's immediate involvement in our first gestures fascinated and frightened me. Before, he had been only a distant figure, but now he was suddenly among us, touching us, chiding us, elaborating on the basics that we thought we had already mastered. He seemed so alert and animated, and he didn't act at all like a man in his sixties. Slender, erect, quick, and energetic, he didn't look like one either. That quiet, impassive figure on the platform high above class was quite unlike the man now in our midst, who was tireless in his pursuit of perfection.

As we began our pliés, he demanded a perfect fifth position, with the heel of the front foot even with the tips of the toes of the back foot. Most teachers would give you a half-inch leeway or more, but he gave you nothing. Overcrossing was just as bad as undercrossing; the position had to be exact.

Then came *battements tendus:* sixteen in each direction, more than we had ever done at one time. While we were doing them, Balanchine was down on one knee, next to various students, repositioning feet and guiding legs. Each successive combination of tendus was faster than the last, and soon we were trying to do them faster than we had ever done them before. It was all so extreme and made our muscles burn with fatigue.

As the barre progressed, we did exercises in which he wanted us to move our limbs as if they were meeting resistance. He would provide that resistance by pushing and pulling us with his hands. But it was when we moved to the center that the real surprise came. Suddenly Balanchine was jumping, landing catlike, executing steps like a dancer half his age. He seemed more godlike than ever.

What a relief when it was over! The class had been terribly stressful—physically, mentally, and emotionally. Fear of the unknown had been the worst part. We had wondered whether he would be patient and understanding or stern and unforgiving. We had feared his high standards, yet he proved to be reasonable. He never raised his voice or got angry, but he was very definite about what he wanted. He didn't praise anybody; the most he said was, "That's right."

Everything I had heard about the difficulties of Balanchine's class was true, but the primary difficulty had never been made clear to me. He didn't just give strenuous exercises; he demanded closer attention to more details in every step than I had ever dreamed possible. The most familiar basic steps became a new challenge. Were his classes like this in the Company, or were they even harder? Or perhaps this was just an intensive course especially for us at the School.

The summer following my second year in C, I was part of a group of students who were chosen to go to Saratoga, New York, where the New York City Ballet has a summer season every July. A special summer course had been organized for the first time, and classes were held in the old Canfield Casino, in a beautiful little park right in the middle of town. We took class in a large room, with a crystal chandelier, that must have been the main gambling hall. As I looked at the gold paint and mirrors everywhere, it was easy to visualize wealthy, elegant ladies and gentlemen strolling from table to table.

One of our teachers was Irina Kosmovska, from California, many of whose students had already joined the Company. She stressed balances and turns—double attitude, arabesque, and *à la seconde* (with the leg extended to the side) turns that were very hard and that other teachers at the School rarely gave us. But it was good to have new teachers. Each one's emphasis was different, making me realize how far I had to go before becoming a ballerina.

Doubrovska also taught that summer but the rest of the SAB faculty had to remain in Manhattan for the regular summer course. We were therefore very lucky to have

Jacques d'Amboise and Suzanne Farrell, both principal dancers at the peak of their powers, as teachers for the Saratoga summer course.

Jacques was a whirlwind of energy and enthusiasm and like Balanchine, he was very firm and insistent about what he wanted. His corrections came through loud and clear, and he had us all quaking in our toe shoes. Yet, when he flashed a smile and turned on his charm, he was disarming. He might say, "If anyone can do this step all the way through without a mistake, I'll treat them to a sundae," and he would keep his promise. He gave very complicated steps very fast, and as I look back on them now, this too seems very much like Balanchine. But Jacques gave long combinations and continually added to the steps he had just given, almost as if he were choreographing a ballet, and that was different from Balanchine. It was a superb exercise for our minds but very hard on our bodies.

Suzanne was altogether different. She was cool and remote in her manner but, at the same time, she tried to convey to us the importance of enjoying ourselves, and *looking* as if we were enjoying ourselves, when we danced. We had to let go and not merely pay attention to the steps. It sounded simple enough, but when the steps you're executing have you stretched to the limit of your ability, it's hard to feel joy, let alone radiate it.

Suzanne taught us the difficult Sugar Plum Fairy variation from *The Nutcracker.* Because of the simplicity of the steps, it is easy for the eye to follow the dancer's feet, and every flaw is thus glaringly exposed. If the feet are not placed beautifully and delicately, and if the dancer is not poised and elegant, the variation is not effective. In addition, there was a series of turns I could not do at all. At the time, well-executed double pirouettes were still a matter of hit or miss. I had a long way to go before I would master this variation.

We all went en masse to the Saratoga Performing Arts Center every evening. Seeing "our" Company and its huge repertory night after night made me love what I was doing more and more. Although I enjoyed watching all the dancers, I couldn't find one who was beyond reproach. I suppose I was hoping that I would become such a dancer one day. Those who didn't execute the steps well held little interest for me, and those with better technique usually showed the strain or had personalities I found unappealing. I tried to find the best in each dancer and form a mental image of the ballerina I might become.

As my fourth year at SAB got under way in the fall of 1967, I had the feeling that all was going well for me. I was continually getting stronger, though I was still very thin. I felt confident that eventually I would be asked to join the Company. If I had any pessimistic moments, I could always tell myself that almost all the scholarship students were admitted. Rarely, however, did such speculation enter my thoughts. I felt I was not yet ready to join the Company and I was sure that several of my classmates would be chosen before me.

Shortly after my D class began that fall, Leslie Peck, Colleen, and I were asked to

In class at the School of American Ballet in 1967. (© *Ernst Haas*)

take part in several special Company classes that Balanchine was giving as a seminar for teachers from all over the country. The three of us found places in the back of the studio where we would be less conspicuous, but from there it was hard to hear or see what was going on. My most vivid recollection is that some of the steps he gave were terribly complicated and difficult, making me feel quite inept. Nevertheless, just being there was exciting.

During this same period, I was called on by John Clifford, a Company member who later became a principal, to rehearse as a member of the corps in a ballet he was choreographing for the School workshop. One evening during one of the rehearsals Gleboff came into the studio and indicated that she wanted to see me in her office when I had a break.

I immediately became nervous. Had I done something wrong? Why did I find dealing with the Russians so nerve-racking? Their deep, resonant voices imparted drama to the simplest utterances, and their gruff manner with the students only reinforced that impression. When I entered Gleboff's office, after putting off the encounter for nearly an hour, I found her with an uncharacteristic smile on her face.

"Mr. Balanchine would like to invite you to join the Company," she said.

I was stunned. It was the last thing I had expected at that point. I had been in D class only three weeks and had heard nothing through the grapevine about Balanchine's taking in new members. People at the School usually got wind of such momentous matters and the word would spread like wildfire. This came as a total surprise.

"Are you all right?" Gleboff wanted to know. I nodded feebly, unable to respond.

"But," she added in a serious voice, "Mr. Balanchine has added the stipulation that you finish high school and get your diploma."

I had never heard of his saying that to anyone else, and wondered why I had been singled out. It made sense, of course, and my parents, heaven knows, would approve. I had every intention of finishing school, but why this proviso? So many people taken into the Company had never finished school. What prompted Balanchine to make this request remains a mystery to me to this day.

I kept the happy news to myself until I got home and blurted it out to my mother. We laughed and cried while I danced around the apartment, planning a celebration.

The Company was not beginning its fall rehearsals for a week, so I had time to bask in the limelight of my newly acquired celebrity at the school and to accept congratulations. I tried to do so graciously and modestly. I felt sorry for those who had hoped to make it, and had failed, but my sympathy was diluted by my own euphoria. It was a week when I could serenely contemplate the future from my lofty perch, heedless of the fact that I would soon plummet into the obscurity of the lowest reaches of the NYCB corps, where I would lose my identity—and my name. For upon joining the company, I found I didn't have a name to call my own.

CHAPTER

2

LINDA ROSENTHAL, who had been a classmate of mine in C class at SAB, had assumed the name Linda Merrill when she had joined the Company shortly before me. I couldn't believe she had done such a thing, since she knew I stood a good chance of getting into the Company and would then be forced to change my name because of her. But what was done was done. I had to find a name I liked and one that was somehow related to my family's name. This problem was always in the back of my mind, nagging me, and whenever out-of-town friends congratulated me, having seen Linda Merrill's name on the Company roster, I was reminded not only of the big decision that was looming but also of the confusion being caused by the "other" Linda Merrill.

Directly after I was taken into the Company, I received a call: "Linda, what name do you want us to put on your contract? We need to know this week." There was no longer any way to postpone the issue.

Should I give up both my first and last names? That might look as though I were turning my back on my family, and I certainly didn't want to do that. I was close to them and owed them so much. So, for a start, I decided to keep the family name, Merrill. I briefly contemplated using one of my middle names, Michelle or Billings, keeping Merrill as my last name. But the New York City Ballet had taken in so many brother and sister pairs that, inevitably, I would be taken for Linda Rosenthal's sister. Balanchine suggested I call myself Linda Merrill II. At first I thought he was joking, but several days later I found myself riding in an elevator with him, and he said, quite seriously, "Oh, there's Linda Merrill II." Obviously, he had made up his mind, even if I hadn't. He had even influenced the ballet mistresses, who also began calling me Linda Merrill II.

If Merrill couldn't be my last name, I decided it should be my first. My father's name was Harvie Merrill IV, and as there was no son to carry on the family name, no one to be Harvie Merrill V, I thought I could at least be Merrill Harvie. I notified the company of my decision, but after about a week I started having second thoughts. The name didn't have the right ring to it.

It was clear I couldn't solve this alone. One day I was sitting with a few acquaintances at the School on the same bench where I had sat waiting for the results of my audition, and it seemed as good a time as any to do a little brainstorming. We decided to scour the alphabet, from A to Z, in search of a suitable last name. *A* wasn't a bad letter to start with, because the Company lists its dancers alphabetically. One of the first names that came up was Ashley. Merrill Ashley. It had a simple elegance that appealed to me and suited the ballerina I hoped to become. Finally I had found my name.

Balanchine wasn't happy, however: "Ashley, okay, but Merrill—as first name?" he sniffed. He never could get used to it, and for the rest of his life he called me Linda, except in public.

I had to break the news to my family, whom I felt I had betrayed. I was even more unhappy when my father told me how, as a boy, he had put together a musical group known as The Merrill Harvies, and how happy he was that I was bringing the name back to life. Nervously, I explained that I had changed my mind, and burst into tears as I blurted out my new stage name. He had a surprising consolation: Didn't I know that Ashley was an old family name? I didn't, but I was very relieved to hear it. Now I could get on with the business of becoming Merrill Ashley.

When dancers join the New York City Ballet there are no formal induction ceremonies, no welcoming committees, no orientation or indoctrination courses. You learn the ropes as you go along, and no one makes things easier for you. The quicker, more observant you are, the better off you are, but the message is unmistakable: "You're on your own; it's all up to you; nothing is going to be made easy."

At first, it was exciting just reminding myself that I was a member of the Company and fantasizing about the glory to come. But soon reality began to bewilder me. I would have welcomed and memorized a handbook with answers to all my questions, spelling out the Company's myriad rules and regulations.

At least I knew my way around the State Theater, a maze of elevators and hallways. My *Nutcracker* experience had stood me in good stead. But I couldn't make a move without being assaulted by doubts, and everything I didn't know seemed of vital importance. I had to learn how to read the rehearsal schedule, what constituted overtime and where to report it, and where to get paid. When I found the toe shoe room, I was told that I had to use someone else's shoes until I received a supply of my own. A supply of my own! An endless supply, at no expense to me—this luxury was practically better than getting a salary. In fact, the price of my shoes (six pairs a week, or a total of $60) very nearly equaled my take-home pay. (My gross salary was $115 a week for rehearsals, $120 a week during the season, and $150 a week on tour.) I proudly gave my specifications to the shoe manufacturer and eagerly awaited the bonanza from the factory.

It was up to me to learn how to put on makeup, how to wear my hair for the different ballets, and how to put on the headpieces just so: sometimes on the right side, sometimes on the left, and sometimes wherever I wanted—and *always* securely. The only help I got came from other corps members, and it usually took the form of criticism after I had made some blatant mistake.

When we were not in class or rehearsals with Balanchine, the only person who provided any guidance—and she did so by laying down the law—was the wardrobe mistress. If she caught us sitting on the floor or even on a chair when in costume (stools were allowed because we could sit on them without crushing our costumes) or putting our hands on our hips or eating or drinking (or smoking, God forbid), we got a scolding.

I also had to learn how to warm up before a performance. It was up to me to decide when my warm-up should begin, how long it should last, and which exercises I needed to do. I watched others to decide what a proper warm-up should be, but everyone took a different approach. It was years before I learned what my ideal warm-up was, and in the meantime I often did no more than ten or fifteen minutes of barre exercises. Balanchine often told us we should work alone in a studio, but he never said a word about warming up. He expected us to solve that problem on our own.

All this learning took place in an atmosphere that was entirely different from the School's. There, everything was strictly regimented and each student's progress was closely monitored. In the Company, I (and all other new members) felt immediately lost in the group. We rarely got a smile, a hello, or even a glimmer of recognition from anyone, much less any other sign of interest or concern for our well-being. No longer significant as individuals, we took on a new identity, that of proud members of the greatest ballet company in the world.

Balanchine's dignified bearing and unfailingly respectful manner toward us set an example most dancers were inclined to follow. In the theater we felt we were on hallowed ground. In fact, we often heard Balanchine say that we should think and act as if the theater were a church. He wanted us to be respectful in our manner and dignified in our dress. He didn't want us to look like "dirty hippies." He particularly wanted the men to be well groomed and clean shaven. We weren't supposed to eat, drink, or smoke in the rehearsal rooms or backstage, and Balanchine had large signs hung on the walls as reminders. Nor did he like to see a piano being used as a barre or a resting place for anything other than music. He said a piano was not a piece of furniture but a beautiful instrument that should be treated with care.

That fall, the rehearsal period was used to prepare not only for the New York season but also for a trip to Chicago, where we were to inaugurate the newly renovated Auditorium Theater. I was disappointed that my debut with the New York City Ballet would not be in New York, but I told myself this trial run would help me get over my stage fright.

Balanchine had taken the final rehearsals in New York, and when we arrived in Chicago he took all the rehearsals there as well. Balanchine looked for the same things in rehearsals as he did in class, but he was even more demanding in rehearsals about how we presented ourselves. He kept reminding us that we were "entertainers." His attitude varied, however, from dancer to dancer. With a few he was matter-of-fact, knowing that what he said would produce results right away. With others he was more insistent, realizing that a little prodding was needed. With still others he was easily frustrated, but he was rarely distant or uninterested. No matter whom he was helping, he always seemed to notice flaws the ballet mistresses rarely saw; and so we never knew what to expect.

Another surprise was having to go on stage without the benefit of orchestra or dress rehearsals. These were luxuries the Company could afford only for new ballets or for ballets with difficult music, such as those by Stravinsky.

I made my debut as one of Hippolyta's hounds in Act I of *A Midsummer Night's Dream,* a role traditionally given to the newest girls in the Company; in Act II, I was one of the members of the court. The next day there was a picture in the newspaper of a line of "hounds" leaping through the air. I was able to pick myself out of the group even though our heads were completely covered by the costume heads we had to wear. My excitement at seeing myself was spoiled somewhat by the fact that the picture showed me out of line—out of line for all eternity.

That week in Chicago I also danced in *Diamonds* (part of *Jewels*) and *Stars and Stripes.* These roles were difficult, and the speed at which they were taught to me was breathtaking. At SAB we had learned roles at a leisurely pace. In the Company we were shown something once or twice and that was supposed to be enough. In an hour I had to learn half my corps role in *Diamonds.* The fiendish opening waltz consisted of four groups of three dancers, each in constantly shifting diagonals and patterns. If a beginner was the middle dancer in a group of three, she could at least rely on the dancers on either side to show her changes in direction and to remind her of what came next. I had the misfortune of being on one end of my group. Marjorie Spohn, who had also just joined the Company, was on the other. We both felt lost. I know that even then we were being watched by the other corps girls, who were making no allowances. By the end of the rehearsal neither of us could remember all the steps we had learned. As no one was eager to rehearse this section, Marjorie and I had mainly ourselves to rely on as we tried to jog each other's memories.

I was in the second campaign of *Stars and Stripes.* We call it the "tall girls'" regiment (I was a "tall girl" in most ballets). It required stamina and technique that I had barely mastered, and I had to go off by myself and practice some of the steps. Some of the older members of the corps snickered at my eagerness. If I worked harder than was considered suitable, I was made fun of for being too conscientious. But this was preferable to being unable to do the choreography properly.

I turned for comfort and advice to my friend Renée Estopinal, who had been in the Company for a year. She seemed simultaneously to be a newcomer and an old-timer and was able to help me put my problems in perspective. Renée, Marjorie, and I roomed together in Chicago in an old hotel in the vicinity of the theater, and every night we stayed up late rehashing the day's events and sharing grand thoughts about our futures, as dancers invariably do.

When I returned to New York the exciting process of learning new roles continued. Fortunately, I had become a fast learner, for I had very little time to learn my corps roles in *Swan Lake, Western Symphony, Firebird, La Valse,* and *Symphony in C.* Each one presented me with a particular problem. I continued to struggle with the opening waltz in *Diamonds,* as I had in Chicago. And my corps role in Balanchine's version of *Swan Lake,* Act II, was literally a painful experience.

Early in *Swan Lake,* the corps girls enter, one by one in single file, all doing the same combination of steps over and over, suggesting the majestic arrival of a flock of swans. Next they execute a series of U-turns and eventually form five lines of four each, arriving at what we call "places in line." At that point the dancers glide about, constantly changing places with each other, skimming weightlessly across the surface of the stage, arms evoking the graceful, undulating movement of a swan's wings. At least that is the way these steps—bourrées—are supposed to look. To make it work, the "swan" has to be able, on pointe in fifth position, to move forward, backward, and to both sides by taking quick little steps, no more than a few inches each. The legs should appear to be straight—the knees bend only imperceptibly—and the dancers must at every moment be in perfect balance: no lurching back and forth; no bobbing up and down; and, above all, no hopping from foot to foot. It's even harder than it sounds. I knew what I wanted those bourrées to look like, but at first, in my eagerness to travel the necessary distance, all I seemed capable of were big steps with the leading leg supporting most of my weight and the trailing leg coming along as an afterthought. After some time, I managed to make the steps smaller and still cover the necessary space, but I did this by picking up my feet and bending my knees, using my legs like a pair of pistons and looking like the wrong kind of bird altogether.

I alternated between these two extremes, as I struggled to perfect this particular kind of bourrée, which crops up everywhere in Balanchine's ballets. It was a long, painful learning process, and my toes took a fearful beating. It was maddening to think that if I had been capable of performing the steps properly, flitting across the stage with those tiny rapid-fire steps that defy the quickest eye, my toes would have been spared some of the banging and bruising they received in my version of the step. In a sense, the hard way would have been the easy way.

The older girls in the corps had had plenty of practice with these bourrées, and most of them executed them better than I did. But no one comes by this step easily. There may be natural turners, natural jumpers, and natural balancers, but when it comes to bourrées, there are no naturals. It takes years of practice to get them right.

It wasn't just in learning steps that I had to be quick. I had to be quick-witted in coping with mishaps in performance, too. In *Firebird* we were dressed as monsters, and our costumes had tails that were made out of wire coiled like a telephone cord. One evening in performance, as I jumped out on stage for an entrance, I saw that the tail of the girl in front of me had become entangled in the telephone cord attached to the stage manager's desk by the first wing. I quickly untangled her, and we both raced out onto the stage, caught up with the choreography, and found our proper places. There were also the more usual mishaps: headpieces coming loose and earrings or bits of costumes falling to the floor. There are ways of dealing coolly with these crises, but a newcomers' instincts are often misguided.

In my first two years with the Company, John Taras, one of the ballet masters, often conducted corps rehearsals before we went through a ballet for Balanchine on stage. He was a stickler for detail, getting us in line and moving in unison—things for which the New York City Ballet is not noted. These were very trying rehearsals because we had to repeat steps over and over. Later, when Balanchine himself took the rehearsal, the emphasis was more on energy and beautifully executed steps. He wanted us to cover space boldly, so that the changing patterns could be easily seen. Because we were so concerned with staying in line or being right where we thought we should be, we tended to be too timid in our movements to suit him.

Balanchine often watched performances from backstage inside the first wing. He stood there, expressionless, with his elbow resting on a little shelf that looked as if it had been built specifically for that purpose. It was hard to tell what he was thinking, but it was easy for me to imagine he was thinking the worst. When I had the good fortune, or misfortune, of dancing right there in front of him, I felt as if I were under a microscope. I saw it as a perfect opportunity to show him what I had learned and to exercise control over my nerves. I was determined that he see me at my best, and I tried to recall any comments he had ever made either in class or rehearsal about the steps I was doing.

The high point of my first season was being selected to be in the corps of a new ballet by Balanchine to music by Iannis Xenakis: *Metastaseis and Pithoprakta.* I danced in the first part, *Metastaseis,* which had only corps members, and I understudied the second part. The ballet began with all of us flat on our stomachs, forming a great shapeless mass

26

The opening moments from
Metastaseis and Pithoprakta, 1968.
(© *1984 Martha Swope*)

in the center of the stage. Slowly, we rose up, little by little, first lifting our hands and then standing. Balanchine chose me to be the first person to raise her hand.

"Now let me see how you're going to do it," he said.

I worried that, no matter how I raised my hand, it would be the wrong way. Timidly I poked up a fist, thinking I might then produce some sort of interesting effect by opening it and showing my fingers.

"No, dear, has to be stronger, like this," he said patiently, as he showed me that he wanted to see all five fingers right away. After I tried again, he seemed satisfied and went on to the next step. Once more, I was the leader. He had two boys lift me high in the air and then he told me to bend forward, as if I were going to do a slow somersault in the air. He may have chosen me and the other girls who were lifted because we were thin and easy to lift, but I didn't think of that at the time. My only thought was, "He likes me."

Slowly the whole group began to move, undulating like a giant amoeba. Most of the time we relied on visual cues rather than counts, which was unusual for a Balanchine

ballet with difficult music. When we saw a dancer reach a certain place on the stage or do a particular step, that was our cue to start the next step. There were obvious musical cues we followed too, because the music didn't have easily recognizable melodies or beats. For example, when a certain distinctive note was struck or a particular instrument began playing, or when there was a sudden change in volume, we knew we had to perform the next step.

Soon after the hand raising, we were all on our feet, little figures in white leotards and tights moving in every direction, dispersing. Then we gradually came back together and formed a compact mass. Again we lay down on the floor, and slowly we assumed the original position. *Metastaseis* lasted about ten minutes, and it was hard for me to tell what the overall effect was, but I had never seen a ballet that looked anything like it.

In the second part of the ballet, there *were* counts. The music was so difficult to follow we couldn't rely on our ears to tell us when to do what. So, as Balanchine choreographed a sequence, he would give us counts to go with the steps, one count or number per beat, though he wouldn't necessarily stop counting at the end of a measure. For example, if the first measure had four beats and the second had six beats, we might count from one to eight and then from one to two, provided the steps fell naturally into two sequences of eight and two beats each. He might also have elected to follow the music and choreograph steps "in a four and a six."

All this was new to me. Learning steps and counts together made the assimilation of the new choreography confusing, and because each dancer often had to do something different from his or her neighbor, there was no relying on anyone else. As the ballet was new to us, we were all groping. Learning an old ballet is much easier because everyone around you is on familiar ground. Fortunately I was only an understudy, so I had more time to let it all sink in. As it turned out, I never danced in the second part, for the ballet had a short life after its premiere in January 1968.

The rehearsals for *Metastaseis and Pithoprakta* took place in December, during the annual run of *The Nutcracker.* The corps in *The Nutcracker* is always divided into two groups, A and B, which alternate performances, but sometimes the newest members are in both groups and do all the performances, as I did, with roles in both Acts I and II. I appeared as the Maid in the party scene and as a Snowflake at the end of Act I, and in the Spanish divertissement in Act II. Since I was doing the same thing every evening, I could focus my mental energies on learning the oddities of *Metastaseis and Pithoprakta.*

I acquired some strength, stamina, and experience as a result of all the dancing I did those first few months of my career, but, while the hard work and long hours did not dull my enthusiasm or pleasure, there was no improvement in my overall technique. Practice was not making perfect. It seemed that all my waking hours were taken up with learning, trying to remember, and then performing all those roles that traditionally go to newcomers. There was enormous variety, and I picked up a great deal that I had never been exposed to at SAB, but few of these roles included more than a smattering of classical steps. The monsters in *Firebird,* the hounds in *A Midsummer Night's Dream,* the party scene in *The Nutcracker,* the run-on girls in *Western Symphony,* and even the corps roles in the fourth movement of *Symphony in C* could not maintain, much less improve, my overall technique.

None of this was then apparent to me. I was so happily engrossed in rehearsals and performances that I didn't stop to think about anything else. Any fatigue, soreness, or minor injury told me only that I was working as hard as could be expected. Balanchine gave me corrections from time to time in class, which meant that at least he was noticing me. I often received compliments and heard that I would "make it." Deep down I too felt confident I would eventually succeed, and in my mind that meant becoming a principal dancer one day. But I still had so much to learn.

I kept pressing on, neither elated nor depressed. I always found pleasure in the roles I had, but feelings of ineptitude and ignorance haunted me, making me feel like a novice, particularly in Balanchine's class. As time passed, I noticed that I was having more and more difficulty with certain steps I had just begun to master at SAB. My pirouettes once again became harrowing experiences. And what had happened to my jump? Big jumps had always been one of my strong points. Some of my confidence had been based on my lightness, energy, and good jumps.

Gradually I realized the simple truth: my daily routine was taking its toll. I was spending endless hours in roles that added little to my repertory of steps, and when difficult combinations cropped up I often found myself struggling and having trouble staying with the music.

I attended Balanchine's classes regularly, partly because I felt I should and partly because I knew that my feelings of relative ignorance were well founded and I needed to learn all I could. In every class, Balanchine brought up many technical points that were new to me, but he rarely explained them in full detail, and my eye was not yet sharp enough to detect the subtleties in his demonstrations.

Another difficulty I faced was his frequent request that the same step be done differently from one day to the next. It took me a long time to realize this wasn't an inconsistency in his demands but was instead his attempt to give us a broad range of skills to choose from. He wanted us to be in complete control, not forced by our bodies' habits to move in one particular way.

One thing was immediately clear to me: Balanchine wanted a high level of energy in every movement. It made no difference whether we were moving slowly, quickly, or not at all. We had to be aware of every part of our body and make it look alive. He tried to make us understand that principle when he taught class at SAB. He wanted to see the energy contained in our bodies even when we were standing still at the barre. He liked to draw a comparison between a cat ready to pounce and one sitting in the same position. There is no movement in either, but one can sense the energy and alertness in the cat that is ready to pounce. We too had to be ready to pounce!

I dwelled constantly on the mysteries and frustrations of class with Balanchine. I took all his classes, except when Stanley Williams taught the advanced classes at the School. It was reassuring to work in a class where I felt in close harmony with the teacher. I began to hear, however, about up-and-coming young corps members who never missed Balanchine's classes. It made me wonder whether I should not be doing the same thing. Soon I realized that my only hope of stimulating Balanchine's interest was to learn to dance the way he wanted, and that could be done only in his classes. They might not be comfortable or reassuring, but that was where my future lay. I couldn't just *say* I was committed to him. I had to *be* committed. It took me a little while to understand the obvious, but finally it became clear. Many never understood.

Company class was given then, as today, in the "main hall," a large studio, supposedly with the same dimensions as the stage of the State Theater. But, since the studio was enclosed by four windowless walls, it seemed a much more confined space. Everyone complained about the dim fluorescent lighting that strained our eyes and gave us a sal-

30   low, sickly look. How nice it would have been to have natural sunlight and a glimpse of the outside world. Balanchine, too, had wanted windows, but the architect would not relent, feeling they would spoil his design. We would have appreciated the benefits of fresh air, too, for the air in ballet studios becomes stale very quickly.

Barres lined the four walls. Space was at a premium, but no one had yet thought to put portable barres in the middle of the floor. When the room became unbearably crowded, tall ladders were dragged in and used as makeshift barres. A few dancers used the piano for support, but Balanchine permitted that only when there was no alternative. The floor was covered with battleship gray linoleum, which I found easy to adjust to after the slippery wooden surfaces of the School, but the main hall lacked the springiness of the stage or the floors at SAB. (This was later corrected.) There were tiles missing from the ceiling, and during rainstorms we would dance around the large plastic garbage cans we had placed in the middle of the studio to catch the dripping rain. (That, however, has never been fixed.)

I always arrived a minimum of fifteen minutes before the scheduled starting time: 11:00 A.M. This was not to get a desirable spot at the barre—such maneuvering by a newcomer would not have been appreciated—but simply to warm up, for we all knew it was foolhardy to launch into a Balanchine barre with cold muscles. His was not like one of those comfortable, leisurely barres given by other teachers to massage the muscles and reassure the egos of their temperamental devotees.

Each dancer had his favorite place at the barre, and as a newcomer I naturally had to defer to everyone. At first I found a place in the middle of a side barre, but from there I frequently had trouble catching Balanchine's words. He spoke softly, for he felt he would lose his voice if he spoke up all the time. Later I switched to the opposite side and moved a little nearer to the front. That was the beginning of my long march to the front of the class.

Balanchine would usually arrive ten to twenty minutes late. When he entered the room, everyone fell silent and was immediately ready to work. He almost always appeared in good spirits—he was not a moody person—and he enjoyed spending a minute or two exchanging words with the pianist or one of the dancers before class began.

He was very fond of colorful western shirts, which he sported in denim, prints, satin, and silk. I was fascinated by the contrast between these distinctive shirts and the nondescript "work pants" he wore when teaching or choreographing. He often wore his regular street shoes during class and rehearsals (when choreographing he wore either his street shoes or light, flexible dance shoes), but, no matter how stiff or heavy the shoes, they never seemed to interfere with his innate grace when he walked about and demonstrated steps. If he had just come from a meeting, he might appear in a jacket with a scarf loosely knotted around his neck. The jacket immediately went over the back of the pianist's chair, but it was a little while before he removed the scarf and rolled up his sleeves to show he was ready to get to work with us.

Balanchine rarely varied the plié combination that started the barre; a simple "and" to the pianist or an expansive thumb-down gesture with one hand, meaning "go down," was all we needed to start our deep knee bends, or *grands pliés*. He wanted us to bend our knees and come back up in one perfectly smooth movement, and he wanted a minimal amount of music to accompany the movement—just chords would do. Throughout the rest of class, if the pianist played music with too many notes in a measure, or played too loudly, Balanchine would stop and remark that the pianist was working so hard that *we* could easily believe that *we* were working hard, too. He would then ask the pianist to play soft chords so he could hear the movement of the dancers' feet. He could tell as much, and sometimes more, from the sound our feet made than he could from looking at them. He could literally "hear the dance." Generally he snapped his fingers or tapped his foot to indicate emphasis or the timing, although he sometimes also slapped his thigh. If he wanted to stop the action at any time, he clapped his hands, but repeated clapping was an expression of irritation.

After grands pliés came many battement tendu combinations. Balanchine believed tendus were the foundation of a dancer's technique. "If you just do battement tendu well, you don't have to do anything else" (*Ballet Review* [Winter 1984], p. 25). At first it was hard for me to grasp how—by merely sliding the foot out from fifth position along the floor as far as it would go to either the front, side, or back, while maintaining contact with the floor, and then returning it to fifth position—we were doing a step that would influence our every move on the stage and largely determine whether our technique was precise or sloppy or something in between. Eventually, I realized how right he was.

Tendus came in several varieties, but Balanchine liked to give simple tendus first. It seems perverse to call them simple, for they were by no means easy, especially the way Balanchine wanted them done. I strained my ears to catch all the details that Balanchine gave so lavishly, if at times inaudibly. At first I thought that he and the teachers at SAB were after the same thing but that Balanchine was just being more emphatic and insistent. Then I realized there was a world of difference: Balanchine pointed out many more details and he meant exactly what he said.

The easiest corrections to understand were those about fifth position and about where in relation to one's body the toes should rest on the floor when the leg was extended out as far as it would go with the foot fully pointed. That was the tendu position, the stretched position, which was not supposed to vary one iota when we did a succession of tendus in one direction or another. For example, each time we moved our foot to the front, he wanted it to go to exactly the same spot on the floor, in line with the center of our bodies. The same rule governed our tendus to the back and the side. The foot and leg had to be well turned out and the foot had to have light contact with the floor as it slid out and returned. And all the while he was scrutinizing our fifth position to see if the heel of one foot was even with the toes of the other foot and to be sure that both feet were nestled together. He would often stand next to a newcomer and say, "Don't you know what fifth position is, dear? Didn't anyone ever tell you? Where did you study?"

Of course, he knew perfectly well that the dancer had studied at his school, but with that question, he made his point, with devastating effect.

The most difficult corrections had to do with everything that happened between fifth position and the tendu position. But at the time, these corrections having to do with the in-between positions were often too subtle for me and they just passed over my head.

Balanchine, like everyone else, knew that perfection was not of this world. Yet what he thought was humanly possible was much closer to perfection than we could ever have imagined. He cared about the most minute details of these tendus. The timing was perhaps the trickiest part of all. I struggled mightily to retain everything he said and hoped that somehow, someday the words would filter through my anatomy and come out looking like perfectly executed battements tendus.

Since at first I had only a vague idea of what the finished step should look like, I watched others in class and tried to learn from them. Many had been there for years, but quite a few seemed even farther from the mark than I. How could that be? Did they not hear what Balanchine was saying, or did they hear but not understand? Or was it that they understood but couldn't be bothered to make the effort?

And what an effort it was—as well as painful. Balanchine taught tendus through the use of extremes: very slow and very fast tempos; many repetitions; and a great expenditure of energy. He took the same approach as one might take to tongue twisters: by starting slowly you have a chance to think about each element, and then build up speed. He normally gave a minimum of sixteen tendus in each direction—that is, a total of forty-eight with each leg—to begin with. These were usually done at an extremely slow tempo, alternating legs all the time: first sixteen to the front with the right leg, then sixteen to the front with the left leg, and so on to the side and back. Then the tempo would quicken with each new combination. We'd have eight front, side, and back with the right leg and then the same with the left. Then faster still: four front, side, and back with each leg. There was no rest between sides or between combinations, so by the time he gave two or one in each direction with each leg, our muscles were burning and dancers were groaning and sometimes giving up altogether.

Throughout all the repetitions at accelerating tempos, Balanchine wanted the mechanics and timing to remain intact; the foot was to be presented in the tendu position as beautifully as if we had all the time in the world. He also wanted us to get used to expending vast amounts of physical energy, and he liked to draw an analogy between energy and money. If you have plenty of money in your pocket, he would say, you have the choice of whether to spend it or save it. But if you have no money, you have no choice. It's the same with energy. If dancers are accustomed to expending energy, then they are free to determine exactly how much energy to use on each step. But if they are always sluggish in class, it's impossible suddenly to become dynamic on the stage when it's needed. The theory was elementary, but it took dogged perseverance before correctly executed tendus became second nature to us. (*See sequence photographs following.*)

While I understood Balanchine's methods, I couldn't help wondering what he was really after as he worked to get us to perfect these tendus. Were all these niceties just a matter of aesthetics? Was it just that he wanted tendus done his way, whereas another choreographer might want them done another way, if he cared about them at all? The answers to these questions came slowly, but I had to be patient and thoughtful.

I gradually realized that each time I made a movement with a straight leg, I was doing something related to a tendu. Whenever I started to move a straight leg either away from or toward my body, it was almost always because I was either about to take my foot off the floor or place it on the floor. My foot then had to make all the adjustments that were necessary between the weight-bearing and pointed positions. That is precisely what happens in tendus, and the tens of thousands that I had done had given me great familiarity with these intermediary positions of the foot. For that reason I was able to present my working foot beautifully and make sure it was turned out as I put my weight on it or transferred my weight smoothly from one foot to the other. Tendus had also taught me how to start and stop the movement of my legs quickly and easily. In fact, it was an ideal step for the development of fast movements in general, because of the relative simplicity of the step.

Whenever I started or ended tendus in *demi*-plié (a small bending of the knees), I was learning how to move from step to step by bending and straightening my knees in the most efficient and beautiful way possible. The only things that tendus did not prepare me for were movements of my leg in the air with a bent knee (*fondus* served that purpose) and movements of my leg in a circular pattern (*ronds de jambe* prepared me for that). Those four basic exercises at the barre, with all their variations, prepared us for practically any movement we would have to make while dancing, and when I finally grasped that simple but elusive truth, Balanchine's great insistence on these exercises made much more sense to me.

We proceeded quickly with the different tendus and other remaining exercises at the barre, which took no more than twenty minutes altogether. There was often a link between the exercises at the barre and what was given in the center. If, for example, Balanchine spent extra time at the barre on demi-pliés and grands pliés, there was reason to suspect that all those knees were being made to bend for a purpose: lots of jumps with special attention to the takeoffs and landings would soon be given in the center.

Throughout the barre, Balanchine walked around the room, eyes darting about, his mind racing; he was noticing our flaws and deciding how to correct them. The steps at the barre were calculated to make our legs move in all the ways they would have to move during the work in the center: front, side, and back; up and down; slowly and fast;

and clockwise and counterclockwise. He might stop by a dancer and adjust the position of an arm or leg, head or foot. If a verbal correction failed to produce the desired results, he might plant himself right by the dancer, who had the choice of either doing the step properly or hitting Balanchine with his leg or foot. It certainly was an effective way for Balanchine to get what he wanted. He did this most frequently when he was trying to get us to move directly to the front, side, or back or to make sure our fifth position was right. Often he used his hands and arms to imitate the movement he wanted us to make with our feet and legs. He wanted them to be as dexterous as his hands and arms, although he never said so directly. The clearest analogy he drew was with an elephant's trunk; our legs were supposed to look flexible, even boneless, but at the same time to maintain their control and strength just as an elephant's trunk does.

When it was time to move away from the barre to the center of the floor, the class, perhaps forty strong (about half the Company), divided into two groups, with the more experienced dancers going to the front of each group. The groups then took turns occupying the entire floor for two or three minutes, in four or five rows of four or five dancers each. Balanchine took up a position in front of the class, walking from side to side to get a better view of everyone, giving corrections as he went. He might concentrate briefly on one dancer, bending over slightly for a better view of the feet. If he had to reposition a part of the body, he did so. If he could correct verbally, he did, but if that did not work he demonstrated the step himself. Many of the subtleties that were so hard to comprehend from verbal instructions alone were plainly visible when he moved. You could learn much just by watching him. He always put us to shame with his grace and finesse. Never have I seen *any* dancer move as beautifully as Balanchine. The quality of movement that he had in every type of dance was extraordinary. But sharp eyes and ears were constantly needed to absorb everything there was to learn.

Class usually ended a little late, around 12:10 or 12:20 P.M., for Balanchine was not a clock-watcher. If he became involved working on a particular point, he wasn't going to stop simply because the clock said class was over. The appearance of a ballet mistress, or gentle prompting from her, sometimes reminded him that he was running into rehearsal time and had better end class. He would always end proceedings a little suddenly, with a "that's enough" accompanied by a sweeping gesture. Brief but appreciative applause would follow for a few seconds—a practice he didn't like but was never able to stop.

Balanchine's classes took place six days a week. With renewed resolve, I attended them regularly. Gradually I overcame my fears and improved my ability to listen to and retain Balanchine's words. My powers of observation also increased, and I became more open to ideas or information about ballet, regardless of the source. I was troubled, however, to find that the few steps at which I had excelled at SAB continued to deteriorate. Balanchine gave few big jumps in class, but when he did give them my tried-and-true techniques for bounding as high as anyone were taken from me: Balanchine wouldn't allow

1

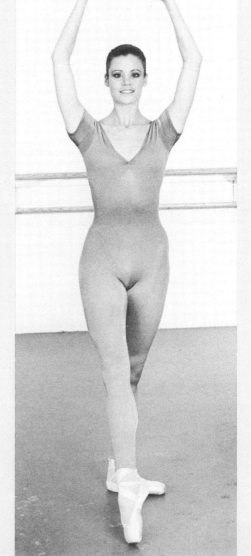

2

1 This is the tendu front position. Notice that the hips and shoulders are even (one not higher than the other) and facing squarely front. The extended leg is straight with the tip of the toes resting lightly on the floor.

2 Here you see the correct tendu position shown facing straight front (*en face*) with the toes of the extended foot in line with the center of my body (in line with the middle of the standing foot). The foot must always reach the same position each time a tendu is done. A common mistake is to extend the foot in line with the heel of the standing leg. Less common but also incorrect is "overcrossing," or extending the foot and leg past the center of the body so they are more in line with the toes of the standing leg.

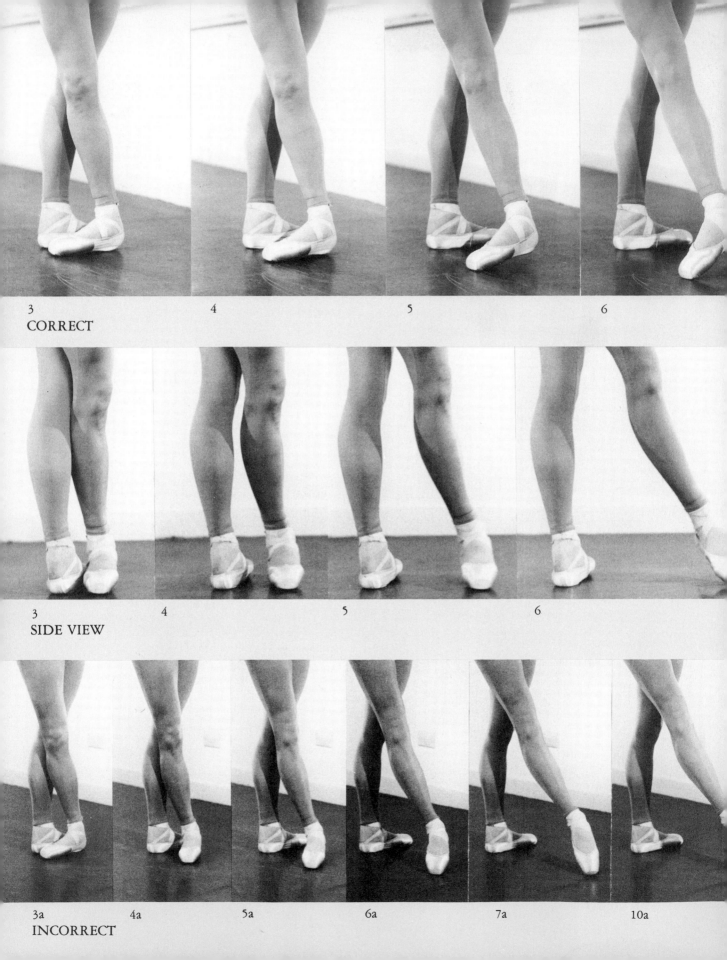

3　　　　　　　4　　　　　　　5　　　　　　　6

CORRECT

3　　　　　　　4　　　　　　　5　　　　　　　6

SIDE VIEW

3a　　　　4a　　　　5a　　　　6a　　　　7a　　　　10a

INCORRECT

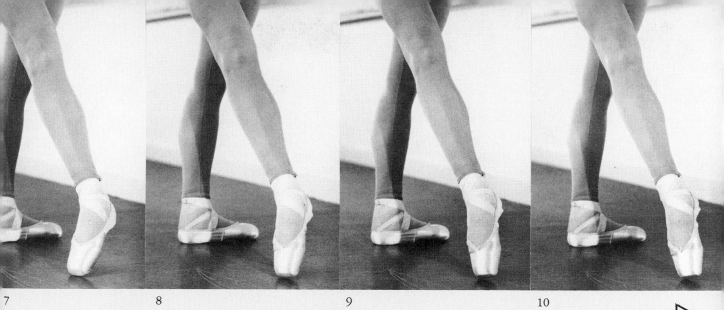

7   8   9   10   ▷

3   Tendus are usually done from fifth position, in which the feet are as close together as possible, with the heel of one foot directly in line with the tips of the toes of the other. The weight is centered on the ball of each foot although both feet remain flat on the floor.

4   The first movement of the working leg toward the tendu position is made by shifting the weight onto the standing leg and guiding the inner thigh and heel of the working foot forward while keeping the toes pulled back. This maintains the turnout of both the foot and the leg. If the dancer does not lead with the heel, the toes slip forward, as shown in 4a, causing the leg to turn in. But she must not bear weight on the moving foot or use the floor to hold the toes back as the working leg moves to tendu. It must be done with muscular strength so the contact with the floor is very light. (Each incorrect picture, followed by the letter "a", should be viewed in comparison with the correct picture of the same number throughout.)

5 and 6   As the leg moves quickly and smoothly toward tendu, the heel continues to guide the leg straight forward and the toes begin to point as the leg moves farther away from fifth position. There is a slight acceleration of the leg as it moves through these in-between positions. The dancer must *create* the momentum needed to do this, rather than *collect* it, as the leg moves outward. The foot must continue to make the necessary adjustments as it points to reach the proper extended position. The dancer must not allow the leg to move slightly to the side when she extends it because this would result in having the toes in line with the standing heel, rather than in line with the middle of the foot or body. Pictures 5a, 6a, and 7a show how turned-in the leg and foot become if the toes lead the leg out of fifth position instead of the heel.

7–9   The leg is barely moving forward; the primary visible movement is that of the toes pointing in toward the final tendu position. Because the leg has moved swiftly (even at a slow tempo) through the previous in-between positions, the dancer must slow the forward movement of the leg at the last moment so the foot will not lift off the floor. A very common mistake is to lift the foot slightly off the floor and then replace it on the floor in tendu.

10   By slowing the leg at the last moment, you not only arrive clearly and beautifully in tendu but you train yourself to stop the movement of the leg suddenly yet smoothly. That way the dancer is in control: she is not overpowered by the momentum created by the opening of the leg. Dancers are often tempted to put weight on the foot in tendu to make the foot look more pointed and/or to stop the forward movement of the leg. There should be no weight on the foot in tendu; it should touch the floor only lightly. In 10a you can see that the leg remains turned-in if the toes have led out of fifth position.

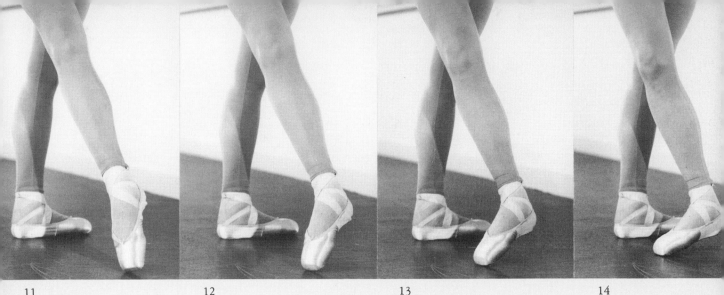

| 11 | 12 | 13 | 14 |

CORRECT

11   Once in tendu, the leg should remain there for an instant before starting back to fifth position. During that instant, the tension must remain in foot and leg. There must be no relaxation of the muscles at any time.

12 and 13   The return to fifth position is the exact opposite of the opening. Just as the toes arrive last in the tendu position, they must leave first. They quickly pull back toward the standing heel, while the heel of the working foot pushes forward. In 12a and 13a, you can see that the heel is leading the foot and leg back toward fifth, again making the leg turn in.

14 and 15   Once the working foot is parallel to the standing foot, the entire leg begins to move back toward fifth position. 14a shows the incorrect movement of the heel as it touches the standing foot, leaving the toes well out of fifth position. They then have to make a fanning movement (15a through 19a) to reach fifth position, which makes the return so slow and jerky it becomes an inefficient way to move back to fifth position.

16 and 17   As the working leg nears fifth position, many dancers, including myself, find it impossible to keep our knees entirely straight, unless we change the position of some part of our body. The position of the hips should not change, for they provide the support for standing up securely, but Balanchine accepted a slight bending of the working knee as long as it occurred as late as possible and straightened again as early as possible. Given this bit of leeway, dancers often start bending the knee as soon as the toes start pulling back toward fifth position. Balanchine did *not* condone that.

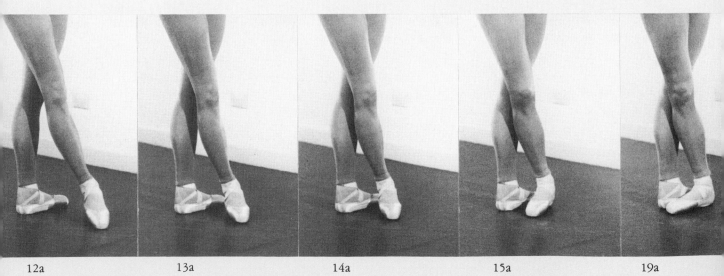

| 12a | 13a | 14a | 15a | 19a |

INCORRECT

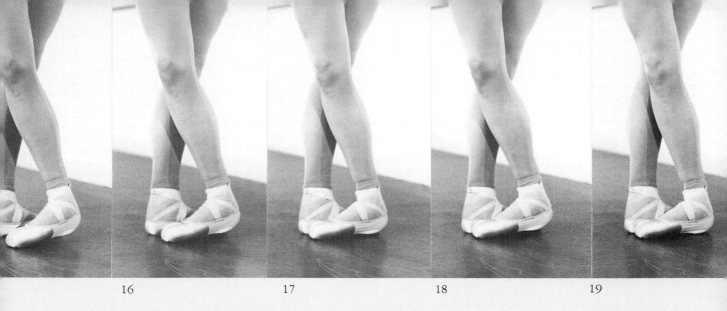

16   17   18   19

18 and 19 Just before the foot arrives in fifth position, the movement must slow down so the working foot does not bang into the other foot. The working foot must be *placed* in fifth position, and the knee straightened to reach the end of the battement tendu. When the working leg is back in fifth position, most of one's weight is still on the standing leg, although the working foot is flat on the floor. This makes it easier to start the next tendu quickly. (Any shifting of the weight back and forth between each tendu would be too time-consuming.) The full weight is transferred to the leg that has just returned to fifth position only if one is going to stand on it while the other leg is in tendu. If a series of tendus is being done, there is a slight pause (without relaxing) in fifth position before the leg starts moving again. The tendus should not be run together, especially if done at a slow or medium tempo. The separation between the outward and inward movements should be clearly visible. When the tempo becomes very fast, it is impossible to stop the movement without going off the music, but the effort should still be made to do so. This effort maintains the proper line and tension of the leg and continues to develop speed and strength in the leg.

20

21

20 and 21 This is the tendu back position, the only direction that requires a shift in the position of the hips. As the leg extends, the hips twist (the degree of this twist depends on the dancer's turnout) in the direction of the moving leg to a more open position while the rest of the upper body remains still. This is to make sure the working leg is turned out when it is directly in line with the center of one's body (21). If the hips did not open at all, the only way the leg could remain turned out would be to extend the leg in line with the standing heel, or even beyond, which Balanchine would not accept.

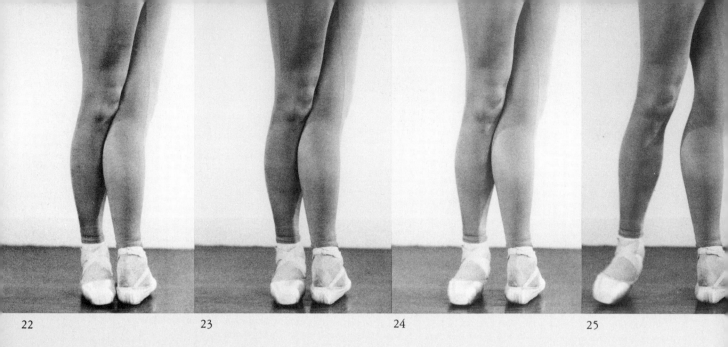

22   23   24   25

22   When standing in fifth position before tendu back, the shoulders, hips, and the weight distribution are the same as for tendu front.

23   The timing for tendu back is exactly like tendu front, but here the toes are the first part of the foot to move out of fifth position. One must not lead with the heel, or the leg will immediately turn in.

24 and 25   The toes continue to lead the leg out of fifth position and the hips begin to twist open. If, as the hips open, the standing leg has to turn in slightly to avoid twisting the knee, that is acceptable, for it is more important that the working leg be fully turned out.

26–28   The toes are pointing and pulling in toward the final tendu back position.

29   30   31

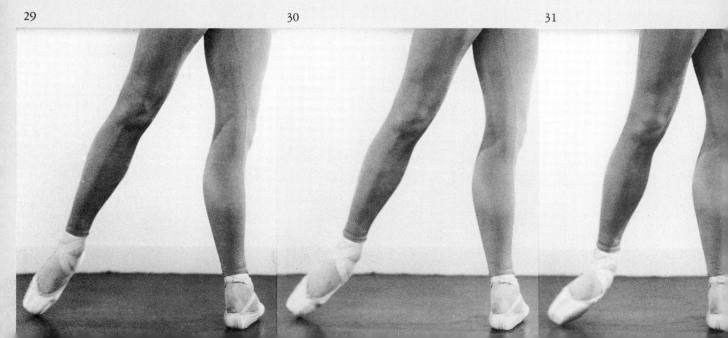

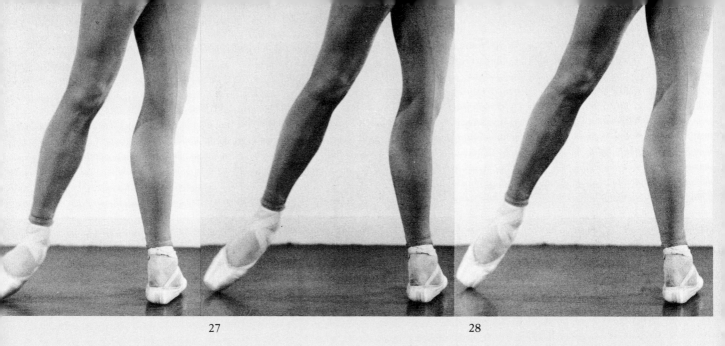

27   28

29   The final tendu position has been reached, and the leg pauses there for a moment before moving back to fifth position.

30 and 31   The heel leads the foot and leg back toward fifth position. If the toes lead, the leg will be turned in.

32–34   As the leg nears fifth position, a knee has to bend to accommodate the closing leg. Unlike tendu front, it is the standing knee that bends slightly, but, as in tendu front, this bending must be minimized.

35 and 36   As the leg returns to fifth position, the heel and toe of the working foot should meet the standing foot at the same time. The foot should be *placed* in fifth position. The hips return to their square position if no more tendus back are going to be done, otherwise the hips remain open until the end of the series.

33   34   35   36

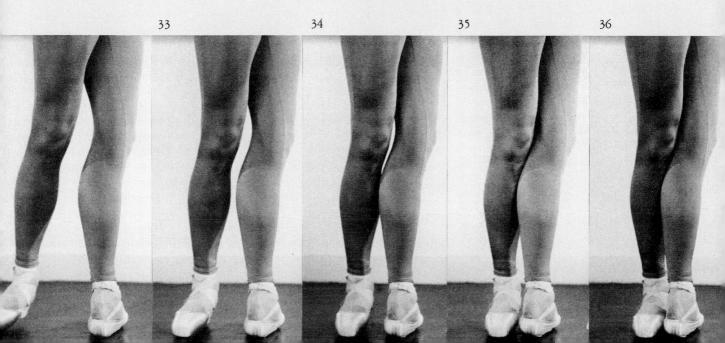

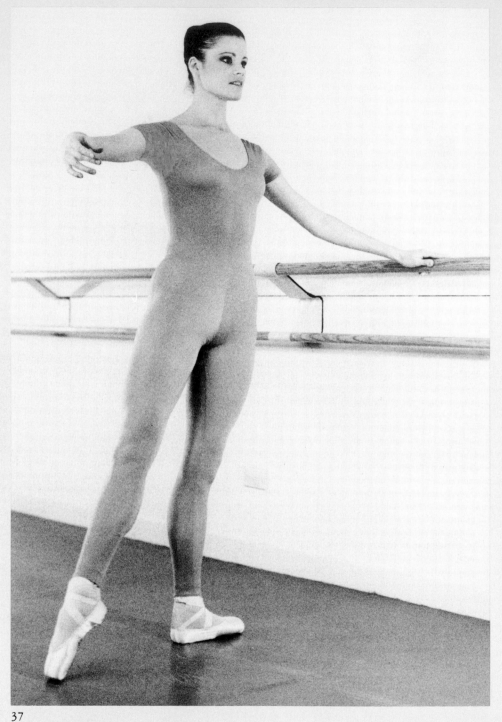

37

37   This is the tendu side position. The extended leg is directly opposite the shoulder and the heel of the standing foot, with the hips squarely facing front. Just as in tendu front and back, there is only one correct tendu side position. The foot should not be in front or in back of that point. As the working leg moves in and out of fifth position, the heel must be in line with or slightly in front of the toes, *never* behind the toes. The leg must move in a straight line to tendu side. There should be no circular movement of the leg.

38 Here you can see (from the lines drawn by the light on my foot) the pattern described on the floor by *correct* tendus to the front, side, and back.

38

38a This is what happens to the working leg when tendus are done *incorrectly*. In tendu front the line moves on the diagonal toward the camera, which means the tendu did not end at a point directly in front of the center of my body. In tendu side, as the leg closes to fifth position with the right leg back, the leg describes an arc on the floor, the foot turns in as it nears fifth position and then readjusts to a turned-out position once it is next to the standing foot. As the leg moves to tendu back, it again does not go to the correct tendu position, but moves out to the side.

38a

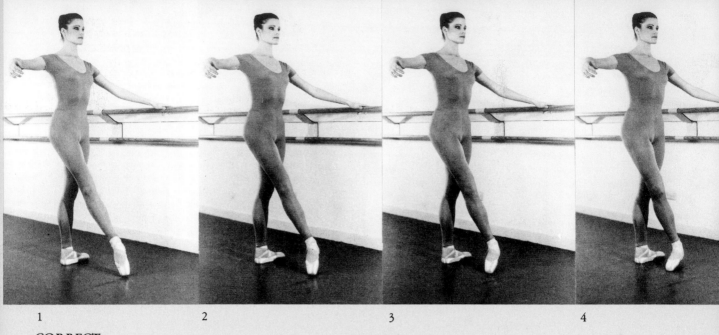

1   2   3   4

CORRECT

BATTEMENT TENDU PLIÉ

1-3   From the tendu front position, the front foot and leg begin to move to fifth position as if doing a simple tendu. Both knees are still straight.

2a   Here, the closing to fifth position in tendu plié begins incorrectly because the moment the toes of the front foot begin to be pulled back toward fifth position, both knees begin to bend.

4   As the leg is about halfway between tendu front and fifth position, the knees begin to bend. The timing so far has been the same as in a simple tendu. It is much easier to move a straight leg quickly. Notice how much closer the front leg is to fifth position than in the related picture (4a). The unattractive in-between positions have also been minimized by keeping the leg straight for as long as possible.

INCORRECT

1a   2a   3a   4a

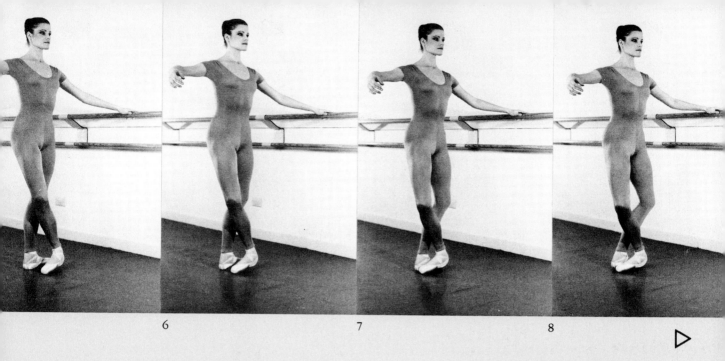

6   7   8   ▷

5 and 6   Now you can see both knees beginning to bend as the foot slows to close in fifth position. The leg must *not* reach fifth position before both knees have started to bend. If this happens, it is a simple tendu with demi-plié added at the end: it is not a tendu plié.

5a and 6a   In comparison to pictures 5 and 6, the front leg is still very far from fifth position. The heel is also further off the floor.

7 and 8   The feet are now in fifth position, and the demi-plié continues downward, with the movement slowing only at the low point of the demi-plié. The body's weight should be evenly distributed on the balls of both feet even though both feet are flat on the floor; the tendency is to put weight more on the heels. The knees should be bending directly over the toes.

7a and 8a   The working, or front, leg is still slowly closing to fifth position, and the heel of the working leg is very far off the floor. The working foot does not even bear weight until 9a.

6a   7a   8a   ▷

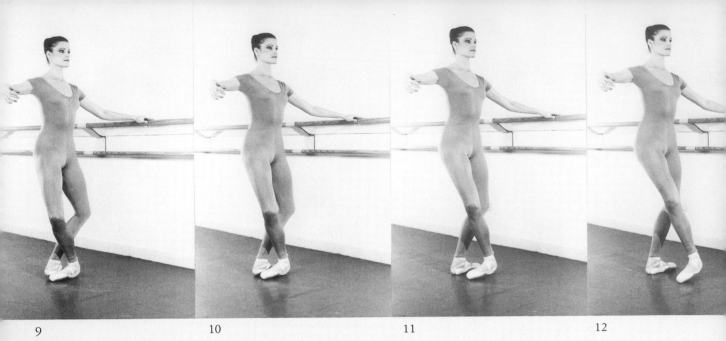

9	10	11	12

CORRECT

9 and 10   After reaching the lowest point of the demi-plié in 9 (which is just before the heels leave the floor, a point that is determined by the amount of stretch in the dancer's calves and Achilles tendons) the dancer must—without stopping—begin to straighten both knees before the working leg starts to move out of fifth position.

9a and 10a   The leg is beginning to move out of fifth position before the knees have straightened at all.

11   It is very hard to define the exact position the legs are in when the working foot begins to move out of fifth position, but it is roughly halfway between the lowest point in the demi-plié (9) and fifth position with straight knees (not shown). In other words, the legs must not be completely straight before the foot begins to extend toward the tendu position.

11a–13a   Both legs are still quite bent even though the working leg is moving out toward the tendu position.

INCORRECT

9a	10a	11a	12a

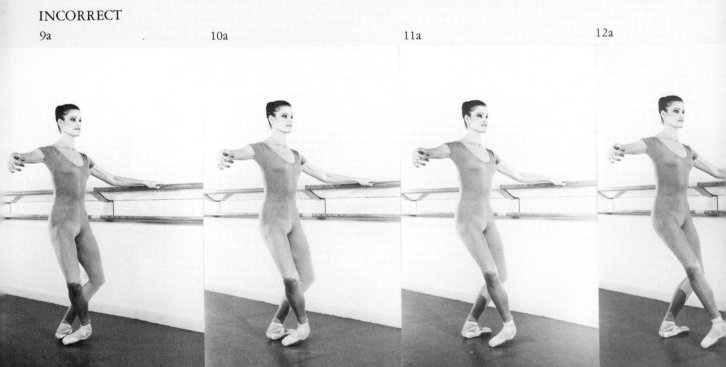

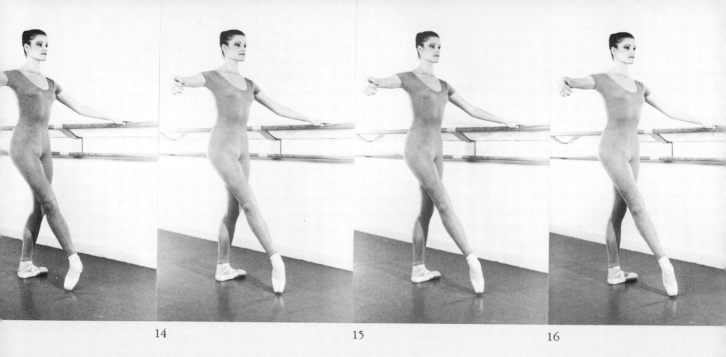

14	15	16

12-14   Both legs are continuing to straighten as the working leg moves toward the tendu position. As in a simple tendu, as little time as possible is spent in these in-between positions. By 14, the legs are almost completely straight.

15 and 16   Both legs straighten at the same moment as the working leg continues toward the tendu position, the movement of the legs once again resembles that of a simple tendu. The working leg slows its forward movement as the toes point and the leg arrives in the tendu position. By practicing tendu plié in this manner, one develops smooth and efficient landings and takeoffs for jumps and relevés on pointe or half-pointe.

14a and 15a   Compare these positions with the positions in 14 and 15. In 14a, although the working leg is almost straight, the standing leg has barely straightened at all. In 15a, the working leg is straight and the toes are fully pointed, even though the standing leg is still bent. One's balance is much more secure the sooner one stands on a straight leg.

16a   Only at this moment are both knees straight in this example of an incorrect tendu plié.

14a	15a	16a

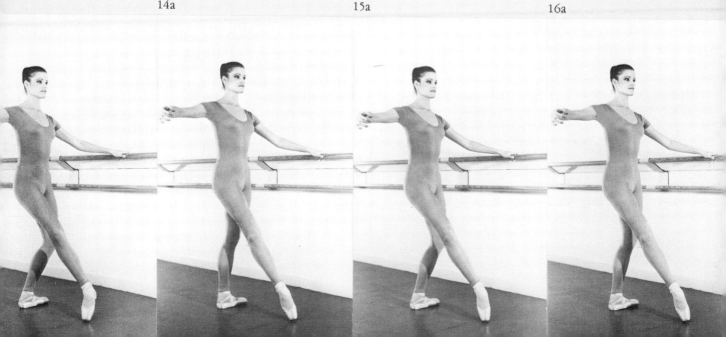

A

B

BATTEMENT FONDU À TERRE (FRONT)

Battement fondu is an exercise to develop coordination of the legs as they bend and straighten; smooth relevés and soft, controlled landings and takeoffs for jumps; and the presentation of the working leg and foot. The most unusual aspect of this step as taught by Balanchine is the manner in which the working foot is presented. Of special interest are the timing and coordination of the movements and the pattern described by the working leg in the air. This pattern may be seen by studying the design made by the light attached to my foot in the strobe photographs. (As a result of the movement caused by the plié in the middle of the step, my upper body is blurred in these pictures.)

A   Here is a fondu as taught by Balanchine. Notice what appears to be an elliptical pattern made by the light on my foot. When the working foot and leg move in this way, the movement becomes much fuller and gives an appearance of lightness, and the leg looks as if it were boneless—"like an elephant's trunk," as Balanchine used to say. As explained in the captions to this sequence, the elliptical pattern, together with the varying speeds of the movements, serves to draw attention to the presentation of the foot and leg.

B   This shows a more conventional fondu à terre. The movement is smaller and less interesting than the fondu shown in A. This is because the foot and knee move back and forth in one plane rather than in an elliptical pattern. This type of fondu is usually done at an even tempo, adding to the flatness of the step. The eye is not drawn to any particular part of the movement.

Sequence photographs 1 through 19 show the mechanics of the fondu à terre. The elliptical pattern made by the working foot (as shown in A) is created primarily by the portion of the movement pictured in 12 through 19. (The knee makes a similar elliptical pattern, though smaller, when a fondu is done in this manner).

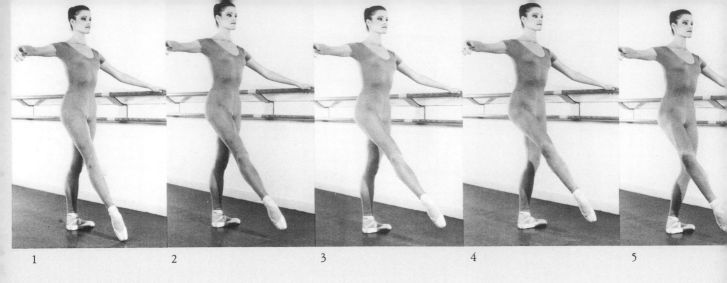

1	2	3	4	5

1   This is the starting (and ending) position of the fondu. The working leg is in the tendu position and the standing leg is straight. Fondu can be done to the front (as shown here), side, or back. There should be a momentary pause in the tendu position between each fondu.

2 and 3   The working leg lifts slightly off the ground to begin the fondu. Once it leaves the ground, the leg never stops moving, although it moves faster through some positions than others.

4   Both knees begin to bend simultaneously as the working leg starts to move back toward the standing leg.

5–7   Both knees continue to bend as the working foot (which remains pointed throughout the exercise) is directed toward the front of the ankle of the standing leg (the coupé front position). There is a slight acceleration through the positions shown in 4 through 7. As the knee of the standing leg bends, it should be directly over the center of the standing foot, and the knee of the working leg should be brought back so that the leg is fully turned out. The toes of the working foot should be pulled back as the heel is pushed forward. By drawing the working foot and knee back in this manner, the elliptical movement of the leg begins.

8 and 9   The movement of the working leg slows as it nears the coupé front position (which is shown in 9), making possible a full, deep demi-plié. In coupé, the toes should be just off the floor and almost touching the standing foot. The heel of the working foot should never touch or come closer to the standing leg than the toes of the working foot.

11	12	13	14	15

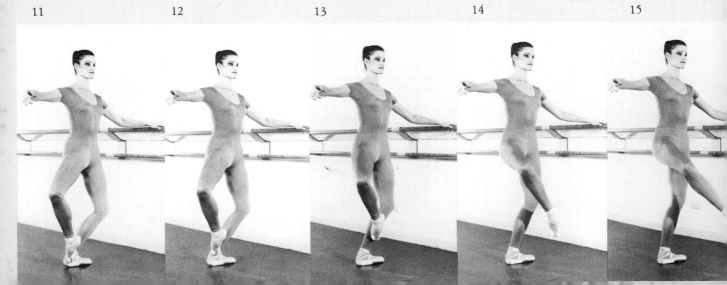

7   8   9   10

10–12   The standing leg begins to straighten as the pointed foot starts to move up the *front* of the standing leg (it should not move up the side of the calf).

13–15   When the toes of the working foot reach the midcalf of the standing leg (13), the pointed foot begins to move away from the standing leg (14) and the knee of the standing leg continues to straighten. The foot, not the knee, must lead this movement; otherwise the leg will turn in. Both legs continue to straighten, but the working leg does not move directly toward the floor as it extends. It continues to open in a forward direction. There should be a noticeable acceleration through the positions shown in 12 through 15 as these awkward-looking positions must be minimized, just as in the tendu.

16   At this point the standing leg is almost straight, while the working leg is bent and still well off the floor. The movement of the working leg begins to slow down again as the foot and leg move toward the floor. This draws attention to the presentation and placement of the foot on the floor as shown in 17 through 19. Every effort should be made to turn out the legs, especially the working leg, as much as possible, during the final extension.

17   The knee of the working leg is straight (the foot is about three or four inches off the floor).

18 and 19   The straight, extended leg moves deliberately toward the floor, and the toes are *placed* lightly on the floor in the tendu position. The movement of the foot must not stop simply because the foot has hit the floor. The movement must be consciously controlled at all times.

17   18   19

D

BATTEMENT FONDU EN L'AIR (FRONT)

Fondu en l'air is a variation of fondu à terre. The working leg may be raised to any height but Balanchine most often asked that the working foot be a half inch off the floor, or that the leg be at a 45° or 90° angle. No matter how high we raised our working leg, Balanchine wanted us to be conscious of its exact level. By asking us to make easily recognizable angles, such as 45° and 90°, he made it easier for us to practice placement in a specific place time after time.

The mechanics of the fondu just off the floor are the same as fondu à terre. Once the leg is raised more than four inches off the floor, however, the mechanics at the beginning and end of the fondu differ from those of the fondu à terre (though the middle part of both exercises is the same).

C   This strobe photograph shows a fondu en l'air as taught by Balanchine. Although the design made by the light on my foot is slightly different from that made in the fondu à terre, it is still elliptical.

D   This is a more conventional fondu en l'air. Notice how the foot follows the same path whether it is being raised or lowered.

Sequence photographs 1 through 19 show a fondu en l'air at an angle slightly less than 90°.

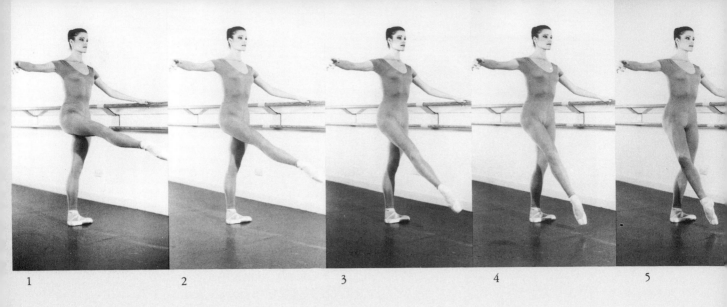

1   2   3   4   5

1   This is the beginning of the fondu en l'air. Both legs are straight and well turned out.

2–4   The working leg begins to lower. Neither knee has begun to bend in 2 and 3. (In a conventional fondu en l'air, both knees would begin to bend the moment the working leg starts to move toward the floor.) The working leg moves quickly through these positions, slowing down only when it is three or four inches off the floor (4). Only then do both knees begin to bend.

5–14   These photographs correspond to photographs 5 through 13 of the fondu à terre. The mechanics and the timing of the movements are exactly the same as in fondu à terre.

15 and 16   The standing leg continues to straighten and the working leg to lift as the pointed foot moves away from the standing leg. The working leg is moving quickly through these positions. A com-

11   12   13   14   15

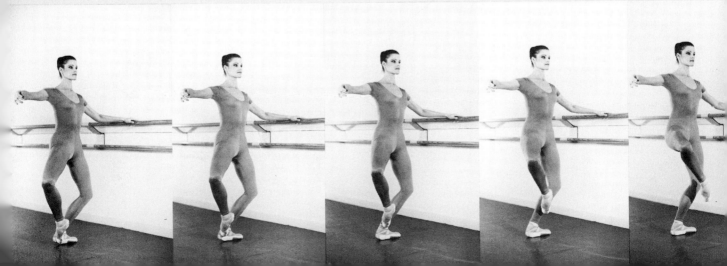

7   8   9   10

mon error is to remain in demi-plié on the standing leg as the working leg lifts, and to straighten the standing leg only as the working leg nears its final position (both legs then straighten simultaneously).

17 The standing leg is now virtually straight, and the working leg is still bent. The movement of the working leg slows down again as it straightens and nears its final position (19).

18 The standing leg is now completely straight. As the working leg straightens, an extra effort should be made to turn it out. At this point, Balanchine, emphasizing the need for an extra effort to turn out the leg at the end of the movement, would often say, "You must be able to balance a glass of water on your foot."

19 The fondu is completed when the working leg becomes completely straight.

17   18   19

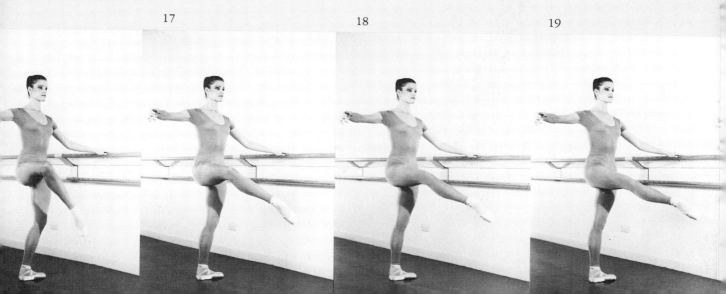

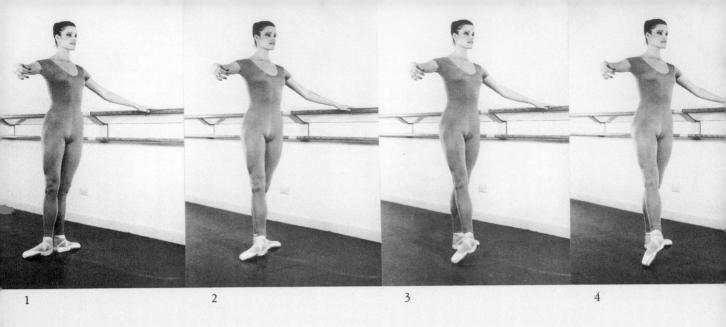

1	2	3	4

ROND DE JAMBE À TERRE EN DEHORS (CLOCKWISE)

1 Rond de jambe begins in first position. (If a series of ronds de jambe is being done, the working leg passes through first position without stopping.)

2 As the working leg moves out of first position, the heel of the working foot guides the foot and leg forward. The toes should not lead the leg out of first position, as this causes the leg to turn in. The foot must not move toward the tendu front position, except when changing directions. (See captions 15 and 16.)

3 The leg is starting to move to the side, initiating the circular movement from the hip.

4 and 5 As the leg continues to the side, the foot begins to point more and more. During the entire rond de jambe, the foot must continually try to point as much as possible, but the amount it is able to point depends on how far the leg is extended to the side.

6 and 7 The foot is very close to being fully pointed, and the leg is well turned out.

8 Now the foot is completely pointed as the leg passes through the tendu side position. There are no pauses anywhere in the rond de jambe.

9	10	11	12

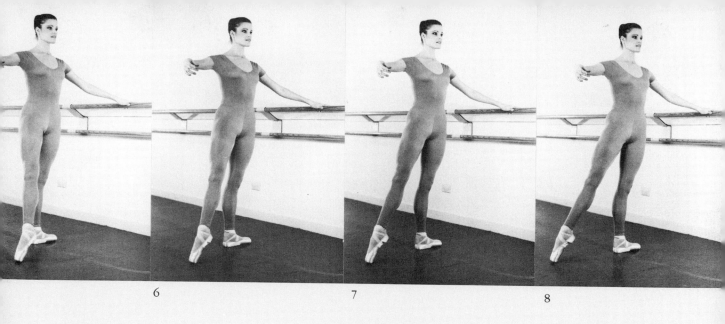

6   7   8

9 and 10 As the working leg continues on its circular path, the foot becomes less pointed again. The leg must continue to stay turned out, and the hips must remain squarely front. At no point in the rond de jambe do the hips open, as they do in tendu back. The more the leg moves toward the back, the greater the tendency to allow it to turn in. This must be avoided.

11 Notice how the heel is still leading as the foot and leg begin to return to first position. The leg and foot must not reach a full tendu back position.

12–14 As the foot returns to first position or passes through it, one must be careful not to roll in on the working foot. The sole of the foot must maintain contact with the floor, as it passes through first position.

15 and 16 The circular movement of the working leg from the hip joint is now completed. This represents one rond de jambe. There should be no feeling of the leg's swinging during this movement. It must be guided in an even and continuous movement the entire time, unless there is a change of direction (in which case the leg moves to the tendu front position and pauses a moment before reversing direction). To understand how a rond de jambe en dedans (counterclockwise) is done, the sequence can be followed in reverse order.

14   15   16

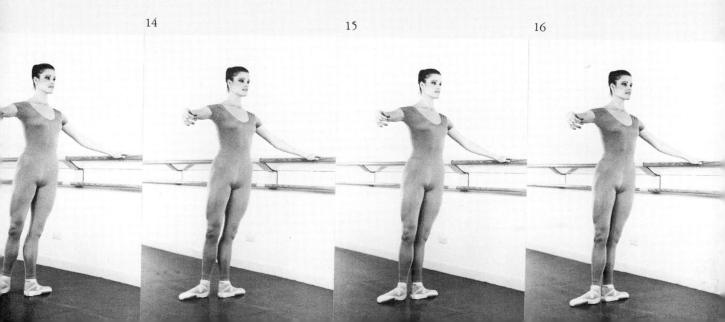

17 This shows a rond de jambe done at a normal tempo, as explained in the sequence photographs. Notice the elliptical pattern drawn on the floor by the toes.

18   This shows a rond de jambe done at a very fast tempo. In order to fit the movement to the tempo, the amount of rotation from the hip decreases. The leg still extends fully to the side but moves less to the front and back, which creates a circular, rather than elliptical, pattern on the floor.

18a   Here the rond de jambe is done incorrectly. The leg goes to the full tendu front and back positions. When this happens, the leg usually swings from front to back. It does not create the feeling of a guided circular movement from the hip. Notice the crescent-shaped pattern the foot makes on the floor.

18a

GRAND ROND DE JAMBE JETÉ (EN DEHORS)

19   This shows a different kind of circular rotation of the hip. The path of the leg is the same as in the rond de jambe à terre, except it is done in the air. The working leg can begin the movement from the tendu back position (as shown here) or from first position. After the leg brushes through first position, it begins to open toward the side and at the same time to lift off the ground. The leg then swings in a circular pattern through à la seconde (a tendu side position in the air) toward the back. It does not return to the tendu back position but should extend only as far to the back as in rond de jambe à terre. The leg brushes through first position and continues without stopping if a series of ronds de jambe is being done. If, however, there is to be a change in direction, the foot brushes through first position to the tendu front position where it pauses for a moment before reversing direction. The circular movement should be continuous but, because of the upward thrust (the jeté) of the leg, the first half of the movement is faster than the second.

   The upper body should remain as still as possible. Ideally it should not rock back and forth. Dancers often fail to move their working leg past the à la seconde position; but when they do move past that side position, they often either allow the leg to turn in radically or they lean very far forward to make it easier to move the leg to the back.

us to stiffen our arms and pump them up and down just before taking off in order to gain a little extra elevation, as so many male virtuoso dancers from other companies do. He found such movements particularly objectionable when the jumps came one after another. Nor would he accept thumping landings. A favorite trick of his was to make us practice jumps with our arms in a position that would make them useless for gaining elevation. We had to work on smooth, deep "juicy"—to use one of Balanchine's favorite words—pliés before and after each jump, as well as soft landings that wouldn't "break eggs." In effect, Balanchine took my jump away from me and wouldn't let me have it back until I mastered a more refined form.

My turns, such as they were, also seemed to disappear. At SAB we had been allowed leisurely preparations for turns, thereby increasing the chances of their being executed properly. Balanchine never let us "sit" in a preparation, and bending the back leg at any point in the preparation was forbidden. The leg could bend only when it left the floor. The arms had to be pulled in toward the body in a more direct way than I had been taught. Although I tried to assimilate his new ideas on turns, there was so little time to think before taking off for the turn that I couldn't coordinate my body well enough to execute controlled pirouettes. It was easy for me to believe that my turns were deteriorating, because they rarely worked.

Other elements of my technique suffered a similar fate. Struggling as I was to assert myself and searching for my identity as a dancer, it took a mighty act of faith in the master's teachings to give up so many of my comfortable old habits. But Balanchine held the keys to the kingdom. All knowledge, all power was his and, as I saw it, I had no choice but to place all my faith and trust in him.

I was perplexed to see that many others did not share my faith. Or were they using different means to achieve their ends? About half the Company didn't take Company class. Perhaps some of them had long since made up their minds that further progress was impossible. Others undoubtedly were sparing their bodies for the evening's performance.

More puzzling than these clear-cut cases were those dancers who seemed to ignore, or even openly oppose, much of Balanchine's teachings and yet remained in his good graces. There were others who took his class and tried their hardest to put what he said into practice but who didn't necessarily get the best roles or advance in the hierarchy. What were Balanchine's criteria? Where did the path to success lie? I looked to the principal dancers for clues. I found in Melissa Hayden a dancer with energy and fire, in Violette Verdy a dancer with beautiful turnout and great musicality, and in Allegra Kent a delicate yet strong dancer with a mysterious and magnetic stage presence. Yet none of these ballerinas was Balanchine's favorite, and I could not understand why. I did not yet appreciate how much Balanchine valued individuality and how ready he was to overlook shortcomings, provided he received enough in return.

Suzanne Farrell was his favorite and she broke the rules both on the stage and, more surprisingly, in class. She was giving Balanchine a great deal in return and at the same time breaking new ground. I am certain that Balanchine learned from her even as she learned from him, but that, too, was beyond my understanding at the time.

So I asked myself what it was in a dancer that truly inspired him? As far as I could see, the few that found favor seemed to grasp the spirit of his laws while violating the letter.

It seemed to be in my nature to want to obey the letter of the law; I believed strongly that every dancer should truly earn whatever he or she was given. I therefore resolved to learn as much as I could from his classes and his choreography—I couldn't be happy with anything less than a strong technique—and then dance as well as was humanly possible.

It seemed that I would have to pursue two parallel careers, hoping that if my courage and body didn't fail me, the success I was determined to have in Balanchine's class would bring success in the greater battle for the best roles. I would pour myself—body, mind, and spirit—into those daily lessons and try each day to come away with more, more, more. Nothing would divert my attention or weaken my resolve.

The long days, filled with Balanchine's classes, constant rehearsals, and nightly performances of sometimes two and even three ballets, eventually took their toll, especially on my ankles, which suffered from chronic tendonitis. I was only just beginning to realize that my body was still not well aligned: I had a bit of a swayback and my feet still rolled in, although I was fighting to conquer that problem. The connection between my sore ankles and my swayback and rolled-in feet, however, still escaped me. I also wore old toe shoes that didn't give me adequate support, placing undue strain on my tendons. I did that in an effort to please Balanchine, who often scolded the girls for wearing new shoes in performance, because of the noise they made. In addition, I failed to warm up well before rehearsals and performance, and that was a sure road to both tendonitis and other serious injuries.

At that time, the Company had only one general physician, who was not always available and usually attended to illnesses rather than injuries. He was an elderly gentleman, inclined to have little memory lapses that shattered our confidence in him. We had no physical therapist or Company orthopedic surgeon, as we have today. From time to time, I sought advice from orthopedic surgeons who didn't hesitate to give me cortisone injections or to put me on Butazolidin for weeks at a time, without warning me of the possible harmful side effects.

My repertory of home remedies was decidedly limited. Moist heat was the treatment I used most frequently. I had never heard about alternating hot and cold treatments. I don't even believe I used ice, today's most favored treatment for the majority of injuries, especially tendonitis. My first trips to the masseur, chiropractor, acupuncturist, and physical therapist were years away, and sports medicine, if it even existed at the time, was generally unknown to dancers.

One day I overheard Melissa Hayden say that dancers had to take care of injuries right away before they developed into something serious. That made a strong impression on me, and whenever I had a new injury I heeded her words and rested completely for a few days, not even doing general conditioning exercises. Then, in my eagerness, I would come back too abruptly and put too much stress on my still weak and stiff body. With all the benefits of rest undone, I was again unable to dance, and so the cycle continued until, by the end of my first year and the beginning of the second, I was out much of the time.

Early in 1968, my second year in the Company, Balanchine began giving an extra class on Mondays, our day off. Although the class was open to everyone, it was an option that most found easy to resist, and only the hard core, about twenty of us—mostly women, but dancers from every level—showed up regularly. I know Balanchine was favorably impressed with those who gave up their day off to attend his class; he took it as a sign that we were true believers in what he was trying to teach. It never occurred to me to appreciate the fact that he was giving up *his* day off, too.

Classes began at the usual hour, 11:00 A.M., but they frequently went on for two or two and a half hours. I have never learned so much in so little time in my entire life.

These classes came at just the right time for me to derive maximum benefit from them. If they had already existed when I joined the Company, I might have taken them for granted and decided I needed the day off more than anything else. If they had begun much later, I might have been too set in my ways, too dependent on what was comfortable and worked rather than on what was right and looked good. As it turned out, the timing was perfect.

In the crowded conditions of regular Company class, I often felt far removed from what was going on and was rarely certain that what I was doing was absolutely correct. It was not humanly possible for one person to give forty or fifty dancers the kind of personal attention I wanted and needed. I was growing dangerously accustomed to my own vague notions of what Balanchine wanted without always being able to formulate sharp mental images of how I wanted the steps to look. I needed a jolt. Every Monday I got it.

The whole feel of the class was different. To begin with, there was no pianist, and this suited Balanchine, who was often frustrated in his effort to get the pianist to play just what he wanted. Instead of music, we often simply moved to the sounds made by the snapping of his fingers, slapping of his thighs, or his clapping hands, which gave us a loud clear beat to follow. Balanchine occasionally felt that music was appropriate, however, and he would sit down at the piano and play, often choosing music he said had been played on the violin in the ballet classes he took as a boy; or he might play some Fritz Kreisler compositions. You could never predict when he would play, but we always found the music a welcome relief because it provided us with extra energy and inspiration.

Balanchine often gave exercises in odd rhythms. He said he didn't want the music dictating to the dancer, and with that in mind he might give us a combination in five or seven beats when the music was in two or four beats, so that we couldn't rely automatically on the music to tell us, for example, when a series of steps in one direction at the barre had ended and it was time to change directions. These unusual rhythms focused our minds and made us think about what we were doing. A striking example of how he wanted the *dancer* to create the music is the variation in Karin von Aroldingen's regiment in *Union Jack.* The dancing there is so vital and the steps change so often that the music seems varied, too, though it is just the same drumroll played over and over again.

With so few dancers in it, the rehearsal studio, the same one that made me feel claustrophobic six days a week, suddenly seemed huge. What a treat not having to jockey for a spot at the barre and not having to worry about crashing into another dancer after one of the long traveling combinations from one corner of the room to the other. Yet the atmosphere was intimate—there were never any visitors watching—and all of us could hear every word Balanchine uttered. That was important, for in this Monday class he indulged his well-known fondness for puns, anecdotes, and catchy metaphors more than usual. His stories ranged from cooking analogies to thoughts on politics, but they always had a moral that was relevant to what we were practicing.

The effort we expended during each exercise was intense, and as there was rarely a moment's pause between exercises, they were even harder than they might have been. Nothing intruded; no rehearsal or performance required that class end at any particular time. And there was no escape until Balanchine said, "That's enough." If the going got too tough and a dancer entertained any notions of disappearing through the side door, the urge was squelched by the sure knowledge that any absence would be immediately noted.

Where the Monday class differed most from regular Company class was in the motivation of those who attended. Each one of us, whether a corps member, soloist, or principal dancer, was wholly committed and eager to learn. Balanchine appreciated that. He needed to feel that his dancers wanted to learn what he had to teach them, and he was well aware that a number of dancers attended his Company classes simply because they felt they had to; or, worse still, because a rehearsal was scheduled right after class and they found it more convenient to go directly from class into rehearsal.

We were, in fact, so eager to learn, and there was so much time available, that endless repetition of the finest points seemed entirely appropriate, even welcome. I received, as did others, more personal attention in one Monday class than I did in a month of regular classes.

By this time my body was beginning to respond to all the hard work, and it was easy for me to get into a perfect tight fifth position without having to look down at my feet or in the mirror to see if everything was correct. Balanchine constantly told us to memorize the feelings of different positions so that we would not have to look to see what we were doing. I still needed to check certain other positions in the mirror to be sure I wasn't being tricked by my memory, but the images I saw pleased me more and more.

I was happy to see that I was making better use of my turnout. My friend Renée Estopinal had always marveled at my turnout, and she loved to tease me affectionately about it: "When you do a grand plié in second position, you're so turned out I can't tell front from back!"

Turnout was an acquired asset, but I had certain natural assets, too, that I no longer took for granted. When I pointed my feet they looked pointed; when I straightened my knees, they looked straight. Not everyone was so fortunate.

But perhaps my most valuable physical asset was a well-proportioned body. When I had been at SAB, I had envied girls with very long legs. Now I was aware that my legs were well shaped and gave the illusion of length, and I was happy to be spared the awkwardness that often comes with very long legs. My delicate ankles contributed to that illusion but were a mixed blessing, because they proved to be susceptible to injury.

Dancers often gained weight during their early years with the Company, but that had not been a problem for me. I was still thin, although my body was changing and developing, and my figure had improved. Renée said that when I was at the School I had reminded her of a white dandelion: one puff of wind and I would blow away. When I joined the Company, Balanchine, who thought every dancer resembled some nonhuman creature, had often said I looked like a mosquito. Perhaps now he would begin to associate me with a more attractive animal.

With those positive thoughts, I began to believe that if I could only understand and master every last thing Balanchine wanted in tendus (which would take long practice and great physical coordination) I would have the foundation essential for nearly perfect technique. And if my technique was nearly perfect, well . . . at that point I let my imagination run away with itself.

The basics of the simple tendus were already firmly implanted in my muscles, and I accepted as quite natural the extreme degree of precision that Balanchine wanted. By now I could extend either foot directly to the front, side, or back with pinpoint accuracy every time, with minimal mental effort, and without my toes coming off the floor even for a split second in tendu position.

My foot, as it went from fifth position to the tendu position—front, side, or back—remained perfectly turned out. Some dancers, in order to turn out their feet in these in-between positions, resort to digging their toes into the floor. I had been warned against this by Diana Adams when I was at SAB. The "digging"—holding back the toes as the heel thrust forward—created a little resistance that made it easier to keep the foot turned out throughout. But I realized that this resistance slowed the foot down and marred the impression of sharpness and lightness we were all striving to achieve. The

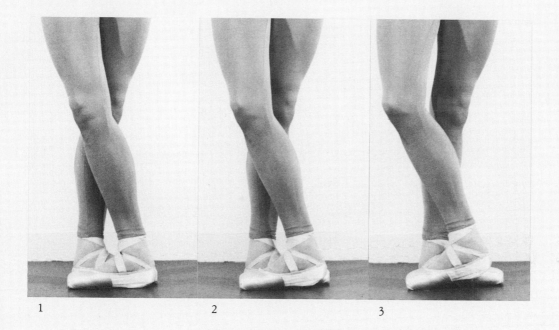

1 2 3

PICKING UP THE FOOT FROM FIFTH POSITION

Balanchine always paid attention to the presentation of the feet and wanted even the smallest movements to look interesting. He taught us a particularly unusual way to pick up the working foot from fifth position, a movement that initiates a number of basic steps, such as passé, developpé, and pas de cheval. This movement, for the most part, is done when the standing foot remains flat on the floor. When the standing foot relevés, the working foot is usually not used in the manner shown in the following sequences.

Frames 1–13 show the front foot, and frames 14–21 the back foot, being picked up from fifth position. These photos give the impression that the movement is slow and deliberate. In fact, an uneducated eye would have trouble following these sequences, which generally take about a second to complete.

1 This shows fifth position with the heel of the front foot directly in front of the toes of the back foot.

2 and 3 As the front foot begins to move out of fifth position, the toes begin to slide along the floor to the side and the knee bends as it too moves to the side, thereby causing the heel of the working foot to lift slightly off the floor. The toes of the working foot, as they move to the side, stay as close to the standing foot as possible.

▷

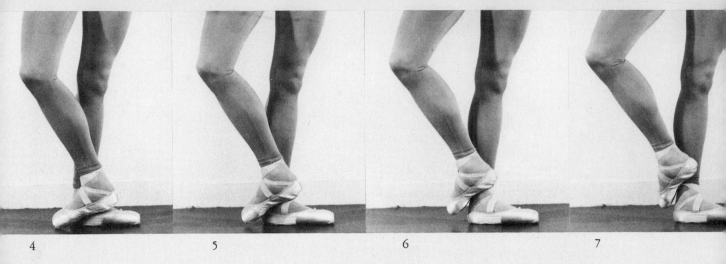

4   5   6   7

4–6   As the toes continue to move to the side, they begin first to wrap around the heel of the standing foot and then to move higher on the ankle. (See below for the side view of this movement.) At the same time, the knee should be pulled back to maintain the greatest possible degree of turnout.

7   The working foot has now reached a position called sur le cou-de-pied. However, the foot should not stop here, or anywhere, but continue lifting.

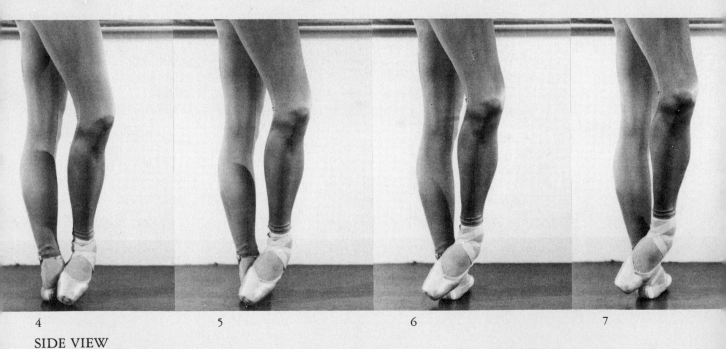

4   5   6   7

SIDE VIEW

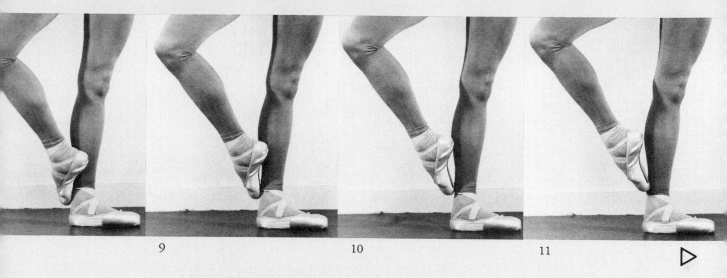

9   10   11   ▷

8-11   As the working foot continues to lift, the toes begin to move from the back of the ankle to the front of the ankle. This must be done within a very small area of the standing leg. The toes of the working foot are just below the standing leg's anklebone when they are in back, and just above the anklebone when they move to the front. The side view shows the toes passing from the back of the ankle to the front.

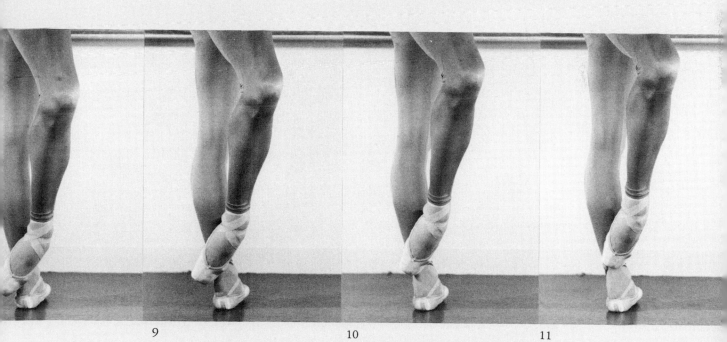

9   10   11

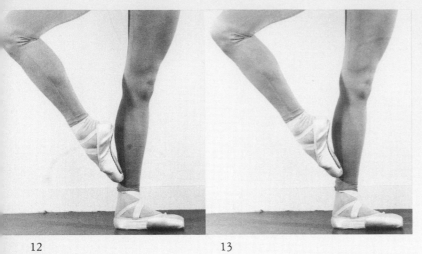

12   13

12-13   The toes are now in front of the standing leg, and the foot is in the proper position to continue moving up the front of the supporting leg to any number of ending positions.

14   15   16   17

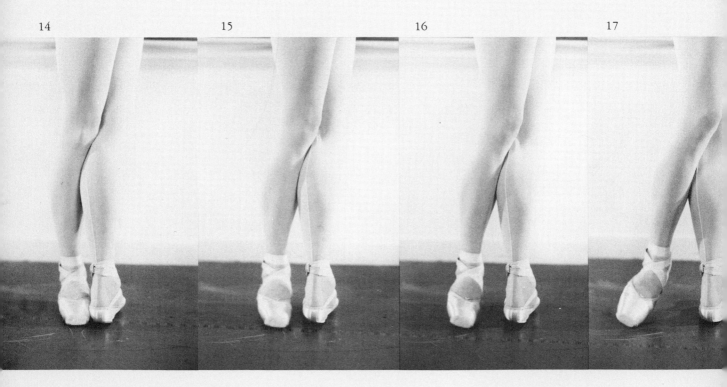

PICKING UP THE BACK FOOT FROM FIFTH POSITION

14 and 15   From fifth position (14) the toes lead the working foot away from the standing foot (15). The working heel must not move away from the standing foot or be lifted before the toes have moved, or the foot will automatically turn in, or look sickled (turned in from the ankle). When this movement is done conventionally, the toes do not lead the heel away from the standing foot but remain right next to the standing leg, as they move upward, causing a turned-in leg or sickled foot in the early part of the movement.

16–18   The foot, led by the toes, continues to move away from fifth position as the knee of the working leg begins to bend.

19–21   The working knee and foot begin to move higher, enabling the foot to point fully (21).

19   20   21

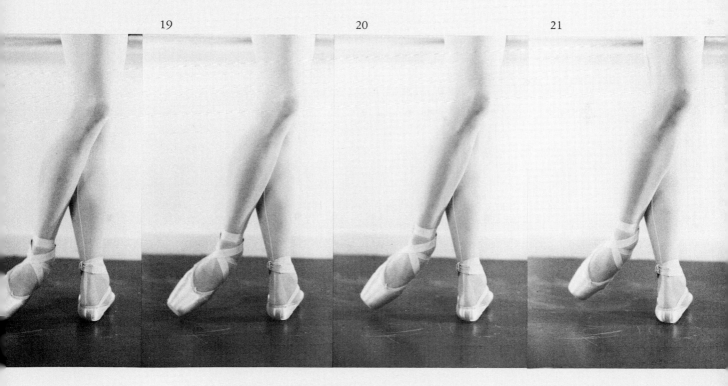

ideal, which I was gradually approaching, was a smooth gliding action with the toes maintaining light contact with the floor.

I was dismayed that in the simple tendus I couldn't keep my leg straight as it moved back to fifth position. In theory, both legs should be perfectly straight all the time. In practice, this wasn't anatomically possible for most people. Balanchine had reluctantly accepted this but wanted us to minimize the length of time and the extent to which the knee was bent. So, my momentarily bent knee having received a pardon, I could still dream of perfection.

Other aspects of the mechanics were easy to understand but rarely easy to execute. In fifth position one's weight is evenly distributed on both feet. At the start of a tendu, the weight had to be transferred to the standing leg; otherwise the working leg couldn't move quickly and freely. The weight remained on the standing leg throughout the series of tendus, even though the working foot returned to fifth position and was flat on the floor. When we had to do tendu front with one leg, followed quickly by a tendu back with the other leg, the weight had to be transferred directly from one leg to the other with no standing in fifth position in between. These weight transfers could be done smoothly only if they became second nature, and tendus were possibly the best opportunity to practice them.

Balanchine was always using analogies to drive home his points. He said that, just as a waiter in a fine restaurant would not bang a dish down on the table in front of a customer, but would place it down beautifully to enhance the presentation of the food, so should we present and place our feet beautifully, carefully, and knowingly. Because the hands and arms are so much easier to control, I thought practicing with my hands would make it easier for me to understand how my legs should move. I asked myself how I would reveal a precious jewel nestled in the palm of my hand, how I would place a fragile crystal glass on a table, and how I would put that glass down without breaking it if it happened to be very hot. Obviously the effects one could produce were innumerable, and, as I experimented, my mind kept coming back to my feet and to those tendus, which were the first and most important exercise in the presentation of the feet. Suddenly, I caught a glimpse of something that had escaped me: that the timing of the step was all-important, that the mechanics of the tendus were nothing without the dynamics. I had to understand the phrasing completely and execute it perfectly.

I tried to understand everything Balanchine said or demonstrated on this subject. The full positions—the fifth position and the tendu position—were emphasized over the interim positions, which, if seen in slow motion or caught in stop action, might appear very awkward. Those split seconds with my knee bent—the cause of so much worry for me—were a case in point. But now I realized that the idea was to leave fifth position and pass swiftly through the interim positions. Then, just before reaching the tendu position, the leg had to be braked, but very smoothly, so that the foot could be carefully directed to the full tendu position without coming off the floor. There the foot paused, pointing elegantly for a brief but precious moment, on display for the eye to behold. Then, the foot went smartly back toward fifth position, with the braking action beginning again just before arriving in fifth position so as to prevent the working foot from slamming against the standing foot. When dancers practiced tendus in this way, they eventually learned to stop and start each tendu (and, in fact, any movement) sharply and clearly, so that an observer could readily perceive the beginning and end of each movement. The natural tendency is to run tendus together, to do them in one long connected series, allowing a certain kind of momentum to take over. When that happens, dancers lose the fine control of their movements that Balanchine wanted us all to have. It was, however, easier to think or talk about that control than to achieve it, especially when the tempo stretched one's speed and strength to the limit.

As I worked more and more diligently on these exercises, I noticed a nearly magical effect: I had the distinct sensation that in these and, astoundingly, in almost all other exercises, at the barre or in the center, I controlled the movement of my legs. It was not the weight, the momentum of the legs, or gravity that controlled the movement. In addition, I found it easier to turn out my feet and legs, and I was more aware of exactly what my feet and legs were doing and exactly where my feet were on the floor at all times. I felt stronger and was excited by my impression that a powerful technique was in the making.

These Monday classes, which continued for about a year, had an everlasting effect on me, and without them I would not be the dancer I am today. They were a unique moment in my career with the New York City Ballet, and I cherish their memory. They came to an end at about the same time Suzanne Farrell left the Company, in 1969.

For about two years after her departure, Balanchine was despondent and seemed to lose interest in everyone and everything. It was as if time stood still while he tried to get over his loss. Dancers kept whatever roles they had, but new roles were taught only out of necessity. How lucky I was to have had two solos to call my own when that period began.

My first year in the Company had been a happy one, despite the frustrations and hard work. I always had a deep feeling of satisfaction as I went home exhausted after a long day, for I had put all my mental and physical energy into my dancing. I knew I could do no more than that. But as I entered my second year in the Company, I couldn't help hoping that I would soon be chosen for a solo, any solo. I needed some sign of encouragement and approval, and I wanted to know what it would be like to be out on the stage all alone, the center of attention. In corps roles it is so easy to be lulled into thinking that no one is watching, that you're lost in the crowd. I realized I wasn't yet strong enough to do properly most of the solos in the Company's repertory, so perhaps what I really wanted was to learn a solo, without actually having to go out on the stage and perform one.

The rehearsal sheet, which was posted every evening, frequently made interesting reading. It was what everyone read to find out which new roles they were getting. It was also a way of keeping tabs on the competition. One day, it read:

NYCB REHEARSAL SCHEDULE

Main Hall / 12–2 / *Divert.* and *Barocco.*
All Principals and Understudies, with Kirkland,
Flomine, Pilarre, Hendl, Ashley.

To me, that meant only one thing: there would be a rehearsal of *Divertimento No. 15* at noon for the principal dancers and their understudies. The rest of us would be in a rehearsal of *Concerto Barocco* that would follow. I hadn't done *Barocco,* so it looked as though I was being given another new corps role, and one of the best in the repertory! That was exciting enough, but I was in for an even bigger surprise.

Since I couldn't be sure that *Divert* would be rehearsed first, I arrived for the rehearsal at noon sharp. Just as I expected, Balanchine began working with the principals in *Divert.* Those roles seemed so many light-years away from me that it never occurred to me to follow what was going on, so I sat down in a corner of the studio and buried myself in a book. At the end of that part of the rehearsal, the ballet mistress told me I had been called to the rehearsal to learn Marnee Morris's role in *Divert,* which included the third variation and the third pas de deux in the ballet. My dream—getting a solo— had come true. I was elated beyond words but at the same time annoyed at the ballet mistress, who had let me sit through the whole rehearsal with my nose in a book while Balanchine was showing and explaining what he wanted in the role I was about to learn. Why had I been treated so offhandedly? Such a waste of precious time—and so embarrassing! Balanchine had certainly been the one to decide I should learn the role. What must he have thought of the little eighteen-year-old who couldn't be bothered to listen to what he had to say about her first solo. Of course, I was at fault, too. Whenever Balanchine was saying *anything* about his ballets, I should have been listening. I soon learned that the treatment I had been given that day by the ballet mistress was typical, and I resolved to be more attentive in the future to what was going on around me.

A few days later I learned that Marnee was going to be away and that I would have to perform the role within a week! How would I be ready in time? The mixture of elation, anticipation, anxiety, and fear put me in a nervous state that was equally harmful to body and mind. At rehearsals I was so on edge I couldn't retain anything: each new step seemed to push the last one right out of my mind. I resorted to trying to write the steps down, something I had never done before. I quickly discovered I didn't have the words or symbols to describe steps or patterns or timing. Those desperate scribblings, which I still have, are an eloquent reminder of my feelings about my first big chance. It was an experience I wouldn't want to go through again.

My mental and emotional problems were dwarfed by my physical ones. I had been suffering sporadically from tendonitis in my ankle since I joined the Company, but the condition worsened as a result of my intense rehearsals for *Divert*. I was terrified this injury would somehow hold me back. It is commonplace for dancers to injure themselves as they prepare for their first solo. Suddenly, there are more rehearsals than before, all done full out at performance pitch. Unfamiliar movements have to be repeated time and again until they are done just right. More risks are taken. I had been doing a lot of rehearsing in soft or old shoes, and I regretted it. Shoes can get very soft very quickly during a hard rehearsal. At that age, I would hardly have dared interrupt a rehearsal and say to Balanchine: "Excuse me, I have to change my shoes." But how often I needed to! And, I hadn't been warming up properly. I didn't know how to give myself a good barre before a rehearsal or performance. At SAB, I had done a barre at the beginning of each class, but I had to discover the hard way why it was so important to be warm before rehearsing. Like everyone else my age, I expected my body to do whatever I asked of it, without complaining. In the long run, we would all be better off if our bodies started complaining sooner and louder. We don't realize the damage we are doing until the bad habits are well ingrained.

Divert, which had always been one of my favorite ballets to watch, had a classical style and was therefore an ideal choice for my first solo. Even then, I thought of myself as well suited to the classical roles and, consequently, I liked those roles most. My taste in music was the same. Mozart's *Divertimento No. 15* was enchanting by itself, but when I listened to the music *and* saw the choreography, I thought they were inseparable. Balanchine had even managed to insert a few jazzy steps into the ballet which, incredibly enough, looked entirely appropriate.

I think Balanchine gave me this role in *Divert* more as a reward for hard work than because I was truly ready for it. It was his way of saying: "I've noticed how well you have been working; here's something fun to work on. Let's see what you can do with it." The variation I had been asked to learn didn't have any steps I couldn't do if taken separately (no hops on pointe, no turns at all, nothing that was beyond me). But putting them all together and achieving some degree of fluidity was the challenge, made even more difficult by the broad, expansive movements that Balanchine wanted done with lots of energy. He always said: "Bigger! Stronger! There are English horns in this variation. You have to match them!" I had no lack of energy, but I didn't always know when or how to use it.

The first time Balanchine saw me in a *Divert* rehearsal was the day before performance, and things got off to a bad start. In the opening moments of the ballet, two of the soloists are on opposite sides of the stage and they switch places by doing a combination of steps with a big traveling glissade in the middle. For the past several days in class, Balanchine had been working on another kind of glissade: a quick, small, low jump to the side from fifth position to fifth position. In the split second between takeoff and landing, we worked on showing second position: a nice inverted V with legs straight,

Balanchine surrounded by his "girls" in 1968. At the time, Merrill was doing *Divertimento No. 15.* These are some of the other girls who were being given opportunities. Directly behind him are Linda Merrill (left) and Renée Estopinal (right); Merrill (third from right) and Gelsey Kirkland (far right). (© 1984 *Martha Swope*)

feet pointed, and only a couple of inches off the floor. We also had to be sure to keep the upper body perfectly still and vertical and do a good "juicy" demi-plié in both fifth positions. The timing for getting out of and back into fifth position was extremely difficult to master even after we understood what Balanchine wanted. One foot had to leave the ground a fraction of a second later than the other on the takeoff; and one foot had to arrive a fraction of a second later than the other on the landing. In the takeoff, we all tended either to allow both feet to leave the ground at the same time or to go to the other extreme, and let the second leg lag behind. On the landing, the second leg inevitably arrived too late. When one leg lagged behind, the result was a rocking-horse effect that Balanchine deplored. When that happened, it was impossible to achieve a precise second position in the air.

Balanchine often used both his eyes and his ears to tell if a step—in this case, the glissade—was being done correctly. "See the music, hear the dance," he often said. If he heard *da-daaah* on the landing, he was happy. If he heard *daaah-daaah,* or if he felt he couldn't "take a picture" of our second position in the air, we were wrong.

All those details were swirling around in my mind as I did the glissade in rehearsal. "What are you doing?" he asked disapprovingly. I froze. "Just glissade, big jump, down, and pose!" I was momentarily bewildered by his criticism. I had been concentrating so hard, thinking with pride that I was showing him I could apply what he had taught in class. He went on to show me how to travel more, how to make the step look like a fuller movement from beginning to end. It was only then that I realized there was more than one type of glissade and that I had better learn the mechanics and the timing of each one.

This glissade in *Divert,* one he used frequently in other ballets as well, started from what can only be considered a demi-plié in an overcrossed fourth position—the front foot way out in front of the back foot and crossed over in the direction I was about to move in. The timing of the actual takeoff and landing was the same as what I had first done, but in between came a long space- and music-consuming jump through the air. It was supposed to be a big, stretched, sweeping movement, ending in the same position it had begun in. What I had done was something closer to the quick little fifth-to-fifth glissade that takes no time at all, and consequently I had found myself having to wait before taking off for the glissade if the subsequent steps were to fit the music. My movements must have looked small and lifeless, even unmusical.

Balanchine used a number of different glissades that were not merely linking steps or preparations for something impressive. He wanted absolutely everything to deserve the attention of the dancers and the audience, and glissades were no exception. We worked on them endlessly, and sometimes a whole class would be devoted to just one kind of glissade, in different combinations and with different tempos. He made sure that, as the tempo quickened or slowed, we didn't change the mechanics of the step. On other occasions, his class might concentrate on different kinds of glissade with subtle differ-

One type of pas de chat
seen in *Square Dance*
(as shown in the
sequence photographs:
*Pas de chat,
Variation II.*)
(© *Beverley Gallegos*)

ences in timing. The same variety existed for other steps, too. I found this one of the
most stimulating aspects of working with Balanchine. He always seemed to find new
details to work on or new touches for an old step and he shared this vast creativity with
us in the classroom, not merely when choreographing new ballets.

Divert was a perfect ballet in which Balanchine could gamble on someone he liked
and wanted to test. There were numerous entrances, so if one part went badly, the
dancer could collect her wits in the wings and come out again and try to redeem herself.
There was also a pas de deux that was short, if somewhat difficult, and it was a good
introduction to dancing with a partner. I had had very little experience working with a
partner and so was grateful for the opportunity. Most young dancers are not so lucky.
Often their solos have no partnering or adagio work, and then, when they go to a more
important role with a long pas de deux, they have great difficulty coping with the unfamiliar problems. This is especially true for the men.

I plunged headlong into the rehearsals, aggravating my tendonitis. But nothing was
going to stop me. During one rehearsal of the pas de deux, Balanchine himself partnered
me. I remember him gently encouraging me: "Don't drop your leg, dear, hold it there,"
he said. "And don't squeeze my hand so hard. Give it to me nicely."

In those days, whenever Balanchine choreographed, he did all the partnering himself. In rehearsals, if there was a difficult partnering problem, he took the man's part, and at times did the woman's part, too. He was a fantastic partner. He could make a woman feel comfortable and secure, and do so with style. His movements had a poetic quality I had never seen in anyone else. Even at that stage in my career I could sense that I was in good hands, but I was scared stiff of appearing clumsy. What if I kicked him?

For the first time in my life, I also rehearsed by myself. I actually requested rehearsals, just as principals do, and in the evenings my name went up on the rehearsal sheet along with the name of the pianist who had been assigned to me. At other times I would work alone with tapes. But I was a poor judge of what looked good or bad, which arm positions I wanted to use, and so forth. My eye wasn't yet trained to see much in the mirror. If a step didn't work, I would do it over and over again, expecting repetition to fix everything. I couldn't think my way through a problem, and I didn't know technique well enough to know what was throwing a step off.

One day, as I was working alone in a studio, Patricia McBride, watching me strike a pose that she liked, said: "Oh, you should do that. That's pretty." I'd never heard of principal dancers helping corps members; they generally didn't even seem to want to help each other. I felt very lucky to have had Patty's comment—but what had I done that was so pretty? Maybe I had done nothing more than tilt my head a little. Although I'd spent years working on my feet, legs, and arms, I was still not at the stage of thinking about my head. Even though Balanchine worked on the use of the head when he taught class, mine still seemed simply to "go along for the ride," responding naturally to the movements of the rest of my body. Patty had suggested a pose, one moment in a role that lasted many minutes. As for the rest, who could help me? Certainly not Balanchine. He never would have had the time to give me that kind of extra coaching; he was busy all day long with class and stage rehearsals.

The day of the performance arrived, and that afternoon there was the rehearsal with Balanchine, who gave me numerous corrections, all so different from those the ballet mistress had given me that I found them overwhelmingly difficult to put into effect. It wasn't that he was disappointed in me; he simply wanted to tell me many things I could not yet have been expected to know. Some of his advice was absorbed by my body; some entered my mind but hadn't reached my limbs by performance time; and some didn't register at all. Balanchine was well aware that no one could do everything he wanted immediately, but I just couldn't accept that some refinements would take months, even years, to learn. I wanted to do everything instantly.

That evening, as I started to warm up before the performance, there seemed to be a nearly miraculous improvement in my tendonitis; and so, after I finished my barre, I decided it would be safe to practice—one last time—a big jump in my variation that I had found awkward. I was in makeup, thoroughly warmed up, and it was about fifteen minutes before curtain time. As I landed on my right foot, I felt a shooting pain that was so

2   3   4   ▷

TRADITIONAL PAS DE CHAT

Pas de chat is a light, springy jump that can be done from fifth or fourth position. Balanchine taught us to do not only the traditional pas de chat but also several variations on that step (see photo sequences that follow). I am not sure whether or not he invented all these variations himself, but he certainly clearly defined the differences among them and used all of them frequently throughout his ballets. Therefore, we had to be able to do all the variations at will, even though the differences were sometimes very slight.

The first sequence, 1–23, shows the traditional pas de chat.

1–3   These pictures show the preparation for the pas de chat, starting from a tendu front position and moving into a large overcrossed fourth position in demi-plié with the weight on the front foot.

4   The pas de chat begins as the back foot pushes off the floor and the back knee starts to move on a diagonally upward path.

2a   3a   4a

CORRECT

5   6   7   8

5–8   As the back knee lifts, the front knee begins to straighten and the front foot pushes off the floor in order to propel the body into the air. When the takeoff for the pas de chat is done incorrectly (as shown in 5a through 8a), the back knee lifts but the front knee stays in demi-plié for too long a time. This not only causes the back knee to move too far away from the leg in demi-plié but makes the preparation heavy-looking and weak-feeling. When done correctly, the lifting of the knee helps create the momentum that will lift the body into the air.

INCORRECT

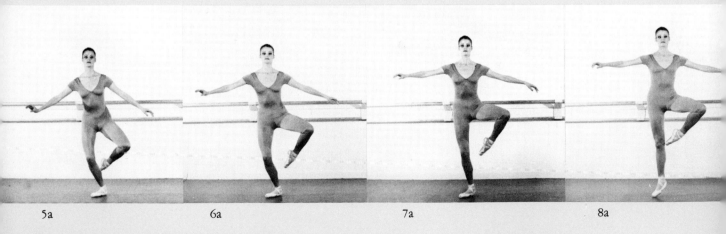

5a   6a   7a   8a

10   11   12   ▷

9 and 10   The moment the front leg (or "second" leg, because it is the second leg to have been lifted) leaves the floor, it begins to bend. The front leg must quickly reach the same level and position as the leg that is already in the air.

11 and 12   In 11, the highest point of the pas de chat has been reached. Both legs are in exactly the same position. In 12, the feet are in the opposite position to that seen in 10. This changing of the position of the legs should take place when the body is at the highest point of elevation. This creates the illusion that the dancer is suspended in the air. In the incorrect pas de chat, this change of position takes place too quickly (10a and 11a), thereby spoiling the illusion of being suspended in the air.

▷

10a   11a   12a

CORRECT

13   14   15   16

13–16 The first leg to have been lifted is the first leg to land on the floor. The second leg follows closely, moving on a diagonal path toward the floor. Notice how much less time was spent in the air in the incorrect pas de chat (four frames compared to six frames—both sequences were filmed at twenty frames a second). Notice, too, the unattractive positions (13a through 16a) caused by the incorrect timing of the landing.

INCORRECT

13a   14a   15a   16a

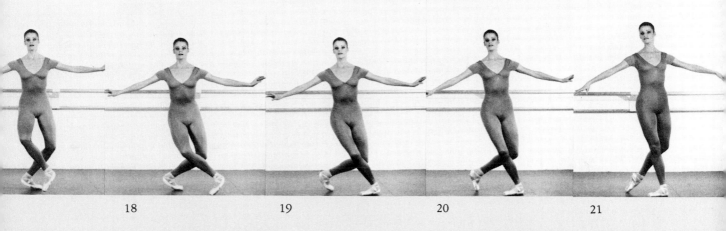

18   19   20   21

17-19   After the first leg lands on the floor, the second leg moves past it and goes to fourth position. The weight is then transferred from the first leg to the second leg in preparation for the next step or pose.

20 and 21   From fourth position, I straighten up into a pose frequently seen in ballet (21) and known in the Company as "B plus," although no one seems to know where that term originated.

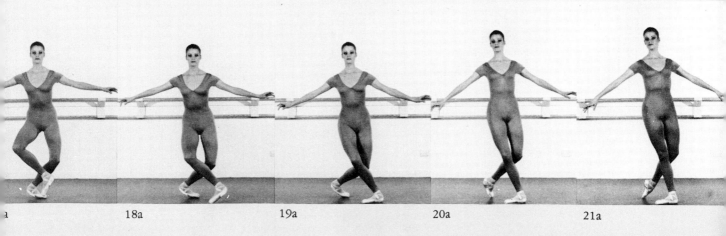

a   18a   19a   20a   21a

1   2   3

PAS DE CHAT—THREE VARIATIONS

Variation I The main difference between a traditional pas de chat and this one is that the feet are brought to the same height in the air and kept there in the same position for as long as possible, creating a "picture in the air" (5 and 6). Unlike 10 through 12 of the traditional pas de chat, the feet should not be seen changing positions. Because the legs have remained together for as long as possible, the feet are much closer together as they near the floor, and there is very little time between the landing of each foot.

7   8   9

5   6

11   12

1   2   3

Variation II   In this pas de chat, the first leg that is lifted off the floor does not remain bent, as in the traditional pas de chat, but begins to straighten as the second leg leaves the floor (3 and 4). At the height of the jump, the first leg should be straight and the second leg bent (6). The timing of the takeoff and landing is the same as in the traditional pas de chat.

7   8   9

5   6

11   12

1   2   3

Variation III   This type of pas de chat is a variation on the preceding pas de chat (Variation II). In this version, the dancer tries to reach the position shown in 5 as *fast* as possible and then to hold it as *long* as possible. In the landing, both feet touch the floor simultaneously rather than one after the other.

7   8   9

5 6

11

A pas de chat from *Donizetti Variations*
(as shown in the sequence
photographs on the preceding page)
(© *Steven Caras*)

sharp and frightening I fell to the floor. I sat there stunned, holding my foot, staring into space, and wondering what I could or should do with the few remaining minutes before the curtain went up. There was only one choice. I had to get up and go on, no matter how much it hurt.

After putting on my costume and performance shoes, I went on stage and continued doing various steps from the ballet, trying to stay warm and also, foolishly, testing my foot to see how bad the pain was. The stage manager called "places," and I went into the wings to take off my leg warmers. As I was putting them down on the table, Suzanne Farrell, who was also dancing in *Divert,* handed me a piece of toasted marzipan and said: "*Merde* tonight" (there is a tradition in the Company in which people give small tokens of good luck called "merdes" to a friend doing a role, even a corps role, for the first time). As I was not a close friend of any of the principals in the Company, and as Suzanne was generally more aloof than most, I was surprised and touched by her gesture and took it as a good omen.

Finally, the curtain went up. Anthony Blum was my partner in the pas de deux and the other principal roles were danced by Suzanne Farrell, Sara Leland, Suki Schorer, Carol Sumner, Richard Rapp, and Earle Sieveling. I remember nothing about the performance except that the pain didn't go away. I do remember the curtain calls, however. We stepped in front of that enormous gold curtain illuminated by the spotlights that shone directly down on us, enveloping us in a golden aura. The stage, the curtain, everything was familiar to me, but for a few brief moments I had entered a strange but marvelous world. My jangled nerves and the terrible pain in my ankle soon brought me back to reality, and when the curtain calls were over I burst into tears—tears of relief that I had made it through the ballet, and tears of pain and frustration that my ankle had prevented me from dancing as well as I might have. Suzanne, probably to comfort me, told me the variation had looked nice, but by then, even though I greatly appreciated her comment, I was so upset I couldn't say "thank you."

After that performance, I stopped dancing for two weeks to give my foot a rest. During that time, I couldn't help worrying about the impression my performance had made on Balanchine. Had it disappointed him or had it been good enough for a "first performance"?

When I started dancing again I was relieved to be cast in *Divert* once more. I still had no idea what Balanchine thought, but was grateful he was willing to let me try again. Being given a second chance was not, however, enough to relieve my anxieties about my dancing. In my next performance of *Divert* as I was waiting in the wings to make my entrance in the pas de deux, I caught sight of Balanchine entering the front wing on the opposite side of the stage, to watch. I must have stiffened, because Peter Martins, who was my partner, tried to reassure me.

"Cool it," he said. "Just dance for yourself."

But how could I just dance for myself when I was desperate to please Balanchine?

More advice came from Hugo Fiorato, one of our conductors. After one performance of the ballet, he simply said: "Don't smile so much in the pas de deux."

I protested: "I want to show that I'm enjoying myself."

"Yes, I know, but in this pas de deux it's not appropriate to have a big grin on your face."

I stubbornly rejected his advice and made the same mistake many times before the truth of Hugo's criticism dawned on me several years later.

Balanchine limited his comments on these performances to specific details. He rarely offered any general criticism, and certainly no compliments. But he must not have been too displeased, because he continued to cast me in this role.

One evening after a performance of *Divert,* I was back on the stage, getting ready for the next ballet in which I had a corps role, when Balanchine came up to me and said: "How would you like to do a solo in *Raymonda Variations?*"

I'm sure I said something stiff and formal like, "Yes, of course, fine." I was so concerned about keeping my dignity that I forgot to show him how deliriously happy he had made me. What I really felt like doing was jumping up and down and shouting like a child. I'm sure even such a spontaneous outburst would have pleased Balanchine more than my repressed enthusiasm.

Raymonda, like *Divert,* was a classical ballet; Balanchine seemed to see me in that vein. And, like *Divert,* it was a good ballet for a first or second solo. Except for my variation, I was part of the corps. The ballet has a series of variations in the middle and, if one is not done well, another comes along right away to erase the unpleasant impression. Fortunately, the success of the ballet wasn't going to depend on me but rather on the principal couple.

Karin von Aroldingen had been doing the role before me. She casually showed me the steps, without benefit of the music, to give me an idea of what it was like. Or so I thought. In fact, she considered she had taught me the role, and I think she let it generally be known that I had learned it. Days passed; no rehearsals were called. I waited, beginning to wonder whether I would ever do it. Then the casting went up just a few days before performance, and there was my name! Once again, I was left with only a very few days to work on my part.

My solo in the ballet was classified as a "big girl" role and was originally choreographed for Gloria Govrin, who was unique in the history of the NYCB: she was very tall, very big, and a very good dancer of whom Balanchine was quite fond. It is known as the "harp variation"—because it is danced to a harp solo—and it contains very basic but difficult steps to delicate music.

Balanchine wanted this solo danced expansively and with perfect control of all the movements. As he rehearsed the variation, he kept telling me, "Bigger! I want to see it. What are you saving it for?" (This was one of his favorite expressions.) But, at that point, I wasn't always in control of my movements. When I was free and expansive, I fell all over the place. When I was careful and precise, the movements were so small they weren't interesting to watch. Either way, I had problems.

The coda was quite different from the variation. It was full of exuberance and contained difficult flashy steps as well as one of my all-time favorite entrances: the two "big girls" (at the time Marnee Morris and I) enter doing jumps and high développés that are so fast they are really high kicks. I think the audience as well as the other dancers were dazzled by the display of energy and the amount of space we covered. I felt in my element as we went flying across the stage. Unfortunately, the coda ended with a series of turns I was barely able to do, and I was certain that they spoiled everything that had preceded them.

I did only one performance of *Raymonda,* the last one of the season, and Balanchine never commented on it to me. When I was not cast for the ballet the following season, I was terribly disappointed and depressed. This was the first bad sign for me, the first setback I had had in either the School or the Company. I knew full well that I had danced badly, but why hadn't Balanchine given me a chance to redeem myself? That season I waited and worried. The following season he put me back in the ballet, and I danced it regularly thereafter.

Balanchine was always giving opportunities of this kind to young dancers, and his attitude toward me in *Raymonda* was typical of his patient approach. Often he intentionally gave chances to dancers before they were ready; he had learned from experience that certain young dancers responded very well to a major challenge. He was willing to take the risk. If the dancer had not been able to cope with the difficulties (be they problems of technique, presence, or the pressure of performing) but had gamely tried to meet the challenges, Balanchine was quite willing to give her another chance later. He hoped that the dancer would continue to prepare for the next opportunity, which would usually come in a few months or even a year, depending on how much the person had improved.

Of course, new roles were also given to young dancers out of sheer necessity. Often the first cast and all the alternates for a role were unable to dance owing to injuries, and no other obvious choice was available to replace them. In that situation, Balanchine had to pick someone from the lower levels of the Company to dance the role, even if the dancer was not clearly ready.

These solos gave me the performing experience I wanted so much and that was impossible to get in corps roles. They also brought me into closer contact with Balanchine, who took more and more notice of me in Company class. This did wonders for my confidence, and, armed with new self-assurance, I started working my way toward the front row of Company class, where I would be able to see and hear everything Balanchine did and said, and where I would always be in his field of vision.

My progress in class and the improvement in my technique, however, far exceeded my development as a performer. The groundwork for the distant future was being laid, but any hopes I had had for a meteoric rise through the Company's ranks had long since vanished.

In my early years with the Company, when the NYCB was not working, I toured the country doing concerts with Jacques d'Amboise. In those days, the Company had long layoffs and Jacques, who loved taking ballet to the general public and had a great gift for making it accessible to everyone, put together a small touring group that provided great opportunities for the young dancers he selected to go with him.

The first time I danced with him was in 1969 in an excerpt from Balanchine's *Episodes,* which was taped in Montreal for Canadian television. I was flattered that he had asked me, but a little bewildered, too. Why me? True, he had been offering me friendly suggestions in Company class, often clarifying whatever Balanchine had been working on. But why gamble on me for television? If a live performance goes badly, there's no record of it; but for television the risks are greater. Jacques must have seen a quality in my dancing that was right for the role. I never saw the tape of *Episodes,* but Jacques must have been satisfied with the way I danced, for he began regularly to ask me to do concerts with him all over the United States.

Jacques was a great virtuoso dancer, noted for his elevation, soft landings, and irresistible charm. He was also a superb partner. He was one of the few men who regularly took Balanchine's class and who understood him and tried to further his teachings.

For his concerts, Jacques as a rule used three girls, including one of the Company's ballerinas: first, it was Melissa Hayden, then Kay Mazzo, and eventually I assumed the ballerina roles. These performances had a very casual format. Jacques came out on the stage, warmed up the audience with a few well-chosen words, and then announced what was to come. The first number was invariably the evening's most difficult pas de deux, danced by Jacques and his ballerina. When they had finished dancing, Jacques would come back out on stage while the ballerina rested, and, still huffing and puffing, would talk to the audience about ballet and dancing, using one of the corps girls to illustrate his discussion. Jacques was a great speaker, witty and informative and so engagingly spontaneous that the audience could have imagined they were in his living room. He liked to stroll about the stage (he never used a microphone), often dancing while he talked. On occasion he would even do a whole variation while reciting a poem, just to show that it was possible to dance while breathing easily—so many dancers hold their breath and then gasp for air without even realizing it—and to show how every step, like every word, had to be well presented. Each moment mattered; nothing could be slurred. His explanations and examples were so enlightening that I learned as much from him as the audience did.

During rehearsals for these concerts, Jacques elaborated on many of the points that Balanchine so often presented only quickly and elusively. I later realized that, if I had taken the initiative and gone to Balanchine with my questions, he would have welcomed a chance to help me. But at the time, I was too timid to approach him. He seemed particularly inaccessible in 1969 because of his despondency over Suzanne Farrell's departure, and so Jacques's help came at a perfect time.

With Jacques, I didn't have to take the initiative. He volunteered a great deal of information and was willing to work with me individually. If I disagreed, I questioned him, and in the end I usually understood both what he wanted and why he wanted it.

Nothing that happened on the stage was alien to him, and he tried to make me aware of the finest points. He was the first to point out to me that, as a general rule, dancing behind the music was a lesser sin than going ahead of it. To begin with, it takes a split second for the sound of the music to travel from the orchestra pit to most of the members of the audience, so even though a dancer may feel she is lagging behind the music, she may actually appear to be right on it. Second, a dancer's delayed reaction to the music can at least be viewed as a response to the music—an interpretation of it—whereas a dancer anticipating the music, reacting merely to what she expects to hear, may appear rushed or, worse, unmusical. I was guilty of the latter until Jacques pointed this out to me.

I tried to put into practice everything Jacques said about performing, but that didn't mean I had anything like his natural charm on stage. I followed all his instructions and perhaps unconsciously copied him to some extent. But by trying to imitate certain of Jacques's habits, such as looking out front all the time and flashing a big smile, I was unwittingly moving in the wrong direction. I did not have Jacques's outgoing personality or spontaneous stage presence, so my attempts to imitate his style looked forced and inappropriate. If I was to have a graceful, pleasing stage presence, it would have to be based on my own personality. Even after I discovered that, I knew that years of self-discovery and careful work lay ahead.

In partnering, Jacques taught me more than I had ever imagined I needed to know. Most of the partnering work I had done had been in the once-weekly adagio class at SAB, where my experiences had not been reassuring. In general, the boys were not interested in partnering. They had become involved in dance because they enjoyed jumping and turning, not because they looked forward to learning the difficult skills of partnering a woman. Because I was so thin and light, I was often paired with the weakest boys in the class. But when two weak and inexperienced dancers work together, neither one learns very much.

Once I joined the Company, I no longer had any adagio classes, and so the only practice I had in partnering came in a few corps roles. My partners rarely had more expertise than I did. So it was a revelation when Jacques, an excellent partner, began to explain details of partnering. Before he started helping me, I had a habit of clenching my partner's hand and keeping my elbow stiff, thinking that would somehow provide extra support. Jacques showed me how my stiff elbow only increased my unsteadiness and how my clenched hand transmitted a feeling of tension to the audience even if there was no visible struggle. He also taught me such basics as how to time preparations for lifts and how to do pirouettes with a partner. It was also reassuring to know that if I happened to be unsteady on any step, Jacques was there to "save" me with his strength and expertise.

At first I didn't have to do the most difficult pieces on Jacques's programs, but I quickly progressed to some very demanding roles. I did Polyhymnia and later Terpsichore in *Apollo,* as well as the ballerina role in Balanchine's *Sylvia Pas de Deux.* Jacques was very particular about these performances and everything was meticulously rehearsed. I knew I was often out of my depth, but I was eager to learn and tried to overcome my apprehensions.

I remember one particularly harrowing experience when I danced the *Sylvia Pas de Deux* in Santa Barbara, California. My family had come to see me dance, and before the performance they visited me backstage. I discovered a tear in the bodice of my costume, which my mother repaired, and as we chatted I lost track of the time until I noticed to my horror that it was fifteen minutes to curtain time, and I hadn't even started warming up. Even in the best of circumstances, the ballet was horrendously difficult. I had never performed it before, and I was terrified at the thought of launching into it with practically no warm-up. Nor did I want my parents and the audience to see an inexperienced and inadequate dancer on that stage.

Everything seemed to go wrong from the start, for my muscles tied up almost immediately because of the poor warm-up. The hops on pointe in the variation went poorly, and the finale was especially rough. I had so wanted the evening to go well and to show Jacques that I had assimilated all that he had taught me for this role, and I was convinced I had ruined the evening for him and the audience. Later that evening, Jacques asked me how I thought *Sylvia* had gone. I said I was unhappy and embarrassed with much of what I had done, but he said, no, it was good. They were nice words to hear, but I found them hard to believe.

Many years later Jacques told me it was that very performance of *Sylvia* that convinced him I was going to make it. He didn't elaborate, but I think he came to that conclusion because, despite the rawness of my dancing, I had tried to incorporate all his corrections. I had kept my head and not given up, even when things were going badly, and I had tried to make my dancing enjoyable for the audience as well as for myself.

I felt extremely fortunate to have the experience of these concerts. I learned how to cope with dancing on small hard slippery stages with poor lighting and taped music. I had the opportunity to dance many roles that corps members in the Company never even had a chance to learn. This meant that when I was asked to dance a new role in the Company I sometimes already had experience dancing it. Nothing could have been better.

Jacques was fond of analyzing and explaining everything. He was easier for me to understand than Balanchine, who was often deliberately vague because he wanted us to discover things for ourselves. I was the beneficiary of both approaches, and during those five years I probably learned as much from Jacques and his concerts as I did from Company classes and performances.

These concerts were interrupted in 1973 when Jacques and I were both injured. Jacques tore cartilage in his knee, which required surgery. A few days later, I tore ligaments in my ankle and was in a cast for two weeks. I recovered fully in three months; but Jacques, although he was still able to dance and charm audiences, was never able to do virtuoso roles again.

Balanchine choreographed *Who Cares?* in 1970, incorporating into it a variation and a pas de deux for each of the three principal women—Karin von Aroldingen, Marnee Morris, and Patricia McBride—with Jacques as the partner for all three. I was Karin's understudy, the only understudy Balanchine used, which was immensely thrilling and encouraging for me as a young corps girl.

Jacques suggested to me that I understudy the other two roles so that I could do any of the three if the opportunity arose. He was also thinking of having me do those roles in concerts with him. Fortunately, by the time I was called on to dance Karin's role (the "jumping variation") for the Company—again on short notice, for Karin had broken her wrist—I had already danced it with Jacques. I rehearsed hurriedly and with more confidence than I had had for my earlier two solos. On the other hand, it was a much bigger part, and I wanted to show Balanchine I could handle a major difficult role.

On the night of performance I was trembling with nervousness, although the familiar music, which was so much fun to dance to, had a reassuring effect. I had only to hear the first four chords of the solo (the first time I was on the stage in the ballet) to know it would be all right. The entire ballet gave me a very special and unusual feeling. I felt in complete control of everything. I finally knew what the phrase "to have the audience in the palm of your hand" meant. The pleasure I got from that performance was indescribable. From *my* point of view, it remains one of the highlights of my career, although I still wonder what it looked like to others. As far as I can remember, Balanchine made no comment.

Marnee's "turning variation," which I do today, was a different story. Marnee had a rare gift for turning, and Balanchine didn't hesitate to display it. In his choreography, he often gave a dancer a chance to show off his or her strengths so that all subsequent dancers taking over the role had to try to match the strengths of the person who originated the role. In so doing, Balanchine, consciously or unconsciously, ensured that each succeeding generation of dancers, in addition to showing off their own particular talents, would have to try to learn the skills of the preceding generation. Constant improvement in technique was thereby built into the Company, as long as the dancers met the challenges honestly and didn't immediately change the steps or otherwise water down the roles. They were challenges I responded to instinctively.

My first opportunity to dance Marnee's part with the Company came on the 1972 Russian tour when, in Marnee's absence, I was cast for every performance of *Who Cares?*

Even before I knew of my good fortune, I was excited about touring the Soviet Union and Poland. Balanchine's roots were in Georgia, and we were going to its capital, Tbilisi. I also wanted to see where Balanchine had studied and performed in Leningrad. I had been greatly inspired in 1969 when the Company went to Monte Carlo, took class, and performed in the very places where Balanchine had created some of his early works, among them *Prodigal Son.* I looked forward to another memorable experience.

My visions of dancing in the famous Maryinsky Theatre or the Bolshoi Theater quickly vanished. The Soviet government knew there would be a big demand for tickets and, therefore, put us in vast theaters that held hordes of people. These old and dirty theaters, with pitted and raked (slanted) stages, were surely not meant for ballet. I had never felt farther from home.

We played to capacity crowds, although the reaction to our performances varied greatly from city to city. Kiev gave us a very cool reception. Moscow was not much better; but Leningrad, and particularly Tbilisi, responded enthusiastically. Poland liked us, too. Ballets without familiar virtuoso steps generally didn't go over too well. *Who Cares?,* with its popular music and virtuoso steps, excited the audiences, who often clapped and stamped their feet in unison to show their approval, especially after my variation, whether or not it went well.

I had done Marnee's role in concerts with Jacques before the USSR tour. It was fiendishly difficult but had to be "tossed off" as if it were nothing at all. The part demanded an individual style that was hard for me to manage, since the troublesome steps required my full concentration. Jacques had asked me to put my "personal stamp" on it, and I tried to do that by using my arms in certain ways and by working on the phrasing, but the steps were so difficult that the "style" had to come between the steps, or in the preparations.

The turning section of the variation begins with a series of double *fouettés.* My turning step in *Who Cares?* was the same as the famous one repeated thirty-two times in *Swan Lake* by the ballerina performing the Black Swan pas de deux, but those thirty-two single turns are much easier than even a short series of doubles. My series started with a normal double pirouette. At the end of the second revolution, I pliéd on my supporting leg (in this case, the left leg). As I pliéd, I extended the right leg to the front, then whipped it to the side. Without stopping, I brought it back into *passé* (a position that looks like a **P**, with the toe of one foot pointing right under the knee of the other leg) as I rose up (*relevéd*) on pointe, thereby creating the momentum to do two more turns if I could only stay balanced. That was my biggest problem: maintaining my balance on pointe.

Balanchine liked the fouettés done "off the music," which made them more interesting as well as more difficult. (In reality, he meant off the melody but on the beat.) The melody of "My One and Only" is in 4/4 time, and can easily be counted: 1-2-3-4;

1-2-3-4, and so on. It would have been easiest for me to do the turns with the plié on the 1 count (in preparation for each turn), because I would have felt supported by the music. But what Balanchine was saying, in effect, was that I should do anything *but* the obvious. I could have done the turns in three or five beats, or even a different number of beats for each turn. I decided to do them in four beats, but those four beats could not start with the obvious first beat: 2-3-4-1 would be fine, for example, and that's what I opted for.

But no matter what timing I used, the doubles didn't work. One day in rehearsal, out of desperation, I tried doing very fast single fouettés instead. I thought they might appeal to Balanchine, but when he saw them he shook his head. "No, dear, not single fouettés. Doubles."

My heart sank. I again tried to do all doubles, resorting to singles only to regain my balance before starting doubles again. But as hard as I tried, I was never able to do repeated double fouettés, and I still can't. Now I start with singles and gradually mix in more and more doubles until I finish with two doubles in a row. That way the series of fouettés builds to a nice climax. It's *almost* what Balanchine wanted.

Another step I spent five years trying, and failing, to master was a series of double attitude *piqué* (stepping directly onto pointe) turns in *croisé*, stepping on the right leg and moving from upstage right to downstage left. Having to hold my leg in a proper attitude position was the hard part. Attitude is really an arabesque with a bent leg. If the leg is carried too low, it is in no definable position and looks sloppy and unattractive. Had these turns been in *effacé* (from upstage left to downstage right) and on the same leg—which is the way it is usually done—I would have had no problem with the step. But, here again, Balanchine had taken advantage of Marnee's fabulous turning ability and thrown in something unusual. After five years of doing this step badly—carrying my leg too low in attitude or falling off pointe or doing something else wrong—Balanchine finally let me do something different. Now I do a completely different step that I choreographed myself, although my inspiration was a turn in another Balanchine ballet, *A Midsummer Night's Dream.*

Balanchine taught me a lesson when he insisted on my doing double fouettés. While he generally was not adamant about keeping the original steps in a ballet, he seemed to prefer that young dancers, in particular, struggle with the original steps and try to overcome their difficulties. He hoped the dancers would learn and improve on their own in the process. But, if after a long and game struggle, like my battle with the fouettés and the attitude turns, a dancer was still unable to do the steps well, Balanchine was more than willing either to change the step or to let the dancer find a comfortable alternative. Dancers should meet such challenges honestly and not give up after only a few rehearsals. Balanchine seemed to sense, however, that the personalities of certain dancers often prevented their working long and hard by themselves to conquer a step. Rather than constantly badgering them, he would let them change the troublesome steps right away, unless they were very important to him.

This was not his approach with me, but he was always very patient and encouraging whenever I had problems. My problem in *Who Cares?* tended to be the same in every performance. If I started a step poorly, I was rarely able to recover well enough to get back on track, and that affected the rest of the variation. If one step went wrong, I would either look very awkward or fall. Therefore I felt I had to do everything correctly from the start to remain in control of all my movements. It was a kind of self-preservation instinct. But each time a step went well, the chances of the next step going well increased. This sounds logical enough, but not all dancers function that way. A few can dance with great abandon and spontaneity, and overcome most missteps very smoothly. When they fail, however, we say that they have "thrown themselves around." I have never wanted to be guilty of that.

Year after year, I rehearsed this variation in *Who Cares?* ad nauseam. The more I practiced, the worse it became. One season, I realized that the variation was executed best the first time I rehearsed it, and then went downhill. A novel idea came to me—not to rehearse. It couldn't get any worse. So I tried one single stage rehearsal before the season's first performance, and, amazingly enough, things went well. This has remained my approach, although it goes against my natural tendencies—but it doesn't work for me in other ballets. There have been times when, because of an emergency, I have had to do a role on very short notice with only one rehearsal, and I rarely feel I dance as well as I might have with more preparation.

Who Cares? Merrill and Jacques d'Amboise. (© 1984 *Martha Swope*)

1	2	3	4	5

FOUETTÉ TURNS

Fouetté turns, which are usually done in a series, are executed on one leg while the other whips in and out, creating momentum for the turns. This sequence shows me in the middle of a series. (Most series begin with a turn from fourth or fifth position.)

1 I have just brought my working leg into passé back.

2 I have now completed a quarter of a turn. Note, however, that my head has not yet turned and that my eyes are still focused on a fixed point to the front.

3 As I continue to turn, my working foot begins to change from passé back to passé front. My body has now turned so far that I can no longer keep my head facing to the front, although my eyes are still focused on the original spot. This is the beginning of the rapid turning of the head called "spotting," which greatly assists in the execution of all turns, especially when done fast. Spotting contributes to the momentum needed to turn well and, in addition, allows a dancer to turn without becoming dizzy.

4 and 5 My head now begins to snap around, allowing me to look to the front again as soon as possible. My body will face directly front well after the head. (Note that in these seventeen pictures, taken at twenty frames a second, only three frames show me with my eyes not on a fixed point in front of me.) By 5, my working foot has arrived in passé front.

10	11	12	13

6 7 8 9

6–8 As I pass the halfway point in the turn, I begin to open my working leg to the front (6) and at the same time my arms start to move away from my body and I roll down off pointe, arriving in 8 with the working leg in croisé front and the supporting leg in demi-plié. The descent from pointe should be smooth and controlled, not a hopping or jerking movement.

9–11 I continue to plié on my supporting leg as I begin to whip the working leg from front to side. At the same time, my right arm moves in a similar pattern.

12–13 As the working leg reaches the side, the supporting leg starts to straighten and the relevé onto pointe, which should be smooth and controlled, begins. The dancer should not jump onto pointe.

14–16 The bending of the working leg coordinates with the supporting foot's relevé so that the working leg is almost back in passé by the time the supporting foot is fully on pointe (16). At the same time, my arms begin to close.

17 My working leg has again been brought into passé back, and I have now reached the same point I was at when the sequence began.

If a double fouetté is to be done, the dancer stays in the passé front position reached in 5 and makes one more full revolution before beginning to open the leg as shown in 6.

14 15 16 17

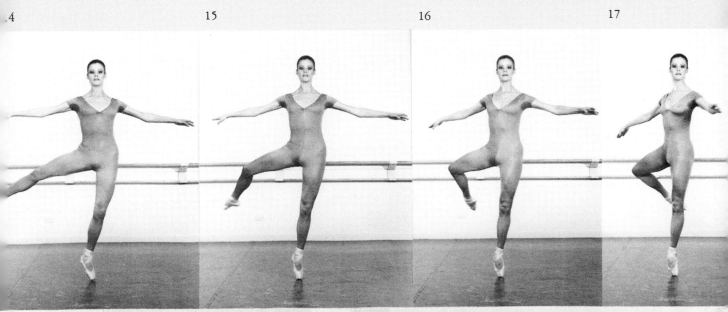

CHAPTER

3

THE MONDAY CLASSES and my increased work with Balanchine did little to help me overcome the inhibitions I felt in his presence. I often had no idea what to say or how to react to his unpredictable opinions or witticisms. If it was a matter of following instructions, my ability to concentrate well and to interpret his sometimes elusive combinations of words and gestures usually saw me through. But if the encounter was more social, I usually was at a loss for words. My problem was compounded by my strong desire to have Balanchine pay attention to me and like me because of the effort I was making to understand and to incorporate into my dancing everything he taught. I didn't want to win him over with feminine guile. I would have felt dissatisfied if I had thought he was paying attention to me only because he found me attractive or charming. Some of the girls flirted with him, but that went against my nature.

With time, I realized that I had unintentionally gone too far in the other direction. I must have appeared cold, or at least aloof, almost as if I didn't like him, when, in fact, I liked him very much. I found him not only charming and witty but also quite an adorable, even lovable man. I knew my inhibitions would not disappear overnight, but I had to make some gesture to show my true friendly feelings.

Again I turned to Renée Estopinal for advice. She too wanted to make a friendly gesture toward Balanchine, so we decided to invite him for dinner. Since Renée didn't want to do the cooking, we invited him to my apartment. Renée did the inviting—I didn't dare—and reported that Balanchine had accepted happily. We also invited three other girls from the corps, all friends of ours, as well as people we knew Balanchine liked and was interested in. I felt there was safety in numbers. Above all, I didn't want to feel that I had to carry the conversation.

Balanchine had quite a reputation as a gourmet cook with very definite ideas about how everything should be prepared, which only added to my uncertainty. But I had heard he loved mushrooms, so I decided on an appetizer featuring Chinese mushrooms. For the main course I served veal with rice and green beans and, because I had also heard that he loved things with plenty of sour cream and sugar, I presented fresh green grapes with sour cream and brown sugar for dessert.

Balanchine arrived in a jovial mood and charmed us with stories. But things took an awkward turn as I was about to serve dinner. "Oh, no, dear," he said when he saw we were going to help ourselves buffet-style and sit on chairs scattered throughout the room. "Isn't there a table we can sit at?"

Luckily there was, although I knew it wouldn't be terribly comfortable. Embarrassed, I pulled out a small drop-leaf table I had intended to use as a serving table and set it up so that we could all squeeze around it. Conversation faltered now and then, but I'm sure it was livelier than I recall. At the very least, Balanchine had an adoring and rapt audience as he related fascinating anecdotes about everything under the sun. But I could tell from his reaction that the appetizer and dessert weren't a big hit. (Years later he told me that he hated anything with brown sugar.) Still, he was the perfect guest and ate everything I served. He was obviously pleased that Renée, whom he had always liked very much, and I had taken the trouble to prepare dinner for him.

Afterward, there was a noticeable change in his attitude: he was definitely more aware of me, as a dancer and as a person. I welcomed this, but I was uncomfortable with the thought that perhaps my invitation or personality had won him over. I wanted my dancing to be what interested him most. I eventually convinced myself that I hadn't overstepped my bounds and that it would be proper to invite him again. But the anxiety occasioned by that first encounter remained vivid in my memory, and I put off inviting him again—for years.

I knew my time in the Company had been well spent. I had poured myself into Balanchine's classes and my corps roles, and was growing from a weak, promising dancer into one of the strongest technicians in the Company. My experience in the solos and the concerts with Jacques had, I thought, polished my dancing to the point where it was more than a display of technique. Yet, I felt my career should be progressing faster. I had been in the Company five years and was twenty-one years old; I felt ready for more prominent roles, and thoughts of a promotion crossed my mind.

The Stravinsky Festival in 1972 brought me hope, for there would be innumerable opportunities—twenty new ballets—and perhaps something exciting for me. No performances were given the week before the opening of the Festival, and every available space in the theater was used for rehearsals day and night. At times, dancers found they had to be in two or even three places at the same time. Union rules were continually broken, but no one complained. We were all exhausted but realized that if one of us faltered the burden would shift to someone else who was equally overworked. We pulled together as never before in the greatest outpouring of collective effort I had, or have, ever seen. Lincoln Kirstein was quoted as saying that the rehearsals were no less than a "miniature Normandy landing."

My hopes were not entirely fulfilled, although my fears were somewhat allayed, when I was put in four new ballets. Jerome Robbins, who upon his return to the NYCB in 1969 had had an immediate success with *Dances at a Gathering,* decided to use Susan Hendl and me in the two leading female roles of *Requiem Canticles,* one of his contributions to the Festival. After Balanchine, he was our most eminent choreographer and ballet master, and I was delighted he had singled me out. There was only one female solo in that ballet and Robbins had choreographed it on Susie, but changed his mind at the last minute and had me perform it.

Balanchine himself used me in the Festival in *Danses Concertantes.* I thought it was a wonderful, sparkling ballet full of quirky, witty movements that were fun to do. I was in the fourth pas de trois, where the music was particularly bubbly, and the choreography, which one reviewer called "fun and a little dirty," had us strutting about, jumping, and thrusting our bodies in unexpected directions. Unfortunately, this ballet and all the other new ballets I was in became lost among the masterpieces Balanchine had created for the Festival, and they did not survive long.

Appropriately, the Festival started on what would have been Stravinsky's ninetieth birthday. Balanchine's primary motivation in staging the Festival was to give audiences a chance to hear some of Stravinsky's lesser-known music. We all benefited from this. I became familiar with many of Stravinsky's less popular works and realized how wonderful his music was for both listening and dancing—something I had never fully appreciated before.

For Balanchine, the Festival was a rebirth. We had all been waiting for something to pull him out of his despondency after Suzanne Farrell's departure, and this had done it. I had never seen him so vibrant, so alive, as during preparations for the Festival, and I'm sure he worked harder than any of us.

I remember in particular the piece of music that closed the Festival: *Symphony of Psalms.* Balanchine requested that the entire Company be on stage, in whatever dress they happened to be wearing, sitting or standing anywhere they wanted around the choir. I had just finished dancing in *Requiem Canticles,* and sitting on the floor on stage right, perspiring in my costume, seemed an oddly casual way to close the Festival. But the music, which I had never heard before, was as exquisitely beautiful and deeply moving as a formal religious ceremony. Balanchine had taken up a position directly behind me, and his physical presence affected all my senses. I shall never forget those moments. As the music, and the Festival, came to an end, tears of mixed emotions came to my eyes and I felt tremendously privileged to have been a part of it all. The most moving part was seeing the satisfaction Balanchine derived from the Festival. After a lifetime of giving joy to others, it was now his turn to receive, to be filled with the joy of this glorious celebration of Stravinsky's music.

It seems to me now that the Festival brought us to the attention of the general public as never before. We had always had a following, a faithful hard core, but now converts had been made; a vast new audience had become aware of us and of ballet. The Festival was the spark that ignited the ballet boom, although the shock waves from it were not felt until a few years later.

The anxieties about my future that I had felt before the Festival were forgotten in all the excitement, but they quickly resurfaced afterward. I kept having a vague feeling that something should be happening to me that wasn't happening, or that perhaps I was neglecting to do something I should be doing. My reaction to those uncertainties was to throw myself even more vigorously into my work. Whenever I felt discouraged, my automatic reaction was to concentrate and expend more energy, and that brought me some peace of mind.

My spirits received a boost in the winter of 1972/73, when Balanchine prepared to bring back *Ballet Imperial* without scenery or tutus and with the new name *Tchaikovsky Piano Concerto.* I had been one of the "tall girls" in the corps of the former version of the ballet, and now Colleen Neary and I were asked to learn the second-ballerina role. It is as great a solo role as exists in our repertory (and is the equal of many ballerina roles, although there is very little partnering) and was the most testing role I had ever learned.

In this ballet all the roles are difficult. Many of the steps are basic classical ones, but they are combined in ways and done at tempos that make them extraordinarily demanding. This was perfect for Colleen and me. By then, we were the strongest of the group of young dancers whom Balanchine seemed to like most.

I rehearsed more intensely than ever. My footwork had to be even faster and sharper, and I had to work especially hard on my pirouettes. At one point in the ballet, near the end of the pas de trois, I had to do a series of double pirouettes with my hands above my head. Not only did I have more trouble than usual, turning with my arms in that position, but I had to execute the movements while my legs felt rubbery with fatigue from all the jumping that preceded the pirouettes. How I feared those turns and how I envied Colleen's natural turning ability!

Since the ballet was an evocation of the Russian imperial court, it required regal bearing, dignity, and elegance. In my mind those qualities were more evident in my dancing than in Colleen's, and therefore I felt better suited to the role. We were, however, equally confident of our abilities. We had to be. Anyone lacking in self-confidence who stepped out on the stage in the midst of so much sumptuous music and choreography would have betrayed that insecurity immediately to the audience.

When we had run-throughs with the corps, Colleen and I never actually talked about who should dance and who should watch, but at the first rehearsal I remember that she, the more assertive one, stepped forward at just the right moment and did the dancing while I watched. I made sure this did not happen at the second rehearsal. We ended up taking turns, rehearsal after rehearsal, but it was never comfortably clear whose turn it was. We must have been a comical duo to all the others watching our silent struggle, but to us the matter was deadly serious, even though on the surface our relations couldn't have been more cordial.

Balanchine was in and out of those rehearsals and had a good look at both of us. One day, as the premiere approached, Colleen and I found ourselves leaving the rehearsal in the main hall together and going downstairs for the first, stage rehearsal. We were only a few feet away from Rosemary Dunleavy, the Company's ballet mistress, when she approached Balanchine and asked point-blank: "Who's going to do the first performance? Whoever it is should do the stage rehearsal." Balanchine looked very uncomfortable. He didn't like being put on the spot like that with us so nearby. Colleen and I waited with bated breath. He hesitated, then answered softly but clearly, "Colleen."

As I tried to recover from the blow, a triumphant Colleen beamed with happiness.

The spring of 1973 brought me the most exciting event of my young career: Balanchine began choreographing *Cortège Hongrois* as a farewell tribute to Melissa Hayden. I thought I was only going to be in the corps of the ballet, but one day I was called to a rehearsal alone with Balanchine, which meant only one thing: he was going to choreograph a variation, the first he had ever done for me. I couldn't believe my good fortune. I felt the occasion called for something extra, so before the rehearsal I nervously fixed my hair as carefully as I would for a performance, put on a chiffon skirt, and dabbed on some perfume. I waited quietly and apprehensively on the side of the rehearsal room near the piano while Balanchine chatted with Gordon Boelzner, the pianist. At last, he turned to me.

"Well, let's see. Where shall we start?"

An answer, thank heavens, wasn't expected. We started at the beginning, and forty-five minutes later he had done the whole variation. The speed and ease with which he worked were uncanny. He included a lot of fast, detailed pointe work—by then I was good at presenting my feet—and many sudden changes in direction.

While Balanchine kept coming up with new sequences, I had to do more than show him the step he asked for: I had to remember everything I had just done, and in this variation the tricky combinations really taxed my memory. From time to time he would pause and ask me to show him what we had done up to that point. For the most part, I managed, but once or twice I needed an extra second to work out the right sequence in my mind. At the end he said, "All right, let's see it from the beginning with music." I knew I would be dancing on very thin ice. I tried my best to do the hard steps in a smooth flow, but I wound up making all sorts of mistakes simply to keep going.

It did not matter at all to Balanchine that at first I could only muddle through the variation. Whenever he sat and watched what he had just choreographed, no matter how many mistakes a dancer made, he knew at once whether or not the piece was satisfactory. Other choreographers insist on seeing the steps done exactly right and in the proper sequence before deciding if they are satisfied with what they have created. Not so with Balanchine. He knew beforehand the image he wanted, where the high point would occur, and when the dance would resolve itself; he did not dwell on each separate moment in rehearsal. Yet, he knew immediately when the individual steps did not look right.

"That's not good," he would suddenly say. "I'll change it." And he would. Steps were like loose change in his pocket or, rather, like diamonds and rubies. Whenever he was choreographing, he seemed able to pull out something on the spot that worked. There were times, while he was making a new ballet, when a dancer would not remember a step from a preceding rehearsal. If Balanchine could not remember it either, he would simply come up with a new combination that was just as good, or better! He was almost never at a loss.

My variation turned out to be fiendishly difficult, but its subtleties impressed the other dancers more than the audience. Balanchine had also choreographed a variation for Colleen that was much more easily appreciated by the audience. Although that spoiled my fun a bit, I nevertheless treasured "my" variation.

Now that I had been in the Company for more than five years and knew its workings, I sympathized with new members trying to cope with Company life and the reality of working with Balanchine. Most had been well trained at the School, but few were prepared physically or psychologically for the stresses of our way of working and dancing.

Before joining the Company, most SAB students assumed they were already true believers in Balanchine. It seemed only logical. Balanchine's reputation as a choreographer was such that one hardly questioned his ways. Newcomers had no idea that the Company had skeptics and numerous nonpractitioners—"believers" in word but not in deed. When I joined, perhaps half the Company, and a larger percentage of the principals, did not take his Company class regularly.

The intensity and difficulty of Balanchine's class was a shock to any new dancer, making the fall from top SAB student to lowly corps member even more dramatic. Many found the shock so unpleasant they didn't stay with Balanchine's class long enough to understand the heart of his ideas. The drop-out rate from his class among Company members was high, even though dropping out ultimately meant leaving his field of vision.

Balanchine would certainly have liked to have every last member of the Company at least try to dance the way he wanted, to take his class and listen and learn until his or her dancing days were over. He was incredibly patient, as long as he felt the dancer was making a big effort to do what he asked. But he wasn't going to force anyone to do anything. "It's up to you, dear. I can't do it for you. When you're ready, when you want to, you'll do it."

In rehearsals, those who hadn't been taking his classes did the best they could. They didn't dance as well as they might have, but even they absorbed a lot by osmosis. They realized, if dimly, that the only way to get through some of Balanchine's harder ballets was to dance the way he wanted.

Even those who felt they were not properly appreciated, or who didn't persevere, admired and even revered Balanchine. No one felt used or mistreated in rehearsal. He was always a gentleman, treating his dancers with love, respect, and concern.

In my early years in the Company, my eye had not been sharp enough to appreciate many of the finer points. I assumed that Balanchine's corrections had to do with his personal aesthetics, which were—or seemed to be—a bit arbitrary. Later, as I did his ballets and came to learn what he liked and what he found unacceptable, my own artistic taste developed. By that time, most of the dancing I saw outside the Company had little appeal for me. I needed to see the stretched positions, the straight back in arabesque, the crossed fifth positions, and the vast quantities of space covered by steps done so timidly elsewhere. Anything else looked quaint to me, at best.

I later realized that, although much of what Balanchine taught had to do with his sense of aesthetics, it also served the very practical purpose of helping the dancer get through his ballets. It became urgently clear, for example, why we had to put our foot directly in front of us in tendu and why each tendu had to be done as a separate movement; why, when doing a *frappé* the leg has to be stopped so sharply and held; why landing and taking off for *changement* has to be practiced from grand plié. We learned the answers to these and innumerable other questions by dancing in his ballets. We began to see how skills learned in his class were so essential for changing direction suddenly, making movements look quick and light or smooth and controlled. The wonder of Balanchine's ballets could dissolve into a grim struggle if the dancers could not do the steps the way Balanchine wanted them done.

Rehearsals with Balanchine could be just as exciting as actually performing his ballets. He was always creating, inventing, tinkering; and if he changed his mind about how he wanted a step done—and he was not above doing so—I knew that it was because his thinking had evolved or because he had made a discovery, perhaps by watching one of us. He could see the different ways the same step could best be done by different dancers. The more I watched and worked with Balanchine, the more my admiration grew. I knew with absolute certainty that I was in the place I was meant to be.

These daily pleasures and cheerful thoughts, however, obscured the fact that I had not been advancing steadily and getting more principal roles, as I felt I should have. In my more realistic moments, I felt as though I were in a holding pattern, and I had no inkling of when, where, or how I was going to land. Even in my gloomiest moments, however, I never lost hope. I always maintained my belief that some day I would be a principal dancer.

At the time, I only dimly understood that my woes were due both to my status as a senior corps member and to the fact I had been taken out of many of my corps roles in a show of confidence. In exchange, I expected to get some better roles, as had happened to others before me. But that didn't happen right away, and I remained for what seemed an eternity in this limbo. Cast infrequently, I watched and waited, wanting only to be on stage. Often I danced less than four times a week. If one dances too seldom, regardless of the level, the stage begins to seem like alien territory. After all, there is only so much one can do in a class or a rehearsal room. Some of the most valuable learning happens on stage.

During performances of my difficult roles, when I felt stretched to the limit of my ability, I imagined my fate being decided on the basis of those few moments, as Balanchine watched from the wings. Such fantasies only made me more nervous and unsteady. Nor was I reassured by the knowledge that what was happening to me had happened to countless others who had risen, either by seniority or ability, to the top of the corps. Regardless of why I was being ignored, I was determined not to neglect my dancing. I wanted to be prepared if an opportunity arose. I would keep improving, no matter what!

When the Company traveled to Los Angeles in August 1973, Jerome Robbins surprised me by putting me in the part of the Girl in Mauve in *Dances at a Gathering*. This role had been created by Kay Mazzo, who had a unique romantic quality, and I was not an obvious choice to succeed her; previously I had been cast in roles with difficult steps that had to be done sharply and clearly. In *Dances*, Jerry often wanted steps to blend with each other. He didn't require clarity, as Balanchine did. Because the ballet was not so much about steps as it was about dancers interacting and having fun with each other, Jerry continually stressed looking at one's partner as much as possible.

At first I pushed too hard, and one of my partners suggested I relax and dance in a more gentle manner. Jerry's corrections, on the other hand, always had to do with specific details, things also mentioned to other people in the ballet.

Jerry also cast me as the Girl in Green in *Dances*, a role created by Violette Verdy. This role relied for effect largely on the presentation of personality, although it had its share of technical difficulties. Jerry coached me and gave me an idea of the type of personality to be projected. He seemed to have a specific type in mind and kept saying,

"Think about Doubrovska, the way she walks around the room, plays with her skirt, the way she is elegant but somewhat eccentric."

Jerry had very clear ideas about how the movements should be made, when they should be sharp and when they should be stretched out. He sometimes even told me where I should look. But every now and then he would say, "Do what you want here, but make it sudden and different from what you have done before," and that gave me some freedom.

I enjoyed the challenges of both these roles and liked moving in a new way that wasn't strictly classical. For some of the steps in *Dances,* particularly in Violette's part, it didn't matter if I was turned in; the gestures were often more important than the steps. It was like "marking" a variation: showing someone vaguely what the steps were without actually doing them full out. Among the more difficult moments for me were those when all I had to do was stand still, while continuing to command the audience's attention. These brought to mind one of Balanchine's more famous culinary analogies: "It's hard to stand facing front and looking straight front. It's like cooking a veal roast with no garlic, just salt and pepper. It's hard to make it taste interesting."

In class, I had worked my way, slowly and discreetly, trying not to offend others, to one of the two positions in the front row, right in front of Balanchine. Because he spoke so softly, he always needed someone in the front of his class who could interpret his instructions. The person demonstrating the step naturally got the first corrections. Few were willing to assume that role and the exposure that went with it, and fewer still were any good at it. Colleen and I shared the burden, and the satisfaction. Sometimes one of us understood one part of a step Balanchine wanted, while the other understood another part; and somehow we'd manage to show the step to his satisfaction. There were times, though, when we were both bewildered.

There were occasions outside of class and rehearsal, when I seemed to pique Balanchine's curiosity. To prepare for my part in "Waltz of the Flowers," in Act II of *The Nutcracker,* I always warmed up backstage, rather than in one of the studios, during Act I. I gave myself a long, hard barre with extreme combinations of tendus, ronds de jambe, and all the rest at very fast and very slow tempos, just as he gave them to us in class. For many steps, the slow tempos were as hard, in their way, as the fast. At times, out of the corner of my eye, I could see Balanchine standing there, watching me from a distance. He never said a word to me about them, but those warm-ups of mine, which had become second nature to me, appeared to interest him.

One day, after a performance of *Who Cares?,* Balanchine came up to me and a strange conversation ensued:

"Is better, dear, better," he said, "but your legs . . ." and then, breaking off in mid-sentence, he drew his hands apart to show that my legs should be more elongated. I thought he was saying my muscles had become too bulky. I couldn't imagine what else he might mean. It didn't occur to me that he was suggesting I lose weight. Although I recognized I had gained weight in the last year, I certainly didn't consider myself over-weight. It was a perfect example of a dancer looking in the mirror and seeing only what she wants to see.

In 1973 the Company traveled to Berlin for six weeks to have a number of ballets filmed by German producers for possible distribution all over the world. I was not used at all for the first two weeks, and so, with free time on my hands, I toured the city, vis-ited museums, and indulged my sweet tooth on rich German pastries. I may not have felt heavy when I arrived in Berlin, but by the end of the six weeks even I could tell I was fat.

The filming studios were forty-five minutes by bus from our hotel, and there was never more than forty-five minutes allotted for class. The studio for class was very small and, unfortunately, had a cement floor. No one, of course, wanted to practice any jumps. Balanchine tried to fit a proper class into the time available, but it was all terribly rushed. What we really needed was a nice slow warm-up to ease us into a long day of filming.

Many of the dancers had killing days on the set: eight hours spent endlessly repeat-ing the same sequence was not uncommon. The directors of the project would not listen to Balanchine, who soon soured on the project, realizing that the results would be worthless. They were bent on "artistic" camera work, filming from every imaginable angle, zooming in and out—the very thing that Balanchine wanted to avoid. Years later I saw some of the results: a perfectly ridiculous rendition of *Stars and Stripes* with the camera right, left, high, and low, nervously zeroing in on heads and feet at the most un-expected moments. It was impossible to tell what was happening. Only the music had remained intact.

I sensed in Berlin that Balanchine was irritated with me because of the weight I had put on. When I returned home, I was heavier than ever before—a shocking 130 pounds. Like many others before me, I had deluded myself into thinking I was still thin, but I soon came to my senses, went on a diet, and lost weight. I later overheard a comment by Balanchine that confirmed he had noticed my unwanted pounds, "Used to be like sau-sage. Now look at her!"

There are often times when dancers feel, rightly or wrongly, that they are victims of injustice. I was no exception. When the Company returned from Berlin, Christine Red-path was put into the principal role in the third movement of *Symphony in C,* and I felt it was terribly unfair. Blonde and beautiful, Chris was definitely someone whose romantic presence made her stand out on stage. Her talent often made up for her technical short-comings, and she was very friendly with Balanchine. But she had a weak jump and that role, first and foremost, demanded jumping ability and vitality. I explained it away by telling myself, "Mr. B likes her and wants her to learn to jump and to be a little more dynamic," but it still hurt.

There were other times when circumstances seemed to conspire against me. One weekend Marnee Morris, who ordinarily danced the first movement of *Symphony in C,* injured herself and a replacement had to be found immediately. Having danced the first ballet in the matinee and knowing I had five hours before I had to return to the theater to prepare for the last ballet of the evening, I had decided to go home, a ten-minute walk from the theater. During those few minutes, Rosemary Dunleavy, on instructions from Balanchine, tried to reach me by phone to tell me to come in to learn the role and dance it that evening. When I returned to the theater several hours later, I felt a stab of envy as I saw Colleen on stage rehearsing *Symphony in C.* I didn't yet know what had happened. Then Rosemary saw me and called out: "There you are. We tried to get you!"

On another occasion, Colleen was thrown in to learn Marnee's part in *Serenade,* another principal role. I was a quick study, but I couldn't learn roles as fast as Colleen. This talent made her invaluable, but each time I was passed over in her favor it weighed heavily on me.

In 1974 Balanchine choreographed his production of *Coppélia* and cast me in Act III as Dawn in the allegorical section representing man's workday. It was the second time he had created a variation for me, and I was so thrilled my anxieties receded to the back of my mind. Once again, he produced something technically difficult by combining fast footwork with large movements that made me change direction all the time. There were frightening turns à la seconde as well as jumps that landed on pointe in plié on one foot. As if that weren't hard enough, he asked me to end the variation with one of those jumps and then balance in that pose before exiting into the wings. Try as I might, it was impossible for me to do it with any consistency.

My problems increased when I tried to do the variation in my costume. It had a very full, three-tiered, knee-length skirt that constantly threw me off balance. Every time I finished a turn, the skirt would sweep around my body a second later, pulling me off balance. The movement of the skirt also tended to knock me off balance on the last jump on pointe. It was terribly frustrating to have the costume add to my unsteadiness.

I did my best in the premiere and continued to work on the variation afterward, but it was no use. Balanchine, realizing how demanding many of my steps were, decided to change the ending to something more secure and reliable. But I still had to worry about those troublesome turns à la seconde. On my own in rehearsal I started experimenting to see if a slightly modified version would work better. I had never changed any choreography before. The steps were his, I felt, and who was I to change them? Even if there were many ballets about which he was not particular, I knew there were works like *Apollo, The Four Temperaments,* and *Agon* that he wanted done just so. He rarely changed his mind about these ballets but, when he did, he wanted those changes to remain. If I was going to alter his choreography at all, I wanted to have his approval. When I went to him to demonstrate the changes I wanted to make in *Coppélia,* I was taken aback when he just smiled and said: "Do what you want, dear. It's yours."

Merrill rehearsing *Coppélia,* 1974. (© *1984 Martha Swope*)

What faith and generosity! Just the same, I would have liked to hear his opinion, for, although they *felt* right to me, only he could judge if they *looked* right.

Over the years, this variation changed each time someone new danced the role. The dancers who performed the role after me found many of the steps so difficult that Balanchine decided to change them. Recently, Rosemary asked me, "Do you remember the original choreography? It would be nice to get it back, at least for the record."

I agreed to try. I worked on it, hoping the music would stir my muscle memory (automatic movement patterns) and bring it back. The variation had been altered so often, even while I was dancing it, that my muscles didn't have a clear memory of it. But with Rosemary's help, I resurrected most of Balanchine's original steps.

CHAPTER

BALLET IS MORE POPULAR than ever, and balletomanes abound. But few, I suspect, have a sympathetic understanding of the rigors of a dancer's life and an appreciation of its rewards. Fewer still would be willing to let their own lives be affected by such uncertainties. And, of those who would, how many would bring such a perceptive eye to performances that they would be able to tell a dancer what her fellow dancers can't or won't tell her, and in a way that inspires rather than offends? They must be rare indeed, but in the spring of 1974 I met one such person.

Kibbe Fitzpatrick was one of those nondancers with whom I had imagined I would have very little in common, but we hit it off right from the start. Tall and slim, he would have been a perfect partner for me, had he been a dancer. A born-and-bred New Yorker, he had traveled all over the world, studied a great deal, immersed himself in many languages, practiced different sports, and led the kind of varied life that dancers so rarely have. I loved talking with him—it was his pleasant voice that first attracted me—and I was amazed at how he brought me out of myself.

Kibbe was a simultaneous interpreter at the United Nations, and that interested me right away. I had always been intrigued by the sound of Russian, which I often heard around the theater. At school I had studied French, but found it difficult and thought I would never learn it properly. It was a pleasure to be in the company of someone who found foreign languages exhilarating rather than intimidating.

Kibbe had been an avid athlete since his days at Kent School. He had been captain of the Yale cross-country team in 1957, and after graduation had continued to run competitively. He had taught tennis and played in tournaments and one year earned a national ranking. His interest in sports and movement led him to ballet, and at first he had seen us only as superb athletes. Later, his piano training helped him to appreciate the grace and musicality of dancers. Most important to me was his understanding of what it meant to sacrifice almost everything in the pursuit of one goal. Whereas he had dabbled in many things, he found my devotion to one thing very appealing.

During our first few dates after performances, I really opened up for the first time in my life. Even around my closest friends, I was more a listener than a talker, but with Kibbe there were times when I felt I was practically dominating the conversation. At first we talked a lot about ballet and the performances he had just seen. His questions and comments always had a provocative twist, which forced me to think about ballet from a fresh point of view.

Soon Kibbe and I were seeing each other every evening. When I was free, we would linger over dinner, discovering to our surprise how much two very different people could have in common. When I was dancing, he was always in the audience, and afterward I would take him backstage and introduce him to all my friends in the corps. I was wary of Balanchine's reaction to my having a man in tow around the theater, since for many years he had had a notorious aversion to the husbands and boyfriends of his female dancers. That July in Saratoga, however, the casual atmosphere around the Saratoga Performing Arts Center (SPAC) made it easy for Kibbe to spend much more time at the theater, and he even watched some of Balanchine's classes there.

Kibbe was obviously enthralled with the world that had become so commonplace to me. He kept searching for parallels between his experience in sports and life, and the peculiar goings-on inside the Company. He was curious about so much that I took for granted. Did dancers really expect to learn anything in a classroom with fifty dancers and one teacher? Why were there dancers on the roster who were never seen on stage? If Balanchine liked tall women, why didn't he have lots of tall men to go with them? Wasn't there an exercise room or a weights room for the men? And no therapist or masseur? Didn't dancers need someone to help them take care of their injuries? High school football teams had better facilities, he thought. Why did toe shoes wear out so quickly? Perhaps someone in Taiwan could be found to make toe shoes that would last more than an hour.

We often talked about the strengths and weaknesses of other dancers in the Company, and I was fascinated by the opinions of someone who had a very perceptive eye but virtually no technical knowledge. It was the first time in my life I had talked at length with a sensitive outsider about ballet, and it made me realize how a dancer's hard work and narrow focus can easily blind her to the general impression her dancing is making on the balletgoer. The more we talked, the greater my curiosity about what Kibbe thought of my dancing, but he said almost nothing about it. When he went off on a three-week vacation after we had been seeing each other for a month, I still had no idea what he really thought.

A little earlier that spring, Jacques had begun work on a new ballet to Vivaldi music called, appropriately enough, *Saltarelli* ("little jumps," in Italian). There were two principal couples, and Jacques had Christine Redpath and me learn both female parts. From beginning to end they required speed and stamina and were filled with jumps and lots of sharp pointe work that I could do well. The buoyant music and playful steps made the ballet fun to learn and rehearse, and I knew I was well cast.

I danced well at the premiere and was sorry Kibbe was not there to see me. I was sure I would have received my first compliments from him. The ballet was a perfect outlet for my energy and enthusiasm, and the fact that I was no longer a sausage helped!

After the premiere, Jacques gave a party at his home. At one point in the evening, I was sitting with Balanchine and a friend of Jacques's, Mrs. Krinsky, an NYCB fan to whom *Saltarelli* had been dedicated. Mrs. Krinsky turned to me and said, "Oh, you danced beautifully tonight. Wasn't she beautiful, Mr. B?"

Balanchine smiled and nodded. "Oh, yes! In three or four years, very good dancer."

I was shocked. I had been basking in the attention paid to me because of *Saltarelli,* congratulating myself on my dancing and thinking it would probably be only a year or so until I would be made a principal. I had conveniently ignored the fact that I was not yet even a soloist, but there was no ignoring Balanchine's comment. Three or four years? "Well, I'll show him," I thought a little defiantly.

After *Saltarelli,* Balanchine seemed to see me in a new light. It wasn't the first time that he had taken particular notice when he saw one of his dancers do well in someone else's ballet. Perhaps he had liked the high energy level I maintained throughout such a difficult ballet, or it may have been all the fast, clear footwork that drew his attention. Whatever it was, shortly after he saw *Saltarelli* Balanchine chose me to fill in for Kay Mazzo in *Diamonds.* This had a very special significance.

After Suzanne left the Company, Balanchine was very careful in the way he replaced her in *Diamonds* and all her other roles, using dancers he genuinely liked or felt were well suited to each role. He certainly had never used corps people. So when he chose me to replace Kay, who was injured, I was astonished and flattered.

The truth was that, at the time, the Company had a serious ballerina shortage, the kind of problem that seems to come to the Company in cycles. Melissa Hayden had retired and Gelsey Kirkland had left to join American Ballet Theatre. Violette Verdy and Allegra Kent were often injured and danced only sporadically. Patricia McBride, who was tremendously overworked, carried the burden of the repertory along with Kay Mazzo, Karin von Aroldingen, and Sara Leland. But Balanchine did not seem to want to use Karin and Sara in strictly classical roles, and so that was the area in which the shortage was particularly acute. It was obvious he would be forced to use younger dancers, and he could easily have chosen Chris Redpath for *Diamonds,* because the role required lyricism, and she was more lyrical than I. Colleen was another obvious choice, and she usually had an indefinable edge over me. I was the lucky one, however, but without this shortage it's unlikely he would have turned to me at that time for *Diamonds.*

Kay taught me the role, but Balanchine spent a lot of time with me and my partner, Jean-Pierre Bonnefous, during the four days that we had for rehearsals. I particularly remembered what he said about a segment in the ballet where I had been taught that the ballerina was to be lifted and put down, four times in succession, on the four corners of an imaginary diamond. That seemed logical and easy enough, but when Jean-Pierre and I did it that way in rehearsal Balanchine intervened: " 'They' always make diamond because they think is more clever. But never was. Lifts should just be side to side. I tell them, but they never do." Whatever had possessed so many dancers to change so many steps arbitrarily, I wondered. True, I had changed steps in *Coppélia* but that was because I couldn't do them. These lifts seemed easy side to side. And why was Balanchine so lenient about points he cared about? Had the dancers ignored his words? I hoped he would always feel he could tell me whatever he wanted and that I would do it.

My first appearance in *Diamonds* provoked the most unusual reaction from Balanchine. As he and I walked off the stage after the bows, he said: "Excellent, dear." That astounded me. Any compliment from him was a rarity, but a superlative of that magnitude was a real event. Surprised that I had impressed him so much, I let those happy words ring in my ears.

I expected at least a similar compliment from Kibbe when we went out for dinner after the performance, but he seemed subdued and evasive and kept the conversation on other subjects. He still had said next to nothing about my dancing, but I hoped that my "excellent" performance in *Diamonds* would elicit *some* comment from him. "You know, that first entrance you make," he finally said. "Well, you looked a little stiff. To tell the truth, I was very uncomfortable watching you." How could he say such a thing? What did he mean? But he quickly changed the subject.

My mind kept going back to the opening moments of the pas de deux. The corps had just exited after dancing the first movement of the ballet, and the stage was empty. Then the music for the pas de deux began. I remembered that in rehearsals, in order to save time, Jean-Pierre and I had always asked the pianist to start where our actual dancing began rather than where we made our entrances. But, as I waited in the wings before my first appearance, I suddenly realized to my horror that, although I knew how much music there was before we started to dance, I didn't know exactly when to walk out on stage. I had planned to watch Jean-Pierre and enter when he did. Since he had done the ballet before, I knew I could rely on him. But when the music began he was nowhere in sight. At the last second, or so it seemed to me, he walked into the wings and straight

out onto the stage. Fortunately, I had waited for him, and I was able to make my entrance when he did, but I realized I must have been a picture of consternation at that precise moment.

Did I recover my composure after that? Did I redeem myself in the eyes of those who, like Kibbe, had shared my initial alarm? What else had he seen? I was afraid to ask.

In Saratoga that July, when we began performances at SPAC, I was pleasantly surprised to find I had received a big raise and was being paid a soloist's salary. But there had been no mention of a promotion. Dancers who had been in the Company longer than I often said that in Balanchine's mind a raise was a greater reward than a promotion. I appreciated the raise and whatever meaning lay behind it, but I felt that only a promotion to soloist would guarantee that I would continue to be given soloist and even principal roles. A promotion seemed essential for my peace of mind.

As soon as the subscription brochure came out that fall, Renée and I put our heads together and studied the programs. We concluded that Patty was impossibly overworked and that other people would have to learn some of her ballets. Since Balanchine had been so pleased with me in *Diamonds,* he might have me learn the ballerina role in *Tchaikovsky Piano Concerto.* Still giddy at that thought as I studied the brochure, I suddenly saw it: my name listed as a soloist! I had been promoted along with Colleen and Chris. Was that the way things were done in the Company? Perhaps one day I would awaken and find my name listed in the program as a principal.

Despite my great elation, I had no illusions that the three of us were really running neck-and-neck. They were both getting more parts than I, but at least the few roles I was getting were among the best. Balanchine undoubtedly enjoyed their company more than he did mine. He loved socializing with his women and Colleen and Chris, with their outgoing personalities, probably found it very easy to talk with him about things besides ballet.

Kibbe remarked to me that most men would have an adverse reaction to anyone as reticent as I was with Balanchine, and he advised me to try to be friendlier to him—to talk more, at least. It wasn't good enough just being attentive and respectful when he spoke to me. I had to show how much I liked him. I wanted to change, and I began to plan things I might say during those chance encounters with him in the theater that usually found me nearly speechless, but I succeeded only in becoming a little more amiable; I could not become more talkative.

One evening, Kibbe and I went out dancing together for the first time. After we had danced for ten minutes, Kibbe led me back to our table with a serious expression on his face. He obviously had something important to tell me: "When you dance at the State Theater, you have basically only two expressions on your face: a pained ballerina look and a forced smile—and they're both unattractive. Neither bears the slightest resemblance to the woman I've been dancing with for the past ten minutes. This is the real

OPPOSITE *Diamonds,* Merrill and Adam Lüders. (© *1984 Martha Swope*)

you. If I had been a photographer, I could have snapped a hundred pictures of you just now and captured a different look, smile, and mood each time. You were wonderful, charming, changing all the time, caught up in the movement, inspired by the music, reveling in the moment, great to watch! That's how you can be on the stage, the way I know you want to be. The audience wants to know who is doing all those incredible steps. That mystery woman with her two masks is no fun at all."

I was utterly dismayed. Everybody had been telling me how great my technique was and what a beautiful dancer I was, and here was Kibbe telling me I was "no fun" on the stage.

Something told me he was right. We had already seen eye-to-eye on other dancers in the Company, and on so many other things. Kibbe's whole approach was so disarmingly cheerful and positive that I couldn't help being swept up by his enthusiasm. It did make sense, and he had put it so clearly. A dancer's innate charm and personality mustn't be left in the wings, no matter how daunting the steps.

That was his initial salvo. Then the whole truth about my nerve-racking entrance in *Diamonds,* and all the other performances he had seen, came pouring out. I often held my breath, he said, pursed my lips, stuck my chin out, and stared blankly while my mind raced ahead to the next virtuoso passage. Or, if I was feeling more confident, my facial expression almost dared the audience to pay attention to me. It was as if I were saying: "Look at me. I'm a good dancer. I'll prove it to you."

It all was gradually becoming clear to me. Without realizing it, I had been suppressing my true feelings and presenting a false image of myself. How could anyone watching me dance have realized what I was hiding? How could they have known I was too insecure to show the exquisite pleasure I experienced while dancing?

Balanchine had always shied away from making critical comments about my stage presence. In fact, whenever he brought up the subject of "presence" with anyone, he spoke in vague, general terms, although I knew he was well aware of it if a dancer did not present herself well on stage. I also knew it was no accident that his favorite dancers throughout the years had all had definite personalities on stage.

He did, however, seem to be trying to convey a message to me. Over and over again I heard the same words: "Too sweet, dear, too sweet—too nice." I couldn't grasp his meaning. He made this comment to other dancers as well, and in an effort to understand I began watching those who received the same correction. I had often made discoveries in this way. My conclusion was that our *movements* were somehow "too sweet." He probably wanted us to be more forceful and dynamic. And yet, I thought my movements already *were* dynamic. . . .

At first I was afraid to ask him what he meant, not wanting to admit that I couldn't understand his point. Nor did I want to run the risk of embarrassing him. He was self-conscious about his English—unjustifiably so—and he might have felt that his poor choice of words was to blame for my lack of understanding.

One day, following a performance of *Cortège,* he stopped me in the hallway. "Your variation . . . too sweet, dear," he said once again. In a feeble voice I finally said, "Mr. B, I just don't know what you mean."

He looked surprised, then troubled. I continued: "I want so badly to understand and do what you want, but I have no idea what you mean by 'too sweet.' "

I paused to catch my breath. He answered with movements instead of words, for movement was often his most effective means of communication. Affecting a forced smile, he began to imitate the way I danced the variation, showing how I tried to draw too much attention to my feet by bending forward as I looked at them.

"Just do it," he added. "Just dance."

He couldn't mean this literally, I thought. Wouldn't I then look like what he often called a "zombie"? What did he really mean? What, in fact, was my problem?

Kibbe had by then seen plenty of whatever my problem was, and he had seen it disappear, as if by magic, the evening I went out dancing with him. If I could just understand what was so different about myself that evening, I could perhaps re-create those feelings on the stage.

My natural reserve had definitely disappeared that evening. I had felt no constraints. There were no specific steps to worry about; there was no role to confine me. I didn't have to worry about what constituted proper stage deportment. It didn't matter if no one liked the way I was dancing. I was enjoying myself just dancing with Kibbe—that was all that mattered. "Just dancing." Those had been Balanchine's words. Had I solved the riddle?

I felt as if I were beginning to emerge from a dense fog. Suddenly I saw how much I had limited myself. Kibbe was right. Basically I had only two approaches to my many different roles. In the quieter ballets I used my serious approach and often wore what Kibbe had called my "pained ballerina look." For the other types of ballets, I thought a smile was required at all times. I was particularly determined to avoid showing that I was being caused any difficulty by the technical demands I was facing. The result was a broad, unchanging, artificial smile. It never occurred to me to modulate my expression. Most important of all, I realized I had rarely been myself on stage, for I had been too busy trying to fit into what I imagined was the proper mold.

With Kibbe's help and a lot of self-discipline, I gradually grew accustomed to putting myself in a frame of mind on stage that was closer to the way I felt when I was happy and relaxed offstage. I taught myself to be aware of small changes in my facial expressions, and then I experimented with when and where to use them. That, in turn, made me more attentive to the music and its infinite moods, for I had always been very responsive to music and knew that a very musical dancer was in me, struggling to break free.

The results of my experimenting were immediate and astounding, even to my very critical self. I not only looked better—I felt better, more at ease. Compliments on my improved "dancing" poured in. People who had never noticed me before discovered me. Old admirers commented on the new me.

Shortly after the rehearsals for the 1974/75 fall–winter season began, my name went up on the rehearsal schedule to learn the ballerina role in *Tchaikovsky Piano Concerto*. Renée and I had guessed right. Now we guessed that I would not only learn the role but also perform it. Every evening *Piano Concerto* was scheduled that season, Patty would have to dance at least one other ballet on the program. Someone would have to replace her in at least one of her ballets, and I hoped it would be me in *Piano Concerto*. Of course, I knew that being chosen to learn a ballet did not necessarily mean I would perform it. If Balanchine came to my rehearsals and was not satisfied with what he saw, then what? Anything could happen.

John Taras taught me the ballet, with the exception of the pas de deux in the second movement. Patty taught me the new version of that, which Balanchine had rechoreographed for her and Peter Martins in 1973. Most of the steps were so classical I had no trouble remembering them, but that didn't mean they were easy to execute. While dancing in the corps, I had often watched the ballerina from the wings or from the stage and, although I knew the role was taxing, it had been impossible to appreciate the degree of difficulty involved, especially in the opening variation.

Once I had finished learning the ballet, I was left on my own to rehearse it. Without any warning, Balanchine showed up a week later at one of my rehearsals. My heart started to pound, but his friendly and patient manner put me at ease. He went through the whole ballet with me, from beginning to end, and showed and explained how he wanted each step done. Nothing could have been more enlightening, or fascinating. Suddenly the purpose behind so much of what he taught in class became clear.

For my first entrance in the ballet, I ran on, posed in fifth position on pointe, and then wove in and out among a line of four corps girls who retreated one at a time after I passed them. I thought I should hold that initial pose, as if to say to the audience, "Here I am." But Balanchine was adamant: "Don't stop there; don't pose. Start running immediately." I did what he asked, but I wanted to understand why. The answer came from the music. My fleeting pose in fifth position was on a high note. This note was at the beginning of the measure and was also the first of a long cascade of notes on the piano. My steps were directly related to what the solo piano was playing. If that high note had not been the first note in a series of triplets, Balanchine might have found an extended pose suitable. Another choreographer, listening solely to that high note, might have thought it was the end of a phrase, instead of the beginning, and choreographed accordingly.

After weaving through the corps girls, I ran in a big circle, ending on center stage with an unusual double turn. Although that turn is similar to a classical turn done on pointe or half-pointe, here it was done with the heel barely off the floor. This was the first in a series of notoriously difficult swivel turns.

The double turn itself, done on a straight left leg, was easy. It was the stopping that presented a monumental difficulty. Balanchine did not want us to use any of the usual means for braking: normally we might put a foot down and plié, or in some way change the position of our body. Here the double swivel turn had to end of its own accord, because the toe of the right foot, which had to touch the floor ever so delicately at the end of the turn, was no help at all in braking. In addition, the straight left leg had to stay straight at the finish. There had to be, then, a perfectly timed loss of momentum. Try as I might, I simply couldn't finish that step perfectly, and so I had to cheat with a little plié. As if that first step weren't enough, it was followed by four more double swivel turns separated by steps that posed their own problems.

The second swivel turn was different: it was on the right leg, in plié, and ended with the left foot pointing back while the right leg remained in plié. There, the same problem occurred. Balanchine wanted the turn simply to end, unaided. There were three more swivel turns to follow, making a total of five, each with its own little oddity. No amount of rehearsing made these swivels work consistently. They seemed completely hit-or-miss, and I was not the first person to feel this way. I realized it would take steady nerves to race onto the stage and face so many steps that seemed to defy my control.

When I rehearsed on stage for the first time, I came across a new set of problems. I seemed to have a knack for stepping on cracks or ridges (caused by trapdoors) hidden under the linoleum. If I missed the cracks, I hit the tapes that held the strips of linoleum in place or repaired the breaks in it. As I worked over and over again on the hardest steps in the ballet, I tried to learn how to avoid all these stage hazards. I found out where I had to begin certain sequences so that I'd find my feet on a smooth surface when the hard steps came. If only I could have looked down.

As I thought about these steps, I marveled at the interplay of steps and music. The match was perfect, but that made it all the more important that they be done correctly. There was no extra time, yet I had to appear totally unhurried. Royalty doesn't rush around, and the ballerina belonged to royalty, Balanchine said. After each turn, my instinct was to pause to collect my wits, and take my time with the preparation, but the pianist's music didn't permit that. Since the pianist was on his own in this piano cadenza—which was not conducted—I tried to rehearse with the pianist who was going to play in performance, which would at least help me know what to expect. At the time, Gordon Boelzner was the only pianist in the Company who played *Piano Concerto* in performance, and he was in such demand for other rehearsals that I often couldn't rehearse with him. It was only during the week of my performance that I was able to work with him regularly; unfortunately, by that time, I was used to the way others played the piece.

The difficulties of these little turns and the steps that followed seemed wholly justified by the music in this brilliant piano cadenza. The music accompanying each swivel turn was a kind of flourish that accelerated to a sudden and unexpected stop. If the ballerina ended any of the turns with the usual braking techniques, perhaps by planting a foot firmly on the floor, the audience would see the end of the turn coming and the surprise effect would be lost.

I learned and rehearsed everything as it had been shown to me and as it had been done in all probability by the many ballerinas who had danced the role over the years. But, as Mr. B went through the ballet step by step with me, I believe he saw an opportunity to reintroduce much that had fallen by the wayside. A case in point was one of the two little solos in the middle of the first-movement pas de deux. This solo contained a step that had seemed quite straightforward when I learned it; but, not surprisingly, Balanchine gave it a novel twist.

My partner had just left me standing alone on center stage. After three sets of two girls each ran around me, I started the step. I relevéd on pointe, hopping slightly to the side as my working leg went from a side extension into passé. Balanchine's idea was to give the impression that the standing leg had been chased away by the foot of the working leg as it was put into passé. The hop is what creates the illusion of one leg's forcing the other to move, and it is what makes the step unique. Otherwise, it would be a plain relevé ending in passé, with the upper body bending toward the passé leg for added interest. As he tried to get me to do the step with the right flavor, he said, "Should be jazzy." It took a sure touch to put a jazzy little step into a Petipa-style ballet such as this.

This moment is followed by a step in which, as I repeatedly piqué on pointe on my right leg, I travel in a small circle in the center of the stage. Each time I piqué, my left foot beats under the arch of the right foot. At the completion of each beating movement, I hold the tip of the working foot up against the arch of the supporting foot—making the accent "in"—until I'm ready to move on. The usual step, one Balanchine often put in other ballets, had the dancers ending these little beats with the accent "out," that is, with the leg opening to the side, as if the beating foot were trying to get away from the supporting foot. Here was another example of a step Balanchine wanted done differently from the way I had learned it.

I thrived on all these little changes. In some cases, he was simply correcting errors that had been handed down from ballerina to ballerina. These "errors" might be steps that Balanchine had previously altered to suit a specific dancer, or a change made by a dancer herself, or even a misinterpretation of the step by the person learning the role. They had most likely been passed on because Balanchine hadn't had the time or inclination to fix them. In other cases, I suspect that new steps, which were little strokes of genius, popped unbidden into his mind. Whatever the case, I was delighted he saw rehearsals with me as an opportunity to demonstrate exactly how he wanted all the steps done. Nothing could have made me happier! I didn't care that I had to unlearn so much that I had been practicing.

Toward the end of the first movement, there is a moment when the corps forms an upside-down V (from the point of view of the audience). I run on and stop just inside the point of the V, and then do a tricky combination, which is the second big trouble spot in the ballet. I start with a piqué on pointe on my right foot while doing a low passé with my left foot; then immediately I plié on a flat foot while the passé leg shoots out into a low développé to the front. That's basically the step: piqué/plié with one foot; then piqué/plié with the other foot, and those two piqué/pliés are done while making one turn. I do this combination again and again as I first travel forward downstage along the side of the V, which is to my right. Then comes a little turn on two feet on pointe (a *soutenu*) before I do the same thing traveling backward along the same diagonal, except with the développés to the back.

The combination is executed at breakneck speed, and clarity can be produced and interest created only by showing the working leg at the completion of the développé. It must be held there, still, for a split second; otherwise, the step is a blur. If the step were done much more slowly, then both the working leg traveling beautifully through passé and the hold at the end of the développé would show nicely. But, at this speed, I have to choose one part of the step to emphasize. By shooting the leg out and holding it there for that split second, I emphasize the in-and-out movement. At the same time, I'm showing an up-and-down movement with the piqué/plié. All the while I'm turning, as well as moving forward, then backward, on a diagonal. To add to the virtuosity, the music, which starts fast, gets even faster. Balanchine put everything but jumps into this fantastic combination.

My greatest challenge was the rapid tempo of the music. As I moved forward along the diagonal for the first time, the tempo was so fast I could barely keep up with the music. Then, as I began to travel backward, the music accelerated, but I still had to go forward and back one more time! If I let the pianist get ahead of me, it would have been impossible to catch up without leaving out steps. I had to know when and how fast he was going to speed up, and the rehearsals were often pretty ragged.

I felt a great sense of accomplishment when I conquered these hard steps, all of which fit the music so perfectly. I could feel that I had it within me to make these steps look and feel like part of the music. It was exhilarating beyond words trying to breathe the right kind of life into them, and I was nearly certain that the results would be equally exhilarating to those watching.

Corps members often stayed to watch my rehearsals and burst into applause when a particularly difficult step happened to go well. I loved it when people came to my rehearsals, although this added to the pressure to do well. Somehow, I never enjoyed it as much when I worked alone.

Balanchine, too, seemed pleased with my general progress, and one day he really surprised me when he commented on that difficult step at the end of the first movement, on which I had worked so hard: "Nobody has been able to do, dear; you're the first one who can do."

"Oh, Mr. B, it's so hard, especially going backward."

"Yes, is true, very difficult," he admitted, uncharacteristically.

Balanchine frequently did not recognize how difficult his ballets were. He did not intend most of them to be difficult. But here Balanchine wanted the ballerina to match the virtuosity of the pianist and the music. Of course, there's so much more to *Piano Concerto,* and even to the first movement, than sheer virtuosity. In the opening cadenza, the ballerina does not, as happens so often in other ballets, first simply present her serene, beautiful self to the audience. Here, she gives a sovereign display of grandeur, with flourishes. The ballerina is royalty in her own realm, as suggested by the way in which, immediately after entering, she dismisses her subjects, who quickly retreat to the back of the stage. Then, in the midst of so much splendor, even without the original tutus and the St. Petersburg backdrop, the ballerina meets the challenges of the music, the choreography, and the audience—without, we hope, looking frantic or frazzled.

As I rehearsed the two big technical trouble spots in the first movement (as well as the rest of the ballet) over and over again, I soon began to strain the ligaments on either side of the bunion on my left foot. The more I rehearsed, the worse it got. When Balanchine came to take the first run-through rehearsal with the corps, I danced the whole rehearsal as if it were a performance. Another rehearsal was scheduled for me alone a half hour after the run-through, so that I could go over any corrections Balanchine had given me. When I got up to go to that rehearsal, after resting for a half hour, my foot hurt so much that I could not even walk. I was finished for the day, but the next day I was back at it. From that point on, the pain never left me as I rehearsed *Piano Concerto* and the other ballets that lay ahead early that fall season.

Peter Martins, who was my partner in these rehearsals with Balanchine, gave me some badly needed confidence. By then he had learned what Balanchine wanted in partnering in general; and his sure hands, great strength, and phenomenally quick reactions made him an inexperienced ballerina's dream come true. In spite of that, I felt very inept and should have liked to rehearse with Peter every day, but I didn't dare impose on him.

Balanchine took as much interest in the two pas de deux in the ballet as he had in my solos. He had specific suggestions about the way I was to be lifted and put down, and he made it clear that it mattered a great deal how I gave my hand to my partner, and held his. He always seemed to be critical of the way a ballerina took her partner's hand. He showed me how a great deal of support could come from mere palm to palm pressure. He did not want to see clasped hands or grabbing with the fingers. It made him furious when he saw partners clasp each other's thumbs, something that often happens since it provides such a secure grip. It is definitely not attractive.

At one point in the first-movement pas de deux, Balanchine even told me where to look. It was a point in the ballet that vividly recalls the earlier *Ballet Imperial* setting. The ballerina is presented by her partner to her "subjects," the corps, who have been standing around the perimeter of the stage during the pas de deux

"Don't look at them! Don't acknowledge them!" he said. "You're royalty. Royalty doesn't have to bow to anyone. They bow to you and you ignore them."

Tchaikovsky Piano Concerto No. 2,
Merrill and Sean Lavery.
(© *1984 Martha Swope*)

I spent almost two weeks rehearsing and practicing steps; learning, unlearning, and relearning; anxiously waiting for the moment I hoped would come soon. It finally came at the end of my second week of rehearsing. There was my name on the casting sheet with the little asterisk next to it to show that I was doing the ballet for the first time.

As my debut approached, I worried more and more about those trouble spots and my toe gave me not a moment's relief. Aside from that, I was as well prepared as I could hope to be, though nothing, of course, could be done about my jangled nerves.

Finally the day came: November 15, 1974. Not surprisingly, I have no recollection of how I danced that evening. My nerves probably blocked out the memory of the thousand and one moments that made up that evening's performance. I cannot believe that it went smoothly, but if it had gone badly, I would have become terribly flustered, and *that* I would have remembered. The really bad performances are somehow more memorable than the really good ones.

But my first performance of *Piano Concerto* ended in a most memorable way. After the curtain came down, I breathed an immense sigh of relief and then, to my amazement, the corps applauded me. I knew they had been pulling for me, that they were all on my side, but this spontaneous expression of—was it admiration?—touched me. Then came the curtain calls, which I will never forget. There was curtain call after curtain call, more than I ever dreamed possible. Time and again I went out with Peter to bow. Even after the house lights came on, I was brought back out again and again. I will never truly understand what inspired the audience that evening, but I feel sure they were applauding more than just my dancing.

After the performance, Balanchine said not a word to me, but I can still see him standing there behind the curtain, through all the bows, watching me.

That season, Patty and I shared subsequent performances of *Piano Concerto.* I remember being terrified before each one, but I also looked forward to them. How fortunate for me that this ballet had not been thrust on me two or three years earlier! What a grim struggle I would have had, trying to cope with something essentially beyond me. There's no telling what the effect would have been. If a fuss had been made over me, would I have been deluded into thinking I was the new wunderkind of the NYCB? If no fuss had been made, if I had been awful, as I might well have been, what would have happened to my confidence? Others given similar "opportunities" too soon have been unable to restore their shattered self-image.

I seemed to have every member of the corps pulling for me that season; I had come to stand for something in their eyes. Every performance brought me notes of congratulation, comments of admiration and encouragement. Several girls told me that I had given them new hope, renewed their belief that by dint of hard work it was still possible to get somewhere. They had all watched me progress over the years, and they believed, as I did, that *Piano Concerto* and I had converged naturally, that the ballet had not been bestowed on me because of my beauty or body type or because I had struck someone's fancy. Their support was surprising and quite wonderful, especially since there seemed to be no jealousy. They all felt I fully deserved what I had been given. Any potential jealousy was replaced by inspiration and hope that they too could advance. In their eyes, this kind of justice hadn't always been at work in the Company. In all the excitement, not once did I detect a discouraging word or disapproving glance from the corps.

My success in *Piano Concerto* brought me an even more daunting assignment. I was given a week in which to learn and rehearse *Theme and Variations* (from *Tchaikovsky's Suite No. 3*). Four years earlier I had done one of the demi-soloist roles in this ballet when Balanchine had revived it for Gelsey Kirkland and Edward Villella. It was Gelsey's first big chance and, although I had always liked and admired her, it amazed me that Balanchine had given such a difficult ballerina role to someone so young. But, she had risen to the challenge and danced very well in *Theme.* Thereafter, I was in awe of her.

I knew from having watched Gelsey that I was facing another one of those terribly difficult ballets; one reviewer called it and *Tchaikovsky Piano Concerto* the Tchaikovsky "gut-crunchers." I soon discovered that *Theme* not only required more stamina than *Piano Concerto* but presented even greater hazards. In *Piano Concerto,* although many of the passages are very fast, the dancer can disregard the exact beat of the music or blur the step, and many in the audience won't know the difference. If a dancer is off balance or out of control on the swivel turns, she might have to hop once or twice to regain control. The audience will notice these adjustments but they will not gasp with apprehension. In *Theme* there are several particularly scary parts where, if things go wrong, I feel I could go sprawling or land in the footlights. And the ballet is filled with turns. My turns were improving considerably but, as far as I was concerned, the fewer I had to do, the better.

I knew my pure dancing style—my turnout, good line, and my natural inclination to follow the tenets of classical ballet without any quirkiness—was ideally suited to *Theme,* as it was to *Piano Concerto,* but even if I had been uninjured, a week would not have been enough to prepare for it. As it was, my increasingly sore left bunion made it hard enough to learn the steps, let alone practice them. Anything more than minimal rehearsing was out of the question. My partner, Jean-Pierre Bonnefous, was in even worse shape. Often he had to cancel rehearsals to receive treatment for his ankles, leaving me to work alone; when he did appear, he was always in great pain. Our performance seemed fated for disaster. If I had been able to see things in the proper perspective, I would have told Balanchine that my foot was badly injured and that I shouldn't try to do *Theme.* But I was so eager to dance as much as I could, to prove myself, that I didn't tell him about it. I just persevered blindly, stubbornly hoping that somehow everything would turn out all right. It didn't, and I'm sure I turned in a rather poor performance. Balanchine didn't comment, but he must have been disappointed because I wasn't cast in the ballet again that season.

Another season went by before I was again cast for *Theme,* this time with Peter Martins. Dancing with Peter was always a big treat. We had ample time to work on the ballet, and I began to feel more confident. Still, I saved my best shoes for it and always kept a good pair in reserve in the wings in case the first pair wore out unexpectedly. I didn't want to have to worry about anything but dancing well.

I rehearsed *Theme* as much as any other role in my repertory, and—unlike *Who Cares?*—it got better with practice. However, in my first few performances as the end of the ballet approached I was exhausted and had nothing left to give. With experience, I learned to pace myself; and as I gained control, I also wasted less nervous energy.

Another new ballet that came my way during that winter season of 1974/75 was *Brahms-Schoenberg Quartet,* the fourth movement. I had done it in concerts with Jacques, thank heavens, so my bunion was spared the hard rehearsing that I had had to inflict on it for *Piano Concerto* and *Theme.* Balanchine had choreographed *Brahms* for Suzanne Farrell, to show the free and uninhibited side of her personality. I enjoyed the Hungarian gypsy dancing, which was a welcome change from all the classical roles I had been doing. But my bunion did not like it. I awakened the day before Thanksgiving, having danced *Brahms* the night before, to find that a large area around my bunion was black and blue. The inevitable had finally happened: I had torn the already strained ligaments. The in-

jury was excruciatingly painful, forcing me to stay out for months, and I was in great doubt about when, how, and even *if* it would heal. Several months later the unhappy truth became obvious: the ligaments had not healed properly, causing my big toe to lose support in the bunion joint. In other words, I had lost all control over the movements of my big toe, and I was certain it would never be the same again. Even the doctors agreed. Now I have to wear a pad between my big and second toes to help keep the big toe from flopping underneath the second. It is essential for me to wear very hard shoes for protection and support. My left foot has not regained its former strength, and it never will, no matter how many exercises I do. Fortunately, I am more handicapped on half-pointe than on pointe; but I would not be of much use in a barefooted ballet.

That toe injury came at a most inopportune time. Balanchine had asked me to learn the Sugar Plum Fairy in *The Nutcracker,* and I would definitely have done it that Christmas season for the first time. Instead, I rested, watched the Company, and reflected on how I had just been defeated by my furious schedule that fall. Little did I suspect that an even heavier workload lay ahead.

The Tchaikovsky "gut-crunchers," and the toll they took on my whole body, convinced me that the work I was doing in class and rehearsals would not make me strong enough to cope with such ballets night after night. I had had some experience with ballet-oriented exercises, and so I knew in which direction to turn.

Back in 1970 I had gone to Carola Trier's studio to do exercises to strengthen weak muscles, improve my body alignment, and thereby get rid of my tendonitis. For the next four years, I went there off and on but usually stopped either when whatever pain I had went away, or when my money ran out, or when I was too busy dancing. I had found one of Carola's assistants, Judy Covan, particularly helpful. A former professional ballet dancer, she had helped me apply what I learned at Carola's to my dancing. In 1974 Judy opened her own studio, and I went there regularly for several years, often five days a week. These exercises, many of which were done against resistance created by springs, accomplished primarily what I had intended, but I never dreamed that as a result I would emerge a much better dancer, with greater strength, flexibility, and control.

Most of the exercises at Judy's were done while lying down, which had many advantages. I didn't have to support my full weight or worry about my balance, and the movements could be simplified in the extreme. All my attention could be focused on one area of the body, on one movement, or even on one muscle. By isolating muscles in this way, a link was forged between mind and muscle, reeducating both. While standing up, many different muscles were at work just to keep me erect, without my being aware of them—which makes it very hard to break old habits.

Judy first focused my attention on my pelvis and lower back. If these were not in the proper positions, every other part of my body would be affected. Once they were in place, I began to be able to use my hips, my inner thigh muscles, and the muscles at the top and back of my legs properly. Then I had to learn how to have straight legs without

OPPOSITE *Tchaikovsky Suite No. 3 (Theme and Variations)*, Merrill and Sean Lavery. (© *Steven Caras*)

completely locking the knees. This developed muscles that not only would protect my knees from injury but would also help keep undue strain off my feet and ankles. This, in turn, made it easier to keep my feet and ankles properly aligned. I learned to bring about similar alignment changes in my upper body. My ribs and chin stopped sticking out, and my shoulders and neck began to relax.

Judy, who worked with many dancers, was happy with my progress and often said: "Why can't I get other dancers to use these muscles?" But that was only the start. Could I reproduce at the barre what I had so meticulously learned lying down? I tried to make myself aware of the feelings and sensations associated with the many exercises I did so that I would be very conscious of what I was striving for both at the barre and while dancing. The new habits that had entered my muscles, that had created muscle memory, must not be allowed to disappear.

The transition was successful far beyond my expectations. Although not as powerfully built as many dancers, I had acquired the kind of strength and control in my movements that we all strive for. Even my turns improved!

These exercises produced such dramatic results in my case that I cannot help feeling they should be as much a part of every dancer's regime as class. They could even be part of the curriculum of the School of American Ballet. No one is too young to benefit, and the sooner one starts, the better.

I started out of dire necessity, and the exercises brought me such benefits that I am now unwilling to give them up. They have been particularly welcome during periods of injury when I am forced to stop taking class; they enable me to maintain some semblance of muscle tone and proper alignment. Then, when I finally go back to class, I do not have to face the terrible feeling of decrepitude that comes when one has done no exercise at all for a few weeks.

These exercises, however, do not produce automatic results. Even if they have been taught well, the hardest task remains: creating a link between one's dancing and the exercises, which—although designed to improve strength and body alignment—bear little resemblance to basic dance steps (many of the exercises are even done turned in). Much intelligence is required to understand how to apply the principles underlying the exercises to ballet steps.

After Suzanne Farrell left the New York City Ballet in 1969, there was much speculation among Company members about whether or not she would ever return. It was generally assumed she would want to return; she had always been so devoted to Balanchine. But would he take her back? And, if so, how would he treat her?

During the 1974 summer season in Saratoga with two days to learn the part, I was cast in another of Suzanne's former roles, the second movement of *Symphony in C.* Suzanne had a home in the vicinity, and though she had never been seen at any Company performances in Saratoga, this season we heard she would be coming to watch. I wanted to show her that her roles were being well danced and that life was going on without her. Was there any truth to the rumor that she wanted to return? Was she attending these performances with the idea of meeting Balanchine afterward?

At the end of that year we learned that Balanchine had accepted Suzanne back into the Company. I knew everyone would be affected but, since no one knew exactly how Balanchine was going to treat her, it wasn't clear what the effect would be.

After Suzanne returned, I and others watched with dismay as Balanchine again cast her in all her old roles and gave her a lot of attention. Gradually he catered to her more and more, as he had done in the past, although somewhat more diplomatically.

I was still recovering from my big-toe injury, dancing less often than I might have otherwise. Even though I was occasionally cast for a performance of *Brahms* and *Diamonds,* it was becoming clear I was not going to dance these roles very often and that I would not be cast for new roles, because they would now be given to Suzanne. The situation in class, however, changed little. Balanchine continued to use me to demonstrate steps in the center, while Suzanne took a place behind me. She did, however, assume my favorite place at the barre.

I felt frustrated by the turn of events, but I watched Suzanne, as I watched everyone, to learn from her. I was intrigued that Balanchine found her unendingly fascinating, and I resolved to discover what it was in her that inspired him. That quality could not be taught in class, or perhaps even described, but such a discovery could only benefit me.

In the meantime, his interest in me didn't seem to flag. He soon cast me in the role of Sanguinic in the important revival of *The Four Temperaments.* I had had only a brief introduction to this ballet in 1967, before it was dropped from the repertoire. At the time, as an understudy in the corps, I had been spellbound watching Balanchine rehearse it. How he had thought up all those original movements was a mystery to me, but it was a joy to watch him demonstrate them. I never had a chance to go out front to watch the ballet, but from the wings I tried to imagine what it must look like from the audience. In any event, I immediately fell in love with the music, which sounded the same no matter where one was situated.

I had learned this role from Marnee Morris, but because Suzanne had done it in the past I didn't expect to perform it that season—much less dance the first performance. And since Marnee was available, I assumed I was third in line. Yet, when the casting went up, there was my name! I panicked; having been so sure I wouldn't be asked to do it, I had rehearsed it very little, devoting all my time instead to the roles I knew I would be doing. Now I had only a week in which to get ready.

Balanchine worked with me and Anthony Blum, who was going to be my partner. Just as he had in *Piano Concerto,* Mr. B went through my part from beginning to end, telling me what he wanted as he went along. Steps that had been bewildering me suddenly made sense.

There was one sequence about which he was particularly concerned. He wanted me to step backward on pointe and then, without traveling at all, put my heel down flat on the floor and let my body fall back—without losing control. Actually the step was meant to make me look as if I had fallen off pointe suddenly, and was therefore falling back. It was very difficult, especially lowering the heel without moving the foot at all. I wasn't able to do it right, but when Balanchine told me that no one else had ever done it correctly either, I felt a little better. Although I come closer to it now, I still move my foot as I lower my heel.

Another difficult moment occurred near the end of the movement. When I reentered after the male variation, Balanchine wanted me jumping and flying forward through the air. At the height of the jump, I was supposed to be traveling through the air with one leg in front of me, while the other was pointed down and slightly back, as if I were falling or being pulled forward. At the same time he wanted my upper body arching backward to emphasize the illusion that the front leg was pulling me forward and off balance.

The problem was that I had to land in the same off-balance position I had struck in midair. My landing leg wasn't perpendicular to the floor; it was still pointing slightly back when my foot hit the floor, and there was tremendous stress in the groin area. It felt as if the ligaments could tear.

Mr. B seemed frustrated that I couldn't do what he wanted. This image of the body arching back while being pulled forward returns in another sequence on pointe, and he wanted the connection between the two to be obvious. His frustration suggested that he hadn't had any success getting other dancers to do this step. Most people tended to land with their body straight and then bend back, but that was not what he wanted. He wanted me bent back in the air before I landed. My solution now is to be in the air with one leg perpendicular to the floor but with my upper body arching back, and then to try to maintain that position as I land.

Of the four temperaments, the bright, high-spirited Sanguinic suited my own temperament best, and I soon began to feel more and more comfortable in rehearsals. I loved the extreme movements in the ballet, the rhythmic steps and all the themes and variations. But my favorite moment came when, in a series of low lifts, like a gazelle bounding through the air, I made a full circuit of the stage.

Many steps seemed tailor-made for my body. Because of my turnout it was easy for me to do all those steps that required leading with the pelvis. At first, I found them so unusual I thought they might be a mistake that had crept into the choreography over the years, but Balanchine reassured me. I was doing the step just the way he wanted it done, and he seemed pleased. So was I.

Though I lost many parts to Suzanne, Balanchine still cast me in some technically demanding and dynamic ballets, such as *Stars and Stripes* and *Valse-Fantaisie*. I felt I was the right person for the roles I received, but I had to admit to myself that I had been in

OPPOSITE *The Four Temperaments,* Merrill and Sean Lavery at the beginning of the low lifts around the perimeter of the stage. (© *Steven Caras*)

the right place at the right time: during this period the ballerinas in the Company were not at their best in roles demanding primarily technique and energy. With Gelsey gone, there was no truly classical virtuoso ballerina among the principals. I thought that if I could just pass whatever test Balanchine was putting me to in all these hard ballets, proving to him that I indeed had that special something that makes a dancer look right in a ballerina role, then I would emerge in a category all my own, as the only virtuoso ballerina in the Company. Finally I felt I had reason to be optimistic about my future.

All the attention I was getting in the Company and the press bolstered my confidence, which in turn brought about an improvement in my dancing. More relaxed and assured, I was better able to savor the pleasure of my frequent performances. I was healthy and felt I had put behind me that frustrating two-year period when I had done so little dancing. The good roles I was getting were more important to me than anything else, but I had my heart set on becoming a principal dancer. Then, suddenly, disaster struck.

It happened one day in April 1976, during a class being taught by André Kramarevsky, a former principal of the Bolshoi Ballet who had just joined the SAB faculty. As I finished a pirouette, the middle step in a fast combination he had given, I put my passé foot down to take off for the next step, and slipped. My right foot sickled and I came down with all my weight on the outside of it. Because of all the momentum I had gathered from the pirouette, I continued to spin around with my foot pinned underneath me. The pain was excruciating and frightening. I immediately packed my foot in ice and was taken in a wheelchair to a nearby doctor's office. There, I had to wait a couple of hours before the doctor, who had been in surgery, could see me. By then, the ankle had become so swollen it looked like an elephant's foot—no toes, only toenails. The diagnosis was torn ligaments on the upper part of my ankle. If I had broken it, I would have been much better off. For the next week I was forced to walk on crutches, and it was four or five weeks before I could walk without a limp. Six months passed before I could perform even my easiest ballets again.

As if this injury weren't enough, my morale received a crushing blow the day after the accident. I had gone to the theater to watch a rehearsal of *Union Jack,* in which I was Suzanne's understudy. As I hobbled on my crutches down the hallway toward the studio, I met Balanchine, who asked how serious my injury was and how long it would take to heal. He was obviously distressed, as he always was when his dancers had serious accidents, but he clearly had something else on his mind: "Dear, that's too bad. You know, we're reviving *Square Dance* this season and I was going to have you do it."

I was devastated, then filled with conflicting emotions. I was thrilled to know that he had wanted me in the first cast in this revival, but tormented at the thought that I was missing my greatest opportunity. My disappointment was so intense that I had to struggle to maintain my composure in front of him. Fortunately the conversation quickly ended and, as he walked away, I was left nursing not only my physical but also my emotional pain. I went home and cried as I had never cried before in my life. I felt utterly helpless, on top of which my foot hurt so much that any movement was nearly unbearable. All I could do was sit in a chair for hours on end. Kibbe tried to console me, but the only positive thought we could find was that I had been Balanchine's first choice. Still, every time I thought of not being able to do *Square Dance,* waves of emotion swept over me and my depression deepened.

My feeling of helplessness became nearly intolerable when rehearsals of *Square Dance* began, but I attended them all in an effort to learn as much as possible about the ballet. I had never seen *Square Dance,* but I knew that originally it had been performed with a small string orchestra and a real square-dance caller on stage. For this revival, Balanchine had decided to dispense with the caller and return the musicians to the pit: I think he felt the caller was a gimmick that took the audience's attention away from the dancing.

Victoria Simon, a former NYCB soloist who had staged the work for other companies, taught it to Kay Mazzo and Bart Cook. From the moment I heard the music Balanchine had chosen (two concertos by Vivaldi and Corelli), I had the urge to get up and dance. The steps looked as if they had been choreographed just for me. The ballet was filled with fast footwork, jumps, and beats, all part of the standard classical ballet vocabulary, but the steps had to be done in a much freer and more spontaneous way than in most "classical" ballets. A joyful I-love-to-dance approach was needed, and I *knew* I could produce that effect.

Since I was sure I would eventually get a chance to do *Square Dance,* I tried to be practical and during rehearsals wrote down the steps and took note of all of Balanchine's corrections. But I had gloomy moments when I wondered whether I would ever recover completely enough to meet the demands of the choreography. I could see the ballet would place more stress on my feet and ankles than any other ballet I had done. What if my ankle didn't heal properly? Would it prevent me from doing this ballet in the future? I had no choice but to wait patiently for my ankle to heal, but as I worked my way back I resolved to be more careful than ever before.

Whenever I had been injured in the past, I had always been so anxious to dance and to improve that I tended to underestimate the time needed to heal, and returned too quickly, often reinjuring myself in the process. But as I grew older and became more confident, I tried to take a wiser approach. This time I forced myself to take my time, no matter how impatient I was to return. Even after I thought my injury had healed, I had to be aware of it in everything I did, working around the parts of my body that were sore or weak as my full strength returned. But even then the injured area remained vulnerable and I had to guard against my natural tendency to try to do everything as before.

I had to become more creative in dealing with each injury individually. What was the proper pace of recovery? The proper therapy? In class, I started to decide for myself whether or not to do a given step, when previously I would have been inclined to do practically anything asked for, especially if it had been Balanchine doing the asking. I no longer felt I constantly had to prove myself, and if I thought a step might aggravate an injury I would modify it or wait for the next step or combination.

As I learned more and more about different therapies, I realized that full responsibility for healing all my injuries lay in my hands, not in the hands of any one doctor. I would have not only to choose which doctor or therapist to see, but also to decide whether or not to agree to the treatment recommended. For me, such thoughts were entirely new.

During my rehabilitation, I often watched the Company from the audience. It wasn't always easy, for I was envious of all the other dancers. What they were doing seemed so wonderful, so fulfilling, and yet so difficult. Maybe too difficult for me ever to do again, I worried.

Whenever I could divorce my emotions from what I was watching, I was struck by how much more I saw from the audience than from my usual backstage vantage point. Technical flaws or inappropriate facial expressions appeared to be just that from the wings. From the audience's point of view, however, they took on a larger dimension: secret glances between corps members were telegraphed to the back of the theater; a furrowed brow looked like neurotic introspection; unstraightened legs seemed like lazy legs; floppy wrists drew attention to themselves, eclipsing everything else; an effortful jump that might have impressed people in the wings looked only like hard work; a dancer's gasps broke any spell that had been created.

Sometimes the opposite was true, however. The serious inadequacies of certain dancers didn't seem to matter at times: a pair of short legs looked fine; an inflexible back could easily go unnoticed; a slip or a fall was quickly forgiven and forgotten. To someone who had spent 99 percent of her time on the stage and in the wings, these "distortions" of what was so familiar were a revelation. If only I could have seen myself as I was seeing others! But at least I could see my ballets as the audience saw them.

Unless I was watching performances or the rehearsals of *Square Dance,* I preferred to stay away from the theater. When I saw others working and enjoying themselves, I felt not only dejected but also like an outsider. I couldn't even keep up with all the minor day-to-day events that inevitably became major topics of conversation. So, I tried to view my recovery period as an opportunity to do the things I rarely had time for: reading long novels, seeing movies and plays, and entertaining friends.

When I finally began dancing again, I know I was not the same dancer I had been at the time of my injury. Undoubtedly, all the performances I had watched and all the changes within myself I had consciously made had had their effect, but something more had happened. Perhaps being forced to stop, to watch and to reflect, had made the difference. I'll never really know. I do know, however, that since then, and after every subsequent major injury, I have returned a better dancer.

When the Company went to Paris in 1976, I danced for the first time in over five months in the role of the Girl in Mauve in *Dances at a Gathering.* It was a wonderful ballet to come back in because I could tone down some of the steps to save my foot without spoiling the overall effect of my performance. The response of the audience and the critics did wonders for my confidence. Usually I was admired for my virtuosity, but this time I was appreciated simply for who I was, and that made a lasting impression on me. I still smile when I think of how one critic described me: *"la délicieuse, la virginale Merrill Ashley avec sa petite tête au nez minuscule."* I had been feeling insecure because I was really not back in shape and wondered if I ever would be, and now it seemed people were saying I was special the way I was.

After Paris, the Company returned to New York for the 1976/77 winter season. Our annual performances of *The Nutcracker* had no sooner begun than our musicians went on strike. There had been strikes in the past, but this one lasted so long that the very future of the Company was in jeopardy. When Balanchine threatened to disband the NYCB and take a few of his dancers to Monte Carlo to form a new Company, I realized I was ready to uproot my life and go with him wherever he pleased. Fortunately, just as there seemed to be no more hope, a settlement was reached and the last part of the season was salvaged.

A highlight of the remainder of that season was the premiere of a new work, *Bournonville Divertissements,* which was staged by Stanley Williams. I was cast in the pas de trois from *La Ventana* with Kyra Nichols and Ricky Weiss. It had the kind of steps and spirit that came most naturally to me. But the opening, with numerous unsupported arabesques *penchées,* scared me every time, just as it will all those who ever have to dance the role. I eventually found a trick that greatly decreased my chances of wobbling around and made me feel a little less insecure. The problem step had me starting in arabesque on a flat foot. From there, I had to lean far forward and simultaneously raise my back leg. Then I had to come back up to where I had started. Throughout the step, which had to be done very slowly to fill all the music, I had one arm extended in front of me and the other behind me, roughly parallel to the leg lifted in arabesque. All I had to do was imagine that I had a partner who was holding the hand behind me, and for some reason that kept my arm in the right place, maintained the angle formed by my back and leg throughout the penché and improved my balance. But even with this mental aide, I often had to make those embarrassing little adjustments with my standing foot—we call them *pancaking*—in order to keep my balance. Amazingly, I had far greater success with the arabesques penchées that were done not on a flat foot but on pointe. These, however, were done very fast, giving me a different set of problems.

At the conclusion of the winter season, the Company went on tour to Washington, D.C., where after waiting more than a year, I finally got my heart's desire. Balanchine asked me to do *Square Dance,* because Kay was injured. I was so excited I didn't care that I had only three days to rehearse.

Everything I had thought about the ballet turned out to be true. Many of the steps seemed to have their own momentum, which swept me along, and I felt in perfect harmony with the music and the choreography. Dancing had never been so exhilarating for me.

Balanchine built a certain rhythm into many of the basic classroom steps, and he choreographed with that rhythm in mind. If a dancer could conquer those basic steps, she was drawn into the musical structure of the choreography, reducing the effort and enhancing the pleasure of even the most difficult combinations. Many dancers, however, failed to realize this and therefore lacked the incentive to work hard in class; but those who did were richly rewarded, as I was in *Square Dance.*

When we went back to New York, it seemed only logical that I would do another performance of *Square Dance* during that season. I was wrong. I tried to be patient but, as the months passed, the urge to do the role again got the better of me. I decided to step out of character and make a special request, something I had never done before. Summoning up my courage, I approached Balanchine one afternoon and said, somewhat apologetically: "Mr. B, I know that you have lots of considerations when it comes to casting, but I would really love to do *Square Dance* again, if it is possible."

"No, dear," he responded quickly. "Is Kay's ballet."

His words were like a knife in my heart, all the more painful since I knew that he had originally intended to use me in the revival. Tears welled up in my eyes. I had to get away from him before I burst into tears.

I lowered my head, mumbled, "I understand," and quickly walked away. We had been standing on stage and I barely reached the wings before the tears started to flow. I don't know if he saw me crying, but nothing was ever said about it again.

Two weeks later Kay was out once more, and I got another chance, again on short notice. Although I would have preferred to be cast regularly for the ballet so that I could prepare it properly, I was thrilled to do it, no matter what the circumstances. Balanchine had seen my *Square Dance* in Washington but hadn't commented. This time, however, he complimented me on my performance. Afterward, Kay and I were both cast regularly for the ballet, and now that I knew in advance when I would be doing the role I could rehearse as much as I wanted.

When Vicky Simon taught the ballet to Kay, she showed her an original and highly unusual step that came in a dramatic entrance across the front of the stage in the middle of the "girls' dance." At the time, my ankle injury had prevented me from trying the step and thus deciphering what Vicky was showing. Kay didn't seem to grasp it either and instead chose to do a series of split jumps with a small swivel turn on the ground in between each jump. Guided by these *coupés jetés* that Kay did, by what I remembered from Vicky's demonstration, and by a similar step that Jacques had given me in *Saltarelli,* I decided to do a large turning jump with one leg bent followed immediately by a coupé jeté. It took me five or six sets of this *saut de basque–coupé jeté* combination to get

Square Dance, the coupé jeté entrance. (© *Steven Caras*)

across the front of the stage, make the turn, and get to the back of the stage where the step ends.

In executing this combination, I wanted to be in the air as much as possible in both jumps. If I stayed in plié too long after landing from either jump or didn't think about taking off at the same time as I landed, the step lost its lightness and surprise effect.

When most dancers take off for the coupé jeté, they are so concerned with the extension of the front leg that they tend to push off too late with the back leg, which means that they can't push off hard enough. The front leg is practically back on the ground by the time the back leg has left it. As soon as I take off for each jump, I try to shoot out both legs into the coupé jeté at practically the same time, so that I can then hold my position in the air for a brief moment. The timing of the takeoff is similar to the timing used in the glissades we practiced so much in class. The speed and control developed at the barre from doing such steps as tendus and frappés the way Balanchine taught them make this possible.

Kibbe offered many suggestions regarding *Square Dance,* once I began appearing in it regularly. He had comments on everything, including the saut de basque–coupé jeté combination I have just described. He criticized the overall pattern I made on the stage as I did the step, noting that after I crossed the front of the stage I tended to cut the far right corner short, as if I were anxious to retreat to the back of the stage where the step is supposed to end. He felt the step would have a greater impact if I made a wider, bolder arc.

I was sure this would be impossible and told him so, but we had long since agreed that Kibbe could make suggestions without worrying about how difficult it would be for me to implement them. That way he could tell me exactly what he saw without having to worry that he was asking the impossible. I at least realized that there was a problem to solve. If Kibbe's suggested solution proved impossible, I would begin to search for another solution.

In my early rehearsals I had made a very wide arc, crossing as much of the front of the stage as possible, but in doing so I found I ran into some of the corps. To avoid this, I would have to make a very difficult sharp turn right in front of them—something I hadn't yet found a way to do gracefully. I knew my solution wasn't ideal, but Kibbe's comments made me realize the problem was bigger than I had thought. If I were going to describe the kind of arc I wanted, I had to find a way to turn the corner sharply without looking awkward or losing momentum. The solution was elusive, but once I had thought of it, the move was easy for me to execute. I overrotated on the saut de basque right where I needed to make the sharp turn; instead of doing only one revolution in the turn, I did at least a one-and-a-quarter revolution so that, as I landed, I was immediately ready to take off in the proper position to redirect my centrifugal force. The rest of the pattern was then easy to complete.

Kibbe made another valuable observation about *Square Dance*. He pointed out that on my first entrance I looked only straight forward and at the right side of the audience, ignoring a whole section of the house. He thought I should introduce myself, as it were, to both the right and left sides of the theater. And so I began to experiment with this opening section until I found places in the choreography where it seemed natural to acknowledge the rest of the audience.

Kibbe and I isolated countless such moments in all my ballets. I usually only had a chance to rehearse some of them, but in performance I often surprised myself by remembering and fixing, on the spur of the moment, the rest of the trouble spots we had gone over.

I always loved dancing *Square Dance* and felt very lucky to have someone in the audience who could help me improve my performances. Technical corrections I might have been able to get from Balanchine or other dancers. But Kibbe's corrections had to do with matters of general aesthetics from the audience's point of view, which most dancers never have a chance to hear.

My success in *Square Dance* and the attention I received because of it from other members of the Company made my confidence soar. Yet, I still wanted to be a principal.

This was not merely because of the honor associated with the title but because Balanchine's failure to make me a principal meant, in my eyes, that he still had strong reservations about my dancing. But all the signs were good. My salary had just been increased to the lowest principal level, and I was sure a promotion was imminent.

I was right. A promotion was soon made, but it was Ricky Weiss who was promoted, not I. Why hadn't we both been promoted? I had been dancing at least as many principal roles as Ricky and, in fact, had been his partner in almost everything he did. Why had I been passed over?

Perhaps I hadn't been passed over, after all, I thought. No one had said anything to me when I had been promoted to soloist, and maybe the same was true this time. They just haven't told me yet, I thought hopefully.

Two days passed with no word from anyone. I went to the press department and inquired, as casually as I could, "Was anyone else made a soloist or principal?"

"No," said the head of the department, with a hint of sympathy in her voice. It was the answer I had been dreading.

I was so upset that I was afraid it would not only destroy my peace of mind but also have a bad effect on my dancing. I had to do something.

I turned to Peter Martins for advice.

"What should I do?" I asked him. "Should I say something to Balanchine?"

Peter looked at me for a second without responding. Then he said, "Swallow it. Just swallow it."

CHAPTER

5

As 1977 PROGRESSED, Balanchine cast me in one principal role after another. *Donizetti Variations* and *Tchaikovsky Pas de Deux* stand out in my memory as the two most difficult of that period. *Tchaikovsky Pas de Deux* was a pure classical ballet, one that Balanchine was not in the habit of giving to young people. I took it as a sign of his faith in me. I loved classical roles such as this one, and felt that if I could perform them well I would really have accomplished something. There was no faking it, no hiding behind personality. Line, technique, stamina, and presence were absolutely necessary to make these ballets look as they were intended, and because I felt well suited to them, I couldn't have asked for a better fate. The more of these roles I got, the happier I was. I was developing an insatiable appetite.

But soon Balanchine presented me with a new kind of challenge. The romantic *Emeralds* (combined with *Rubies* and *Diamonds* to make up *Jewels*), danced with restrained ardor in a flood of green light, was a ballet I had always enjoyed watching. It was the first principal role I'd ever had where the whole focus of the choreography was on the movements of the head, arms, and upper body, and the phrasing of these movements. It was clear to me as I watched the ballet that it was unlike anything I had done before and I felt I could be good in it. But I hardly anticipated the difficulty I would have in acquir-

151

OPPOSITE   *Emeralds.* (© *Steven Caras*)

ing the fluidity or suppleness needed to perform these movements effectively. Gradually I understood that Balanchine had given me *Emeralds* largely to make me think about this area of my dancing.

This emphasis on the upper body is most unusual for a Balanchine ballet. As a rule, he allowed us to be creative in this area and choose the movements that best suited our bodies and ways of moving. I welcomed this latitude and, because my proportions did not rule out any head and arm positions—for example, I didn't have a short neck, which would tend to look even shorter with my arms above my head—I felt free to adopt whatever positions came most naturally to me or seemed most suitable for the ballet.

This freedom given to us by Balanchine (not all choreographers work that way) helped us preserve our individuality—different dancers inevitably wish to use their upper bodies in different ways for the same steps. With this leeway, we sometimes discovered a way to do a step that would otherwise have been impossible. That, in fact, was my hope when I tackled those "impossible" attitude turns in *Who Cares?* I tried every conceivable combination of arms—both arms out to the side, both over my head, the left or the right arm up, one hand on my hip, and others—but nothing made those turns any easier. If the position of the arms had been predetermined, my search for a solution would have been frustratingly limited.

Balanchine welcomed this experimenting with the head and arms, for his dancers often came up with good ideas of their own. He understood, too, that we were often unaware of the effectiveness of our innovations and that, unless he commented on them, we might never repeat them.

I do not think any dancers have equaled the original principal dancers—Violette Verdy, Conrad Ludlow, Mimi Paul, and Francisco Moncion—who had first danced *Emeralds* ten years earlier. I regretted not being able to learn the role from Violette, who had by then already left the Company. In fact, whenever the original cast of a ballet is available, I believe they should always coach newcomers in their roles, though in practice they seldom do. After all, those who worked with Balanchine learned his steps and heard all his corrections and comments, and even if they are no longer able to do what he wanted, they know what his original intentions were.

To add to my difficulties in *Emeralds,* I had an inexperienced partner; consequently, most of the rehearsal time—and most of Balanchine's corrections—were devoted to partnering. The little that Balanchine said about my variation had to do with steps and patterns, not with the use of my upper body.

Time and again, I asked myself what it was about this ballet that I found so mystifyingly difficult. In the past, my greatest problems had usually been difficult steps. Here, I had to learn to use my head and shoulders more expressively. I had always heard that arm movements should "come from the back," but I had only a vague idea of what that meant. At least I knew I didn't want my arms to look like appendages stuck on a body. But I couldn't make my body fit my mental image of how I wanted to look.

I also found it difficult to match the ebb and flow of the music, which so often seemed to be played too quickly for the number of steps I had to do. Balanchine, too, favored a slower tempo, but the performances weren't always conducted at the tempo we wanted. (One evening after a performance of *Emeralds,* Balanchine told me that if he could have one wish granted in his life, it would be to have "perfect tempos all the time.") Whenever I felt rushed, it was all I could do to fit in all the steps and be in the right place at the right time. If I rushed, the movements stopped being as full as I wanted them to be.

Emeralds has never been fully appreciated by audiences. Perhaps the transition from the hectic New York pace outside the theater to the dreamy, rhapsodic pleasures of Fauré's music and Balanchine's choreography is too abrupt for most balletgoers, whose attention is more easily captured by the jazzier *Rubies,* which Balanchine always placed second on the program. If *Rubies* had come first, then the tranquillity of *Emeralds* would have been a welcome change of pace, and the ballet might have received its due. Coming first, as it does, it has become a "dancer's ballet," meaning that the audience's lack of response does not detract from our pleasure in performing it.

Late one afternoon a crisis developed in the theater. Patty McBride, who had been cast to dance the leading role in *Rubies,* was out with an injury. Sara (Sally) Leland, the only other dancer who knew the role, was suffering from severe tendonitis and felt that her ankles would not survive the whole ballet. It was impossible to do *Jewels* without *Rubies;* and to replace *Jewels,* which made up the whole evening's program, was equally unacceptable.

Rubies is so complex that no one person, no matter how quick a study, could possibly learn all the steps in a couple of hours. The part had somehow to be divided. Balanchine decided that I should learn the pas de deux, which came in the middle, to give Sally a rest. Since *Rubies* had always been the part I wanted to do most in *Jewels,* I was thrilled to have this opportunity.

From 6:00 P.M. to 7:00 P.M. I was on stage learning the pas de deux from Sally and rehearsing it with Ricky Weiss, who was going to be my partner. Normally, I would have been in my dressing room at that time preparing my makeup for *Emeralds,* which I also had to dance that evening. At seven, I rushed to my dressing room, hurriedly put on my makeup and did an abbreviated barre. At eight, I was on stage and ready to go in *Emeralds.* But my mind kept going over what I had just learned, straining to remember all those convoluted steps that didn't fall into any recognizable category. During *Emeralds,* whenever I was in the wings I tried to remember what I had just learned, but there were a few spots where I predictably lost track of the sequence, and I knew I would have to ask Ricky to "talk" me through the trouble spots. This, in fact, saved me. Without Ricky's whispered instructions, like "tango step" and "walks," I never would have made it. It's no way to dance, with your attention totally absorbed by each and every step, but the style of the ballet felt so natural to me that I think it went quite well.

Afterward, Balanchine seemed quite pleased, and as he put his arm around my waist while we walked off the stage, I decided to be bold and say what was on my mind.

"I enjoyed dancing that so much, Mr. B. I would love to do *Rubies* again, all of it."

"Of course, dear," he said quite convincingly. "Why not!"

I really thought he meant it, but a month later Heather Watts was taught *Rubies,* and I was terribly disappointed. I considered reminding Mr. B of what he had said, but whenever an opportunity presented itself my nerve failed me, and to this day I have not danced the role again.

As the months passed, with no change in my status as a soloist, a certain desperation set in. I had been traumatized when Ricky was made a principal and I was passed over. Although I reminded myself over and over that I was getting the roles I wanted— the most important thing to me—nothing brought me solace. Had I known for sure that I would eventually be promoted, I could have waited patiently. But there was no such certainty. In spite of my growing mastery over my dancing of all the marvelous roles Balanchine saw fit to let me do, I remained helpless in the face of my powerful desire for the recognition of being named a principal dancer.

I looked around me and saw a different kind of helplessness and frustration in some who had only rank and in others who had neither rank nor roles. These realizations helped me count my blessings. I was being given the best parts, and I had no thankless roles. Every evening was a new challenge, and my future looked bright. I felt genuine sympathy for those who had worked so hard and yet had so little to show for it.

In an effort to rid myself of my prevailing desperate feelings, I applied all my mental energy to whatever criticism I received. Any comment or idea that would bring about the slightest improvement in my dancing had to be seized, examined, used. In class and in performance I tried even harder to pay attention to the slightest detail. I listened carefully to every correction I was given, no matter how trivial or minor it seemed.

All this hard work notwithstanding, I continued to dwell on the reasons Balanchine had promoted dancers in the past. Every dancer was a special case, of course. Many were rewarded for merit, and some for long and faithful service, but the timing of the promotion often seemed to depend on matters that had nothing to do with the dancer's progress. In certain cases Balanchine appeared reluctant to risk a premature promotion for fear a dancer might rest on her laurels or become demanding. He might also go to the other extreme and grant a promotion prematurely, in response to the need to have principal parts danced by principal dancers.

Balanchine had said in interviews that he often knew very early on who would make it and who would not, and that, for him, it was just a matter of timing. As he had already shown his confidence in me by giving me many demanding roles, what, I wondered, was he waiting for?

My reasoning was that perhaps he had always planned to promote Colleen Neary and me at the same time. We had practically grown up together and had long vied for the same roles. But Colleen seemed to be faltering, and Balanchine was casting her less and less frequently. He did not want to promote her until he was sure her progress would resume. To promote me first would be a cruel and devastating blow from which she might not recover, so he would wait until what Colleen would do became clear. I found my explanation plausible, but I continued to be beset by doubt.

During the summer of that year, the Company traveled to Nashville to videotape some ballets for the television series *Dance in America.* One afternoon, while we were taping, Balanchine came over to me and started to make conversation. Uncharacteristically, he asked me for advice.

"What do you think, dear? Which man to put in a virtuoso ballet?" he asked. "Peter [Martins] is too busy, and [Peter] Schaufuss is gone. Maybe Ricky?"

What was I supposed to say? Did he really want me to tell him whom to use in a new ballet? Which new ballet? (Or was it an old ballet?) Utterly tongue-tied, I found myself simply agreeing with his suggestion, and he seemed satisfied with that. This strange interlude came to an end when we were called back for the taping, and I didn't give it another thought.

During the break between these weeks of filming and the autumn rehearsal period, Kibbe and I flew to Bermuda for a vacation. It was so beautiful and we were so happy we decided to stay longer than originally planned. The only reason to go back before the rehearsal period began would have been to get in condition for rehearsals. But since I was never needed early in the rehearsal period, which is primarily used to rehearse the corps de ballet, I decided not to rush back. I knew a few extra days would make me feel much more refreshed and eager to work. It was an easy decision to make, because I had stayed in good general condition.

Whenever I'm on vacation, especially if I'm by the sea, I'm very active. I try to get a hotel room with a terrace I can use as a miniature ballet studio, where I can give myself a good barre. At the very least, I do some of the floor exercises that I started doing with Judy. Kibbe is a good influence, too, because rain or shine, wherever we are, he has some form of exercise planned.

In Bermuda, the best exercise—and the most enjoyable for me—was swimming and sometimes I went on hour-long ocean swims. I would have loved to go horseback riding, try some of the more adventuresome water sports, or go for runs on the hilly golf courses, which seemed so inviting, but wisdom prevailed. Well, not always. Kibbe got me out on the tennis court from time to time, perhaps with fantasies of bringing my tennis game up to the level of my dancing.

On one of my long ocean swims in Bermuda, when the sea was particularly choppy, I was swept by the current onto some coral rocks. I was lucky to escape with only some painful scrapes on the knuckles of my right foot. But they were very slow in healing, and that made wearing shoes of any kind very uncomfortable. When I got back to New York, I found pointe shoes still too painful to wear, and so I couldn't work in class as I would have liked. I was in no condition to start rehearsals, but since I didn't anticipate being called to any right away, I wasn't worried.

On the Monday afternoon before rehearsals began, I was on my way to the theater and I ran into someone from the Company who said, "Merrill, congratulations!"

"For what?" I asked.

"Didn't they tell you? I hear that you've been made a principal."

I felt my heart pounding. Had my dream come true? I was bursting with excitement—but still wary. I didn't want to take anything for granted until I heard the news officially. When I arrived at the theater, I met the head of the press department, who greeted me with: "Hi, Merrill. When you have time, can you come up to the office so we can do a 'bio' on you?"

"Don't you already have one?" I asked.

"Yes, but we need to redo it now that you've been made a principal."

"What?" I gasped.

She looked startled. "Haven't they told you?"

She acted as if she had just betrayed a secret. In my mind, it was still not definite; I wanted an official announcement. I didn't want to get my hopes up, as I had when Ricky had been promoted. I had received congratulations then, too.

That same afternoon, another surprise was in store for me. No sooner had I left the theater than I ran into someone else from the Company.

"I've heard the great news, Merrill. Isn't it wonderful?"

"Thanks," I said warily.

"Well, when do you start working with him?"

"What?"

"Don't you know? I hear that Balanchine is doing a new ballet for you. I wondered if you knew when he was going to start."

I was dumbstruck! Was it possible that my two most cherished dreams were coming true at once?

The next day at SAB I saw Balanchine for the first time since I had heard the news about the promotion and the new ballet. I didn't know what to say and had no time to think. He saw me on the other side of the room and gave me a big smile. I immediately went over to say hello, and before I could say anything he gave me a huge hug and kiss and asked how I was. I said I was fine and had had a wonderful vacation. Then he said, "Good, dear. You know, I was thinking maybe tomorrow we start working on a new ballet. You and Ricky. Something virtuoso. Wonderful Verdi music."

He proceeded to tell me something about the music, which was from Verdi's opera *Don Carlo,* and about the scenario of the original ballet: a fisherman searching for a perfect pearl in an underwater grotto. He said he wanted to re-create the underwater motif and to try to give everything a mother-of-pearl sheen.

It all sounded marvelous to me, but I didn't know how to express my excitement.

Everything that came to mind sounded trite. I finally ventured, "Thank you very much, Mr. B. You've made me so happy." The words may have been inadequate, but I hoped that the sound of my voice and the expression on my face conveyed what I really felt, not only about the new ballet but also about the promotion, if indeed it was true.

No one ever did inform me personally about the most momentous event in my life. My official notice, so to speak, was once again the brochure for the winter season. Later, piecing together the evidence, I found that my promotion most likely had come ten years to the day after my joining the Company on September 23, 1967.

After hearing Balanchine's description of "my" new ballet, it took a little while to come back to reality, but when I did, I realized that I was in no condition to start working on anything, much less a virtuoso ballet. I had begun every other rehearsal period in good shape but with nothing to do. How ironic that the one time I came back out of shape, I needed to be in top condition for the most important ballet of my life. One way or the other, however, I knew I would manage.

The next day Balanchine, Ricky, and I began work on *Ballo della Regina* in one of the studios at SAB. Since the New York City Opera season was in full swing, the main rehearsal hall at the theater was unavailable. Balanchine seemed in excellent spirits, full of enthusiasm and ideas. He had known the music since his youth, he told me, and had been waiting for the right occasion to do something to it. He had written a piano reduction of the orchestral score himself, since none other existed. He also had made up his mind where the entrances and exits of the principals, soloists, and corps would be.

I found him in an experimental mood, and soon after we started working on my first variation, he said: "You know, I try before, but no one could do, so now we will do."

Then Balanchine showed me the step he had in mind. It reminded me of those little ballerinas on top of music boxes. As the music plays, the figure, whose legs are wide apart in second position on pointe, bobs up and down while turning. Did he really expect me to get well off the ground as I jumped on pointe with straight legs in second position, turning all the while? When I tried the step, I was surprised to find I wasn't riveted to the ground. But, as I turned, my toes got no more than a fraction of an inch off the ground. There wasn't even a suggestion of a jump. And little jumps were what he wanted. I could have done them with a small plié, but that would have showed that I was about to go back up in the air, thus losing the surprise effect. I told him I would work on the step. My hope was that I'd manage it when I got in a bit better condition. Very often, the first time a dancer tries a step, it seems impossible or impossibly awkward, but when she repeats it over and over and experiments a little, she finds she can do it and feel comfortable. I prayed that would happen on this step. Balanchine paused for a few moments and then seemed happy to go on to the next step, leaving the problem unresolved.

Next he had me jump forward into attitude plié. This, I knew, would be interpreted by the audience as the end of the variation. It would be a chance to play; to convey with my facial expression, a slight tilt of the head, and a sudden opening of the arms that the variation had ended, only to reveal a moment later that there was more fun in store. If they had liked what they had seen so far, more surprises were ahead.

We went on. Soon Balanchine came to a point where he wanted a big jump, one that would come as a surprise, like a sudden flash. He said I could put in anything I liked. I tried to think of something original but could come up with nothing better than a grand jeté—a big jump with my legs forming a straight line high in the air—but the element of surprise was missing. It had been seen a thousand times and my big preparation signaled that a jump was coming.

The following day I remembered that, as a student, I had (for fun) practiced a big jeté with a back bend and with my arms curved back over my head, reaching for my back leg. It was like Maya Plisetskaya's famous jump in *Don Quixote,* and I wondered if it would fit in here. This jump was an old-fashioned Russian virtuoso step, and, given the context, I thought there would be an element of wit in it. I tried it and Balanchine liked it, but the timing was tricky. Just before the jump, I had to negotiate a hairpin turn and then hide the preparation. I found that if I took off a split second too soon or too late I would not hit the high point of the jump on the high note, and much of the brilliant effect would be lost. Although the jump itself posed no problem, the timing took a great deal of rehearsing.

For the end of the variation, Balanchine decided on hops on pointe while turning; some on two feet, some on one. Hops on pointe on one foot had always given me trouble, and now I knew I had to work on them. Balanchine must have known this, too. On the same day he began work on *Ballo,* Balanchine gave hops on pointe of every conceivable kind in class. For the next two weeks, not a day went by without our being subjected to this step, which we all would have been only too happy to neglect. We knew the hops would lead to bruised and blistered toes, especially if one was not in shape, as was true for so many of us. Although we needed to work on them, Balanchine's primary motivation in giving them was to stimulate his mind and to discover the possibilities inherent in the step. The results of his discoveries during that time are apparent today in *Ballo.*

Things proceeded even more quickly in the second variation, until Balanchine turned to me and said: "We need a turn here, dear. What do you want to do?"

"I don't know, Mr. B," I said. "*Anything* but fouettés."

I could practically see the various possible steps racing through his mind. The choice had to be either traveling turns or turns in place. Which would he choose?

Then, he said matter-of-factly: "Well, maybe piqué turns each ending in arabesque plié?"

I did a few without music, at my own pace. They seemed fine. This was another one of those very difficult steps that suited me, suited the music, and looked impressive.

160 That, after all, was precisely what Balanchine had set out to accomplish when he said he wanted to do a virtuoso ballet.

Balanchine nodded. "Okay, dear, now with music."

The music hadn't sounded unusually fast when I had listened to it but, when I tried to fit in the turns, I suddenly found I was behind the music. Yet, I sensed the steps and the music were a perfect match. I just needed to shift into a higher gear. I tried again and it seemed to get better. He asked me to do four such turns before I went on to the next step. But after four I had generated so much momentum I couldn't stop in control and go on to the next step. I told him this and he said, "Just do three and end with piqué arabesque."

Every time we came to a trouble spot, I worried that I might fail Balanchine, that somehow the little trick that could make a sequence work perfectly would be beyond me. A few of the steps he gave me were, in fact, beyond me. Many others were marvelous, but what it was all adding up to or which approach I should be taking escaped me. I knew, however, that Balanchine did not need to wait to see the steps from the audience's perspective before judging their effectiveness. He could see steps close-up and visualize their total impact in a ballet yet to be completed. I was sure he could even see the total effect of steps he had not yet created! It was as if he could visualize the whole before the parts existed. Maybe this explains why he wasn't concerned when we had minor difficulties with one step or another. He knew where he was going, and he could find any number of ways to get there.

Ricky, too, was getting his share of difficult virtuoso steps in his two variations. They emphasized his lightness, his beats, and his turns. I know he would have liked more opportunities to "spin" (to do numerous pirouettes at one time), but Balanchine wanted to avoid what is so often seen in male virtuoso variations. Instead, he gave Ricky several steps of multiple pirouettes in rapid succession. In the last set he let Ricky do as many turns as he could. That was much more exciting and difficult than endless turns preceded by a careful preparation.

After Balanchine completed work on Ricky's and my variations, he started on the pas de deux, which comes near the beginning of the ballet, before any of the variations. He hadn't yet decided from which side of the stage we would enter. He asked us what our preference was, but we said we didn't have any. At that point no one knew that the preceding section would end with our exiting downstage right. Had I known, I would have asked to come in from stage right. As it happened, Balanchine had me begin the pas de deux by entering upstage left, which meant that I had to do a quick sprint using the backstage crossover in order to be on time for my entrance in the pas de deux.

The music for the pas de deux begins with a violin solo. Ricky entered first, running, posing, and searching, then exiting. Balanchine said to him that this was a "Nureyev entrance." I think he hoped Ricky would work on his carriage and try to look a little more noble if he gave him such an entrance. He guessed that the mere mention of the name Nureyev might inspire Ricky, whereas telling him to work on his upper body might produce the wrong effect.

After Ricky exited, I entered, also running and searching as well as doing many small, quick steps on pointe—one for every note. These were made particularly difficult by the unpredictable tempos of the solo violinist, who tended to race through certain passages, sometimes preventing me from producing the effect I wanted. These tiny steps on pointe were tricky because they contained many quick changes of direction, and I had become so used to the way Gordon Boelzner had played the music on the piano in rehearsals that I had difficulty adjusting.

When Balanchine choreographed, he did all the partnering himself. He had always taken great pride in the fact that he never asked his dancers to do any partnering that he himself was incapable of doing. Although his knees and back often troubled him, he didn't hesitate to lift and support his ballerinas.

The pas de deux itself began with Ricky's reentering and joining me on the stage. Balanchine often started by taking Ricky's part and simply telling me what I should do. Then, if he felt I had missed something, he would take my part and let Ricky partner him. At one point while Balanchine was partnering me, he asked which leg I would prefer to lift in à la seconde. I told him my right leg. If he had asked which leg I wanted to lift to the front or back, I would have answered my left leg. This kind of consideration, rare among choreographers, was something all his dancers especially appreciated.

After finishing the pas de deux, Balanchine started work on the variations for the four soloists. It became obvious that he was building a very fast pace into this ballet. Speed was everywhere. He took advantage of the fact that much of the music was continuous, allowing one variation to flow into the next. This rapid succession of variations was tricky, and Balanchine consulted Gordon, who is also now our assistant conductor, to see if he had any other ideas about how to divide the music for the solos. Balanchine liked to have him at the piano whenever he was choreographing and, because he had such respect for Gordon, he often followed his suggestions.

Once these solos were done, Balanchine turned his attention to the corps. He felt no compulsion to choreograph the various parts of the ballet in their proper sequence. Rather than starting with the opening of the ballet, he began with the coda, which came right before the stately processional at the end of the ballet. This coda was filled with surprise effects and challenges for everyone. But, for me, few of the virtuoso steps in this section tested my technique. My major challenge came just after I entered and ran in a big circle around the middle of the stage: it was a rapid-fire sequence made up of very simple steps put together in an unexpected way. I grasped the combination easily with my mind, but I couldn't make my body do it unless the tempo was very slow. I called it the "leg twister" step because it does to my legs what a tongue twister does to the tongue. I rehearsed it repeatedly, trying to get faster little by little. Soon I found if I relied entirely on my muscle memory, just as one does when walking or riding a bicycle,

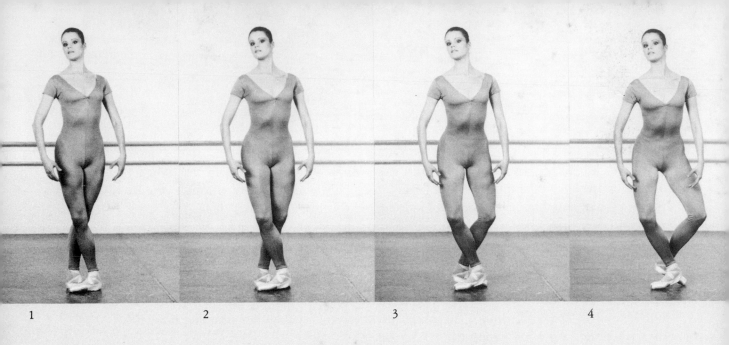

1   2   3   4

ASSEMBLÉ

Assemblé is a jump in which the dancer takes off from one leg and brings both legs together (or assembles them) in the air in fifth position and then lands in fifth position on the floor. This sequence shows "assemblé side" from fifth position *without traveling*. (Assemblé can also be done to the front or back, traveling or turning).

1–3   Assemblé starts in fifth position (1). As the demi-plié begins, all the weight is on the front foot, so the back foot can begin to slide along the floor (2 and 3).

4 and 5   The back leg brushes to the side very quickly as the demi-plié on the standing leg deepens (5).

6 and 7   As the back leg nears the extended side position, the standing leg begins to push away from the floor and straighten for the takeoff. The momentum for the jump is created both from the quick movement of the back leg and the push of the standing leg.

8–11   Even before the standing foot leaves the floor, the leg extended to the side begins to move back

9   10   11   12   13

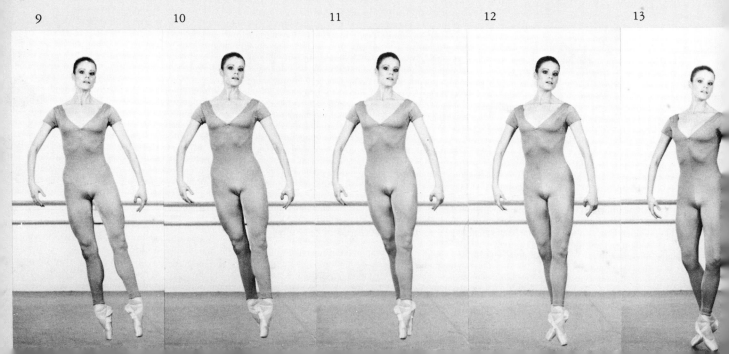

6   7   8

toward the center of the body to form a fifth position in the air (11). In a traveling assemblé, the standing leg moves toward the extended leg during the jump (instead of the other way around, as shown here). In both types of assemblés, Balanchine wanted us to create the illusion of being suspended in the air by bringing both feet together quickly so that a still fifth position could be seen at the height of the jump. The ability to perform this movement is, moreover, essential if beats with the legs or a turn are added to the assemblé: both require that the legs come very close together very quickly. If assemblé is practiced in the more traditional manner, with the legs coming together only as the feet touch the floor, the more complicated variations of assemblé become much more difficult and require a much higher elevation.

12–14 Once the legs have come together in the air, they remain there for the landing. The feet make whatever adjustment is necessary to reach fifth position on the floor. The feet should help control the rate of descent into demi-plié to prevent the landing from being jarring.

15–18 After the landing the demi-plié should continue to deepen without a momentary stop as the feet flatten on the floor.

15   16   17   18

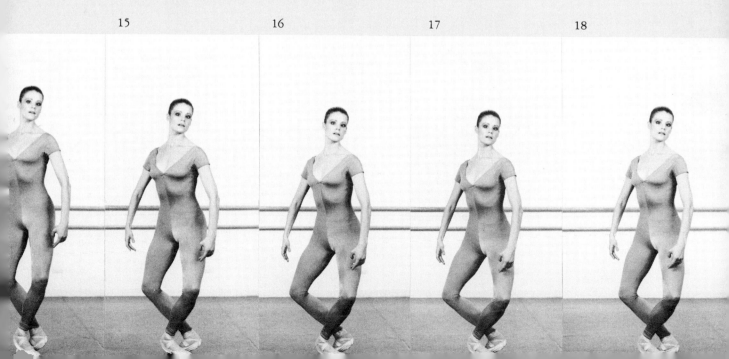

1   2   3   4   5

ASSEMBLÉ EN TOURNANT TO PLIÉ ON POINTE
(from *Ballo della Regina*)

Assemblé en tournant (turning assemblé) is a traditional step. But when Balanchine choreographed *Ballo della Regina*, he created a variation on this step that was the result of his experimentation with jumps on pointe in class: he had me land in plié on pointe in fifth position rather than with my feet flat

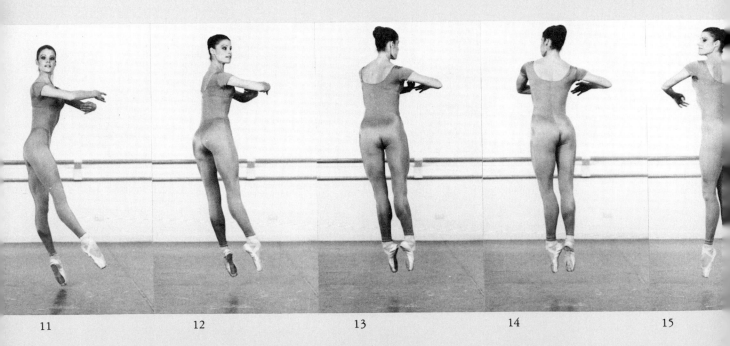

11   12   13   14   15

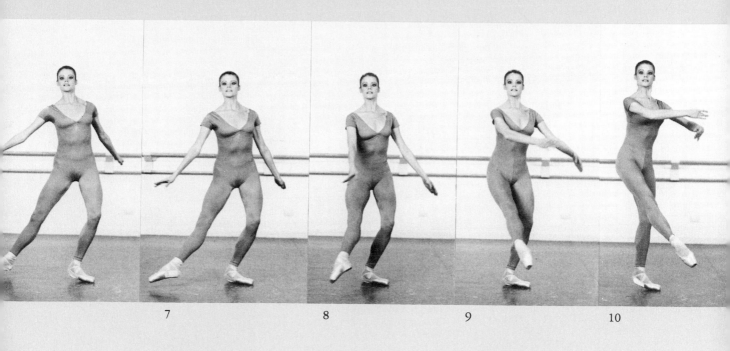

7   8   9   10

on the floor. Even though I had to land on pointe, Balanchine still wanted to see me suspended in the air with both legs together (13 through 16), as they would be in a traditional assemblé en tournant. I also had to land on pointe from a higher elevation than usual, which is one of the more exciting aspects of the step. The impact of the landing is absorbed by a smooth, continuous demi-plié (17 through 20) similar to those we practiced in regular landings from jumps.

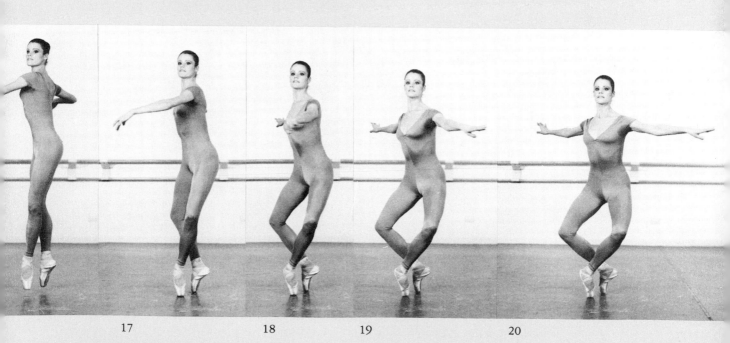

17   18   19   20

Raymonda Variations, Merrill doing a *traveling* assemblé. (© *Steven Caras*)

I could do it. But if I started to think while I was doing the step, I would make mistakes. Even now, I rely entirely on muscle memory, which is the most reliable form of recall for most dancers. I can't even explain the combination to anyone unless I have first actually done the sequence.

The sequence consists of four sets of three little steps, or "walks," done on pointe. Done more simply and more slowly, they are often seen in Balanchine choreography. In *Ballo*, the walks are done at top speed and keep changing direction. If I bend my knees or fall ever so slightly behind the music, the crisp image is lost. The legs have to move from the hips, and there must not be a hint of strain. I drew attention to the leg movements by looking down in delight, as if to say to the audience, "Isn't this clever? I hope you enjoy it as much as I do." As I worked on this step I couldn't help remembering something Danilova once said about a step in the pas de deux for Aurora and the Prince in *The Sleeping Beauty*. Aurora is on one knee and the Prince offers her his hand to help her get up. She places one foot on pointe and takes his hand at the same time. Then she gets up by putting her full weight on the foot that is on pointe. It's not difficult, but to a nondancer it looks that way. Danilova used to say: "Make it look difficult; make them think it's hard." My attitude to my "leg twister" step is the same.

As he reached the end of the coda, Balanchine became very quiet and stared at the floor, as he so often did when he was searching for new steps. Suddenly he looked up with a gleam in his eye as if to say to me: "Aha, what a lovely thing I have for you!" At that point the music had been racing along toward its conclusion and I had just done two double pirouettes, each ending in a sudden pose. Balanchine then had me do a supported triple pirouette that ended in a high développé à la seconde. Then the real wit of the step began. My leg went from that high à la seconde position down through passé to a kneeling position, but in between I did four staccato movements that matched the music perfectly. I appeared to have been caught in four stop-action images in rapid succession. Everyone watching giggled with delight at Balanchine's creation. Later when I rehearsed the step, I saw in the mirror that, in order to make each image sharp, there had to be a tiny, quick reopening of the leg, a barely perceptible little upward movement before the leg went down into its next position. Without this, the sequence would be blurred and might pass unnoticed. Now, during performance, I love to hear the audience react to this step with delight just as the other dancers had done when Balanchine choreographed it.

The coda, which Balanchine had finished choreographing, was preceded by the first processional for the corps and soloists. As he neared the completion of the processional, he found that all his dancers were nowhere near where he had placed them at the beginning of the coda. How could he get them there? He was faced with one of those little puzzles he had such a genius for solving on the spur of the moment. He could have re-choreographed the opening of the coda, but instead he chose not to be concerned with symmetry or even any recognizable pattern. He simply had everyone bourrée at the end of the procession to where they had to be at the beginning of the coda. It worked perfectly.

It took Balanchine only a week to choreograph *Ballo.* It seemed incredible that he could create something that was such a natural expression of the music, and of Ricky's and my talents, in so little time. I had listened to the music beforehand and had liked it but was quite incapable of imagining what he would do with it. How would he get dancers on and off the stage during all that continuous music? And what about the solemn processional? How do you end a brilliant virtuoso ballet with a stately march? I'm happy I had the experience of listening to the music before Balanchine began work, as it forced me to confront the problems before being given the answers and this gave me a special appreciation for how ingenious the choreography is. So much of what Balanchine did seemed to spring so naturally from the music and from us, the original dancers, it was very easy to forget that an "outside" hand had intervened.

Throughout the week of rehearsals that followed, Balanchine invited friends and longtime Company supporters to view his latest effort. Often he would simply watch us run through the whole ballet nonstop, and not utter a word. His face, which normally revealed so little, betrayed pleasure and satisfaction, and I had the distinct impression he was not only delighted but also anxious to show off his handiwork. That, in turn, thrilled me. I had strived for so long to please Balanchine and now I felt I'd finally done it. In addition, I had my own ballet, one that suited me perfectly and was exhilarating even to rehearse. Confirmation of the pleasure I had detected on Balanchine's face came when Peter Martins told me how much Balanchine had enjoyed working on *Ballo,* that it had been something of a game for Mr. B. He would devise step after step, Peter said, thinking I might not be able to do them, and then I would fool him. Hearing that made me treasure Mr. B's gift to me even more.

In fact, Balanchine seemed so happy with what he had done that he forgot there was some unfinished business: the "doll step" in the first variation, which had to be changed, as well as the ending of that variation, with which he was not happy. I felt a little foolish as we did these run-throughs, because I didn't know how to fill in those trouble spots, but my main concern was the lack of time to rehearse new steps. Judging from the rest of the ballet, whatever he thought up would be difficult and would take some time to get "into" my muscles. Trying to be patient, I waited for Balanchine to take the initiative. The last thing I wanted to do was push him into changing things.

At last, sensing that time was running out, I reminded him that I still didn't have a step in the middle of the variation. He looked at me, surprised. "Oh, where, dear? Show me." I showed him the "doll step" again, with music. He lowered his head and thought for what seemed a long time but was probably not even a minute. Suddenly he looked up at me with that elfin expression of his and happily said, "What about this, dear?" He showed me with his hands what he wanted. Interpreting his gestures, I started from plié in fifth position and jumped into first position on pointe, my toes not quite a foot apart.

From there, without bending my knees, I immediately did another little jump into second position, still on pointe. Balanchine liked what he saw and asked me to do a series of these double *échappés,* turning slightly each time I closed in fifth position. That meant I would make two complete turns during the entire sequence, and I didn't anticipate any problems.

It amazed me how reminiscent this was of his original "doll step." Instead of producing a new and unrelated step, he had kept his original idea of staccato straight-legged jumps on pointe. He simply changed the emphasis from the elevation of the jumps on pointe to the sudden opening of the legs on pointe. He had done it again! He had understood my difficulty with his first step and replaced it with one that suited me, the music, and the ballet.

Ballo was previewed for a gala audience on the opening night of the fall/winter season, November 15, 1977. The New York City Opera had just ended its season and we had not had access to the stage until the afternoon of the fifteenth, when we had to squeeze in the placement, orchestra, and dress rehearsals, which are always necessary whenever a new ballet is put on. Opening days are hectic enough when current repertory is being performed, but getting *Ballo* ready in time, without prior access to the stage, was a real feat. There simply wasn't enough time to make sure all the details were right, especially the lighting. The underwater effects that Balanchine wanted were missing, and the rest of the lighting didn't satisfy him either.

We dancers had had sufficient rehearsal time in the studios, but dancing on stage presented new difficulties. We didn't have the opportunity to make the adjustments necessary to feel comfortable, and we had to think too much as we danced. That, on top of the nervousness we all felt, made the first performance less exciting than it might otherwise have been. The response of the audience, as I remember it, was enthusiastic but not overwhelming. It was hard for us to judge if that was just a "gala reception" for the ballet (gala audiences are notoriously unresponsive) or if it was a true reflection of how the ballet would be received in the future. At any rate, it had not yet all come together.

The world premiere came more than eight weeks later, on January 12, 1978. This time the lighting was just right. Big sheets of Mylar had been hung against the back wall of the stage, and lights of different colors were directed toward them. The reflection of the lights hit a white plastic scrim a few feet from the Mylar, creating a dappled effect suggestive of underwater light.

By then, Ricky and I had had more time to rehearse on stage and to think about what we were doing, so we had a much better feeling for what the total effect of the ballet should be. For the gala preview, I had worried about my stamina because I knew my nervousness would add greatly to my fatigue. This no longer worried me. On the night of the premiere I was more sure of myself—and sure, too, that Balanchine's inventiveness would be appreciated.

The premiere went smoothly, and the audience gave us an enthusiastic ovation. Bal-

Balanchine demonstrates two sequences in the pas de deux from *Ballo della Regina* during the dress rehearsal, as Robert Weiss watches, 1977. (© *1984 Martha Swope*)

anchine remained very happy with his creation. After the premiere and some other performances of *Ballo,* I actually heard the word *fantastic* pass his lips. I found *that* fantastic! It was in such contrast to the reserved way he usually expressed himself. There were many flattering comments in the reviews about Ricky and me. It was generally thought that Balanchine had "broken new ground" and that, in me, he had found someone with whom he could "try the untried." But the general impression conveyed was that the ballet was only a divertissement, albeit a brilliant one, and that it might not last long in the repertory. Perhaps it was felt that once the novelty wore off, once people who had seen the ballet several times knew what to expect, the virtuosity would stand bare and seem superficial.

That view might apply to virtuosity straining for effect, but in my case the virtuoso steps and all the rest quickly became second nature, freeing me to revel in the music and in Balanchine's "fantastic" creativity. Some might have underestimated the inspirational power of the pure joy I felt dancing *Ballo* and the audience's joy in watching it. But I felt the same kind of carefree delight that I'd had many years before when I had taken my first ballet classes and been able to enter a world of fantasy and improvisation. It was the joy that I had always felt in so many of Balanchine's ballets, only now it could be seen more than ever before. In *Ballo,* Balanchine had captured everything I loved most about dancing.

Ballo stayed in the repertory season after season, and I looked forward to every performance. It became the NYCB's curtain raiser par excellence. People told me that watching *Ballo* was their favorite way to start an evening at the ballet. It seemed to produce what has been called a "kinesthetic response": it gave people the urge to imitate what they saw me doing, or at least to try.

In 1979, we videotaped *Ballo* for presentation on public television in the *Dance in America* series. As in the past, we rehearsed in New York before going to Nashville for the taping sessions. A hand-held video camera was brought to these rehearsals so that a "work tape" could be made for the Nashville cameramen to study and so that Balanchine could see what sequences were distorted by the camera's lens. Whenever Balanchine saw such distortions, he would rechoreograph the sequence to make it look effective on television.

One such place came at the end of the coda, where I had a series of piqué turns in a circle. On television any step in a circle looks flat and uninteresting. The camera follows the dancer, who stays the same size on the screen, obscuring the fact that you're moving in a circle. Balanchine asked me to do fouetté turns in place rather than the circle of turns. Unfortunately, I had sprained my left ankle a week earlier and it was too sore and weak for me to do fast fouettés on my left leg. Reluctantly, I gave him the news. Balanchine knew that few people are comfortable turning to the left, and so he assumed, correctly, that I would not want to do fouettés on my right leg turning to the left. His next idea was *en dedans* fouettés, which would have me turning on my right leg, but to the right. They are much more difficult than regular *en dehors* fouettés, especially at a fast tempo. When it was finally time to tape *Ballo,* I was able to do these fiendish turns, but only if I was not tired and breathless right before beginning them. Fortunately, we taped the coda in several different takes, which ensured I would be fresh for these turns.

After the shooting, Balanchine found he preferred this change to the original steps and asked me to do the same thing on stage. I did several performances this way, but the turns were always very precarious. I had very little energy left by that time, and as I struggled to do the fouettés I found myself moving dangerously close to the edge of the orchestra pit. When my left ankle was healthy again, I decided to go back to Balanchine's idea of regular fouettés. But even today my dislike of fouettés still surfaces and makes me long for those original easy piqué turns.

When I saw *Ballo* on television, I was disappointed. Although I was captivated by the ballet, which I was *seeing* for the first time, I wondered where all my energy and joie de vivre had gone. I hoped it was just that the little screen had blurred the dynamics of my dancing. I was happy, however, with my general approach to the ballet, which Balanchine had never discussed with me.

It's tempting to think that *Ballo* is indestructible, that its appeal will prove everlasting. People often say that Balanchine ballets somehow survive bad dancing. It's true that I have seen some of his masterpieces dulled by sluggish dancers and disguised by acting yet remain beautiful and satisfying to watch. But I fear little *Ballo* won't stand up to such punishment. Some steps, the easier ones, will of course still look wonderful, but if the tempos are slowed to accommodate dancers unable to cope with the speed, then the brilliance will be lost. If the timing is not exactly right in many of the steps, the impression of clarity, the image of the step reinforced in the mind by the sound of the music, will be lost. In the ballerina role, the added element of joy—not to mention musicality—is essential. It's hard to imagine a ballerina with no experience in the Balanchine repertory finding any joy in virtuosity at *Ballo*'s tempos. For me, however, it will be a joy forever.

"Fantastic," Balanchine said to me once again after one of my early performances of *Ballo.*

It was the chance I'd been waiting for to express my gratitude for his patience and his confidence in me, for making me a principal and giving me *Ballo,* for teaching me to dance—for everything.

"Oh, Mr. B, thank you so much. I owe everything to you."

"No, dear, you did it yourself," he responded quickly, as if he had already thought the matter through.

"But I couldn't have done it without you. I wouldn't have known what to work for."

"Yes, but you had to do it yourself."

Coming from Balanchine, that was a very special compliment. He wanted self-reliance in his dancers. His style of teaching was designed to make us think for ourselves. Yet he knew that, for many, independence and independent thinking were unwelcome burdens. He had seen some of his most talented dancers abandon him in search of the kind of daily private coaching on the most minute details that he felt he shouldn't give.

"You had to do it yourself" meant that he recognized I had had to work hard for what I had accomplished. I had not been one of those raw talents to whom everything comes easy. I had been very weak and had had to overcome a certain awkwardness and stiffness that came when I tried to do things that were too difficult for me. I had persevered; I had welcomed criticism and remembered corrections; I had kept improving, and above all I had remained devoted to him and his teaching. None of this had escaped his attention.

In spite of my steady progress over the years, Balanchine had not been convinced of my devotion. Too many others in the past had shown promise and then abandoned him or given up entirely. Others had fulfilled their promise but then looked elsewhere for coaching. Balanchine seemed to have wondered if I was really the person I appeared to be; whether beneath my quiet exterior, there was not lurking another one of those strong-willed ballerinas bent on doing things her own way. It had taken me ten years to build my technique; it had taken Balanchine ten years to become confident I would remain true to him.

After *Ballo,* however, any lingering doubts he might have had seemed to disappear, and he was ready to start enjoying whatever qualities he liked in me. In all probability, it was my technique that appealed to him most. I not only knew what he wanted; I could do it. Countless others had aroused Balanchine's interest because of their raw talent, beauty, body type, or a special look. Then, if they couldn't cope with the difficulties of his ballets or the pressures of Company life, Balanchine's interest might wane. I was now confident this would not happen to me.

Aside from my technique, Balanchine may have found something in my "all-American look," as some people have called it, that appealed to him. He might also have liked my straightforward but quiet manner and uncomplaining nature. The Company had always had plenty of flamboyant and outspoken types who required diplomatic handling. He may have considered me a welcome relief in that respect.

Yet, I still felt shy and awkward in conversation with him and regretted my inability to come up with a witty line—or *any* line!—in our chance encounters in the hallways. When I had found out that Balanchine was going to do a ballet for me, I ardently hoped that our close daily contact would bring about a miracle cure for my reserve. Perhaps I would suddenly open up and find myself chatting away with him as did some of the corps girls, whose nonchalance in his presence stupefied me. No such miracle occurred, but our working relationship continued to bring both of us immense pleasure.

As Balanchine and I worked together on *Ballo,* a noticeable change occurred. Before, he had been the teacher, I the pupil. Suddenly, it seemed we had also become collaborators, partners. In addition, he seemed to be growing fond of me, not just as a dancer but as a person. He made small gestures of friendship that represented both a change in our relationship and a show of interest. His face would light up when he saw me unexpectedly. He would embrace me and then put his arm around my waist and leave it there in obvious pleasure. Sometimes he would invite me to have tea with him when we both had a few free minutes. My confidence grew, but my awe of him remained. *Ballo* had not cured that.

It was as if the challenge posed by Balanchine's personality was greater than the challenge of his choreography, and I struggled to understand why he had such an inhibiting effect on me. With him, small talk often turned to big subjects—politics, religion, world affairs—on which he had many strong opinions. Although I too had my opinions, I had no desire to force my views on anyone, especially Balanchine; when the conversation became serious, I was only too happy to listen. Balanchine greatly enjoyed conversing with his dancers and regaling them with his comments and stories, which were not always easy for me to follow. My practical mind, always expecting one point to lead logically to the next, was often bewildered by the mosaic of impressions Balanchine fashioned. More than once I thought that listening to Mr. B tell one of his stories was a little like watching one of his ballets: they were often plotless but never pointless. They were marvelous, but I wouldn't have been able to explain to anyone the logic of what I had just heard or seen.

Balanchine's pithy and concise use of the English language and his predilection for quick, precise movements seemed to spring from the same incisive mind. Just as his ballets were known for sharpening the audience's perceptions, so his little quips and unexpected metaphors stuck in our minds and made us think. Though we didn't always immediately understand the underlying message, at least the surface meaning of his words was perfectly clear.

Just as Balanchine redefined the vocabulary of classical ballet to suit his taste, he revised many of the rules of English grammar and created a style uniquely his own. His "incorrect" English, about which he was a little self-conscious, was almost never marked by obvious grammatical errors. The missing articles and pronouns were closer to clever innovations than mistakes, and they contributed to his catchy turns of phrase, which never would have occurred to a "native." So many of his utterances defied translation into conventional speech. How could anyone render his wonderfully eloquent "ballet is woman" into more standard English without destroying the meaning of the original? What would have happened to his intriguingly succinct and very effective "dear, just do!" if the missing pronoun were restored or, worse still, if the "dear" were dropped? Balanchine wouldn't have been Balanchine if he had simply said: "Just do it!"

There is probably no word more closely associated in our minds with Balanchine than his use of *dear* to preface almost all his comments to dancers. Depending on the tone in his voice, he could invest it with whatever meaning he pleased, from the sternly scolding to the clearly affectionate. To him, the word did not have the usual intimate connotation, and he used it with all the dancers in the Company, men and women alike. Any comment prefaced by "dear" immediately took on a more personal and direct tone. Perhaps for that reason he preferred to address almost all of us as "dear," even though he knew everyone in the Company by name.

Balanchine was no less fascinating to watch than he was to listen to. In my effort to understand him, I became intrigued with his facial features. Those same features that were so expressive and eloquent in mime revealed so little in real life. His eyes darted about, seeing everything. He seemed to sniff the air for something beyond our senses; and, as he talked or listened, he pursed his lips and tilted his head back slightly. Were these mobile features an unconscious disguise, I often wondered, or were they merely tics? Were his senses simply so acute, his powers of observation so great, that his features could not remain in a state of repose under such powerful stimuli? With Mr. B anything seemed possible.

In contrast, his whole demeanor was relaxed. He spoke without nervous gestures or shifting from foot to foot. He always seemed at ease with himself and, when not engaged in conversation, he would often quietly observe whatever was going on around him. He never appeared absent-minded and rarely conveyed the impression that he had more important business elsewhere. As he watched others, his attention was so absorbed by the appearance, movements, and speech of people around him that it was easy for me to believe he learned more from a few casual observations than most of us did after hours of careful study.

Balanchine made a lasting impression on everyone. No one who had even the briefest contact with him was left untouched; those who knew him well were changed forever. Many people, upon meeting him for the first time, expected to find a man full of false airs, but his disarming lack of pretension and his natural modesty made them feel more important in his presence. If strangers became too effusive in their praise of the masterpieces he had created, he liked to say: "Only God creates; man arranges." He simply thought he had certain God-given talents and a duty to use them.

After *Ballo,* although I was still too shy and quiet with Balanchine to make our relations truly comfortable, I grew more confident with him. That new confidence helped my dancing but did not make me complacent. I had no time or inclination to relax and enjoy my newfound freedom from the frustration and anxiety I had felt before my promotion to principal status. For a long time I even found it difficult to think of myself as a principal. I did not feel I had arrived; I was simply beginning a new phase. Even though I knew my dancing was at a high level, I also knew I had much more to learn. There were new ideas to be put into practice and old ones to be discarded, but I enjoyed the thought of the years of learning and work that lay ahead.

Kibbe greeted the news of my promotion with mixed emotions. He knew what it meant to me, but feared it would change me, and not for the better. He disliked what he felt was the self-satisfied attitude of a few of the other principals, and he worried that the promotion might make me that way. Principals, after all, rarely heard anything but compliments. He felt that, exhausted after the years of struggle, I might rest on my laurels. He soon realized, however, that I planned to continue my great adventure in the NYCB with the same spirit I had always had. I was not going to change.

Throughout the rest of the season, Balanchine gave me more and more new roles, including *Raymonda Variations* (the principal role), *La Source, Allegro Brillante,* and the central role in *Divertimento No. 15.* In addition, Robbins cast me in two of his ballets: *The Goldberg Variations* and *In G Major.* The best and most demanding roles in the Company were still coming my way. I danced as many as twelve ballets a week and was often exhausted as much from the endless rehearsing as from an evening's performance. But I was so happy and satisfied with my life that it was not hard to tap hidden reserves of strength and energy.

As my confidence grew, I became less inclined to worry about myself, and more alert than ever before—to the other dancers around me, and to the effects produced by the music, lighting, scenery, and costumes. It was also easier for me to pay attention to the corrections Balanchine gave to the other dancers in each ballet, and thus I became familiar with his ideas about almost every step in each ballet. (Since I had never been in the corps of *Divert* or *Donizetti,* there was much that was new to me.) This in itself was valuable, but it was only the beginning. My thinking was stimulated about my own roles, the individual ballets, and about Balanchine's choreography in general. If he tried to achieve a certain style or add a type of gesture to the corps work, I would reexamine my own part to see if that same style was appropriate. Could I add more of that flavor to my dancing or had I already caught the spirit? In this way I often found solutions to my problem spots. A little gesture could change so much.

As I thought more about the different styles of the ballets, I began to want to dance in some of our dramatic ballets, such as *La Valse, Bugaku,* and *The Cage.* I felt I was as well suited to these as to the virtuoso ones. Still, I was dancing in some of the greatest masterpieces in the history of ballet, and it was deeply satisfying knowing that I did not have to look beyond the horizons of the NYCB, for our repertory was a universe unto itself.

The more I saw Balanchine at work, the more I appreciated how frequently he drew on his vast knowledge and his varied background. As a boy he had studied music, dance history, pantomime, and folk and character dancing. His was the kind of education that, in retrospect, I wish I had been given at SAB. Later on, he was exposed to other styles of dancing as well as to painting and sculpture, all of which affected his choreography.

Balanchine was not only a great choreographer; his rare gifts for acting, gesture, and graceful movement enabled him to portray even women's roles. He was incapable of making an inappropriate or awkward gesture—unless he was imitating us. To me he was the greatest of all dancers, although he was well known for saying that Fred Astaire deserved that honor.

Even more surprising was Balanchine's rare knowledge of pointe work. Most men, because they have never danced on pointe, have little understanding of the difficulties involved in getting on and off pointe. But Balanchine wanted to understand everything about the way a woman danced, so that he could enhance her beauty in his ballets. On countless occasions his women would accidentally do something unusually interesting on pointe and he would notice it, remember it, and use it at an appropriate moment. But he also analyzed the basic techniques involved in pointe work and taught his dancers the smoothest, most articulate way of doing these steps.

There are two basic ways of getting onto pointe. One is to relevé, or roll from a flat foot up onto pointe. The other is to piqué, or step directly onto the tip of the shoe with a fully pointed foot. Balanchine had very specific ideas on how to do both these movements; he wanted every part of each movement to be smooth and controlled. Most dancers tend to jump slightly as they relevé, as if they don't want to bend their foot as they rise onto pointe. Their foot is either flat on the floor or straight on pointe, and they do not show anything in between. In an effort to eliminate the jarring appearance of a dancer jumping onto pointe, Balanchine had us "roll through the foot," almost as if we were going onto half-pointe. But, instead of stopping in a full half-pointe position, he had us use our toes to push us the last little distance onto pointe. This gave us the control to relevé in slow motion, which produces marvelous effects in slow adagio work. The same idea applied to coming off pointe. Once again, he wanted us to roll through the foot, controlling the rate of descent rather than just dropping suddenly down onto a flat foot. In Mr. B's eyes—and, therefore, in our eyes—any dancer not controlling her ascent or descent looked careless and unrefined.

Balanchine made us pay attention to the different problems associated with piqués on pointe. Whenever a dancer piqués on pointe, except in the few cases where the choreography specifies otherwise, the leg must remain straight. The urge is to step directly onto the flat tip of the shoe, but if one is stepping more than just a very few inches from a point directly beneath oneself, this is possible only with a bent leg. Therefore the dancer must first step on one of the edges of the tip and roll from there onto the tip itself. The only other way to get directly onto pointe with a straight leg is to jump, but that is another step. Stepping onto pointe with a bent leg that is supposed to be straight is a cardinal sin in ballet.

Balanchine taught us which edge of the shoe to step onto, depending on which way we would be traveling. Sometimes the weight first went onto the little toe; at other times, onto the big toe; and at still other times, on the top or bottom edge of the shoe, where all the toes could support the weight. As with the relevé on pointe, this gave us a smooth, controlled ascent onto pointe.

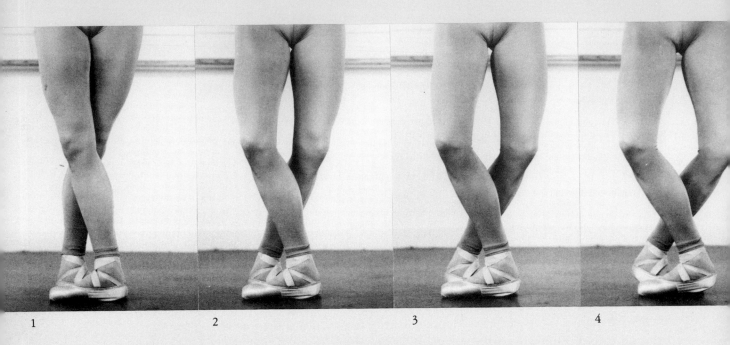

1   2   3   4

PASSÉ RELEVÉ FROM ONE FOOT

Passé relevé is traditionally started by pushing off with both feet simultaneously from fifth position (see following sequence). Balanchine taught this traditional type of passé relevé, but he also developed a passé relevé that pushes off with *one* foot, although it, too, starts in fifth position. A great deal of coordination, strength, and control is required to do this type of passé relevé, which is generally executed at a very slow tempo.

1-3   The passé relevé starts in fifth position (1). As the demi-plié begins, all the weight is on the back foot so that the front foot is free to move.

4-6   In 4, the front foot begins to move toward the toes of the back foot and continues to move in this

8   9   10

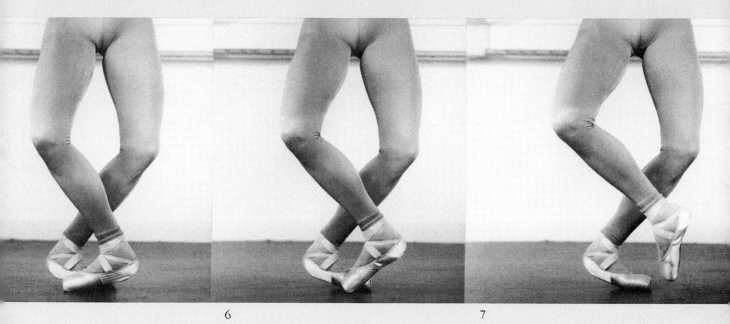

6   7

direction as it begins to point. (The foot will not be fully pointed until 9.) At the same time the demi-plié on the standing foot deepens.

7–10   As the front foot leaves the floor (7), the relevé on the standing foot begins and the knee of the front leg begins to lift. The moving leg accelerates during this part of the movement (8 through 10). If the movement of both legs is coordinated properly, the action of the knee being lifted makes the relevé easier.

11–13   As the standing foot moves from a low half-pointe (10) to full pointe (13), the movement of the front leg slows as it nears the passé front position (13). The toes of the passé leg should arrive in the passé position at the same time the standing foot reaches full pointe. The toes of the passé foot should not rest on the standing leg at any time, even if the passé position is held for a long time, but should be held, as Balanchine said, so that "you can put a piece of paper between the knee and toes."

▷

12   13

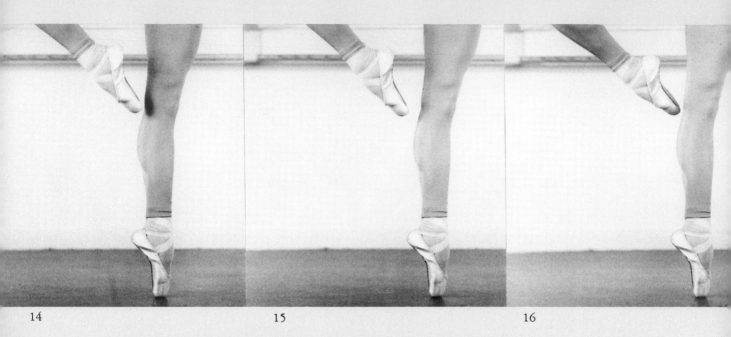

14   15   16

14–17   As the passé leg continues to move toward fifth position, the knee lifts and moves backward, causing the foot to move slightly away from the standing leg (14 through 16) as it changes from passé front to passé back (17).

18–20   Without stopping in passé back, the passé leg continues to move toward the floor in line with the center of the standing leg. The standing leg remains straight and on full pointe as the passé leg is lowered.

21 and 22   When the passé leg nears the floor, the foot begins to move sideways away from the standing leg as it makes the necessary adjustments to reach fifth position.

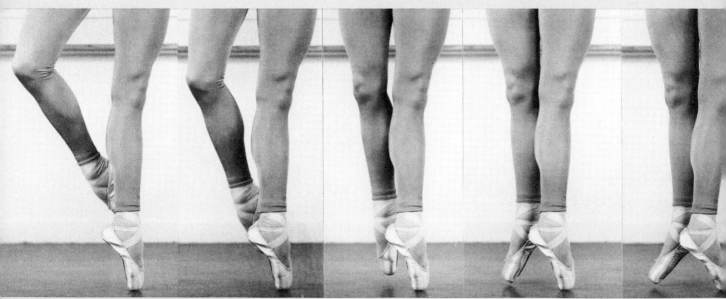

20   21   22   23   24

18   19

23-25   Once the passé leg is very near the floor and the knee is almost straight, both feet begin to move toward fifth position (23 and 24). The dancer must be able to judge exactly how far away from the standing leg to place the toes of the passé leg in order to ensure a correct fifth position at the end of the movement (25). Once both feet are on the floor, the knees begin to bend in demi-plié

26-28   Even after both feet are on the ground, the descent must remain controlled. Notice how slowly the feet continue to roll down off pointe and move to a flat position on the floor in demi-plié.

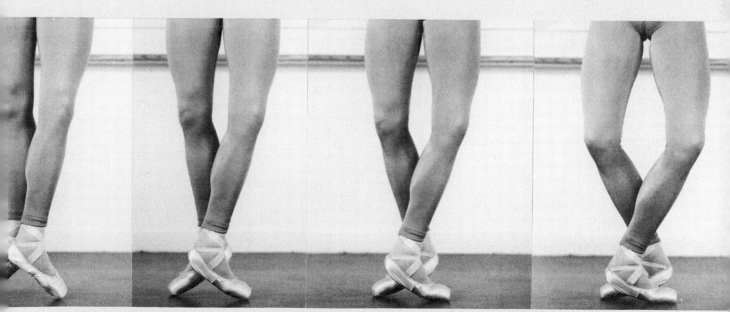

26   27   28

1   2   3   4

PASSÉ RELEVÉ FROM BOTH FEET

Balanchine usually asked for this type of passé relevé when he wanted the passé movement to look crisp. This step is therefore often performed in his choreography at a quick tempo (as shown here) requiring that small adjustments (compromises with an ideal version of the step) be made. This sequence shows only the ascent to passé, because the descent is the same as in the preceding sequence.

1–3   From demi-plié in fifth position (1), with the weight equally distributed, the feet push away from the floor with equal force while the knees begin to straighten (2 and 3).

4–6   As the standing foot nears the full pointe position, the working leg leaves the floor (4) and begins to move to the passé position (5 and 6). Ideally, the foot of the working leg should move directly up the front of the calf so that no space can be seen between the working foot and the standing leg. But, since this passé was done at a quick tempo, the working leg moved slightly away from the standing leg to accommodate the speed.

7 and 8   In 7 the full height of the passé has been reached. From there the working leg moves, without stopping, back toward fifth position by changing (passing) from passé front to passé back (8). The leg will then move down the back of the leg to fifth position as shown in 17 through 28 in the previous sequence.

5   6   7   8

Each time we did a piqué onto pointe, Balanchine wanted us to be aware of the foot in the air, as it moved toward the floor, and as it actually touched the floor. This awareness was intended to make it possible for us to put our foot on pointe deliberately and delicately. He also wanted us to step at least as far as the extended tendu position, and even beyond if there was time, to make the movement look unconstricted.

Balanchine understood the problems inherent in being on pointe that are generally so difficult for men to grasp. When a man stands on half-pointe, his weight is distributed over a relatively broad area. He also can make small adjustments in his balance by raising or lowering the height of his half-pointe. A woman on pointe does not have the luxury of these adjustments. Her weight is distributed over a much smaller area and she cannot use her toes to grip the floor for balance. The area she stands on is at most the size of a half dollar, and if she is on the edge of the tip it can be smaller than the size of a pea. That means her foot can easily slide out from under her if the floor is the least bit slippery. Many times, men expect that a step done on half-pointe can also be done on pointe, and that is often simply not true.

In addition to understanding the limitations of pointe work, Balanchine also made full use of the possibilities inherent in it. Many steps, for example, are easier on pointe: a woman can do quick walks on pointe with relative ease, since her feet are already pointed; all she has to do is make her legs move. A man on half-pointe has to point his toes each time his foot lifts off the floor. That takes up precious instants and means he can't make the movements as quickly as a woman. For example, a man trying to do my "leg twister" step in *Ballo* would either have to slow down the tempo to do the step properly or resign himself to having flexed toes throughout the course of the step, thus losing the effectiveness of the step.

A choreographer without this knowledge and all it implies will find it difficult to understand women's classical dancing, and such a choreographer will often have trouble creating new inventive steps for women. Balanchine acquired his knowledge as a result of his fascination with women and was able to use it to create steps that made them look unique and beautiful.

While it may be difficult for men to appreciate pointe work, they have a great advantage over women when it comes to understanding partnering. The man is usually standing behind the woman or in another position where it is easy to watch her. He can study various positions and the effects they create. As a woman, I have great difficulty understanding what a man does in partnering. I know what feels right, but that is all. When a man is partnering a woman, he can feel her weight and may have ideas about other possible movements. He sees how her body falls and constantly has to adjust or fix things that go wrong. His job is to react and relate to what he sees. The woman is in a more passive stance. This may be one of the reasons so few women choreograph classical ballet.

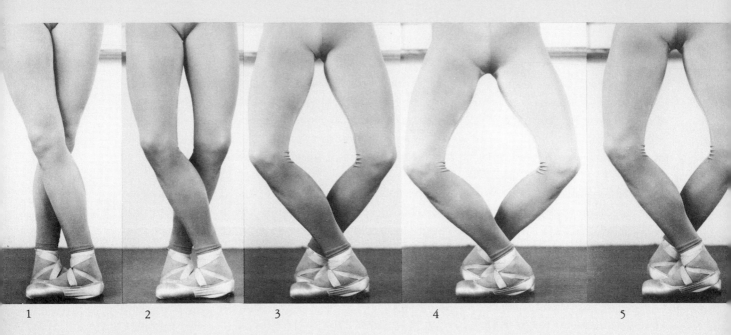

1   2   3   4   5

SOUSSUS

Soussus is a springy but controlled relevé from fifth position to fifth position on pointe.

1–4 Soussus begins with a demi-plié in fifth position.

5–7 As the knees begin to straighten (5), the toes of both feet begin to slide along the floor as they move closer together (6 and 7), causing the heels to lift off the floor. Both feet should move simultaneously, covering the same distance at the same speed so that the body does not have to move sideways. The most common error is to relevé on one foot and bring the other foot over to meet it, causing the body to move sideways. Notice how early the knees straighten; they are almost straight before the feet are even half-pointed (7).

8–10 The toes maintain light contact with the floor as they continue to point (8 and 9). By 10, fifth position on pointe has been reached and the full body weight is equally distributed on both feet. The toes

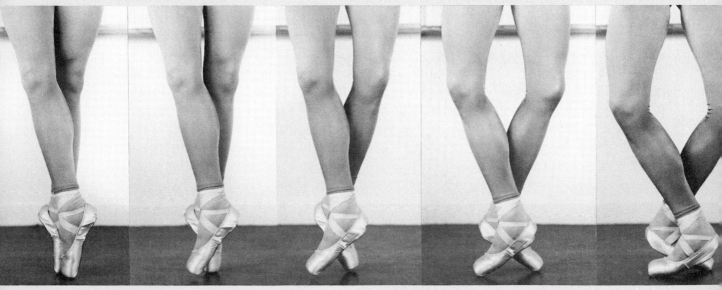

11   12   13   14   15

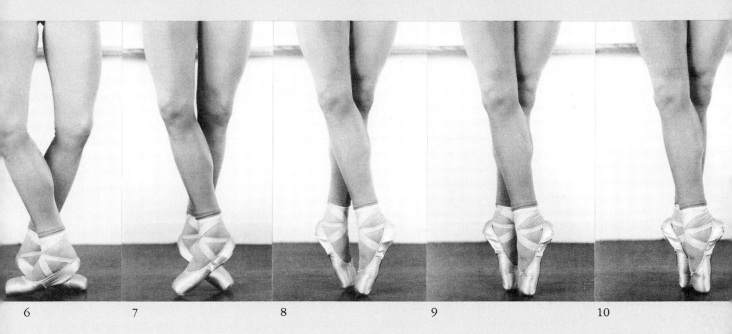

6   7   8   9   10

are very close together and the feet are well crossed. Balanchine stressed these two points the most.

11–13   Ideally the descent from fifth position on pointe, which begins in 11, should be the exact reverse of the ascent, but as there is no plié on pointe, it is very difficult to lift both feet off the floor at exactly the same moment. Any discrepancy must be minimized. In 12, which represents one twentieth of a second, the front foot has begun to move while the back foot still is supporting my weight. By 13, the discrepancy between the movement of the feet has practically disappeared.

14–17   Now the feet are in the same position and moving in the same way (14). The toes have light contact with the floor as they continue to slide toward fifth position, and the knees bend in demi-plié (15 through 17).

18–20   Fifth position in demi-plié has been reached (18) and the knees straighten to end the movement (19 and 20).

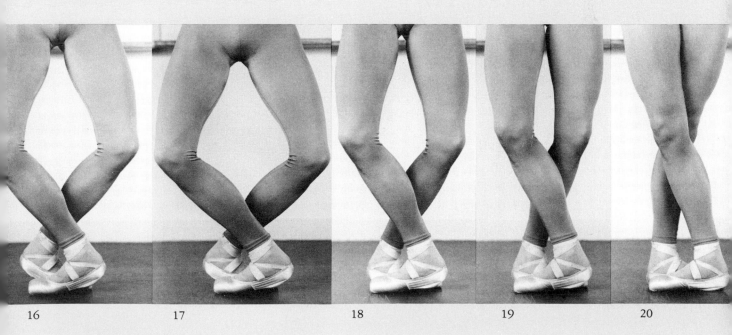

16   17   18   19   20

Balanchine's keen interest in pointe work rubbed off on me and became one of the strongest elements in my technique. The fact is that the shape of my feet is not ideal for pointe work because my toes are not of equal length; my big toes are quite long in comparison to my other toes, which makes it difficult for me to distribute the weight in the middle of the foot, where it belongs. Instead, all the weight goes onto my big toe, which I'm sure has contributed a great deal to the problems I have had with my bunion joint. I also have very small feet, but that has turned out to be an advantage, since I have a much shorter distance to cover when I relevé, and therefore I can spend less time in the stressful in-between positions if I am moving slowly. For the same reason, I can make quick movements more easily. Although Balanchine may have preferred the look of a long foot, he certainly liked what my feet could do.

Despite all the emphasis Balanchine placed on pointe work, and the control of all the various movements the feet and legs make, what was most important to him was the use and coordination of the entire body. This was what made us dancers instead of robots. If the feet and legs were moving crisply, the head and arms often had to be doing just the opposite, while still maintaining a relationship with what our legs were doing. The body had to bend as well. In class Balanchine worked on using the whole upper body, but it was easiest to see how his corrections applied while we were rehearsing his ballets. It was also during rehearsals that he was most adamant about seeing the body work as a whole. Balanchine would often make rehearsals run overtime if he felt the dancers were still not using their upper bodies the way they should. He would finally get them to move in a freer manner but then the lines often became ragged. If he had to choose between dancers' dancing with their whole bodies and precise, accurate steps and lines with very little "dancing," he would always opt for the dancing.

Balanchine continued to explore different facets of speed and energy after he choreographed *Ballo.* A few weeks later, he set to work on *Kammermusik No. 2,* a modern and cerebral ballet; but one that, like *Ballo,* was packed with steps done at top speed.

Colleen was given one of the two female leads in *Kammermusik.* I think Balanchine hoped that this gesture of generosity and concern would encourage her to persevere. But she seemed unable to surmount her various problems, and when Balanchine took more of her roles away from her, she finally left the Company in 1979.

Chris Redpath, too, had been given numerous opportunities, but when she didn't live up to Balanchine's expectations he cast her less and less frequently, leaving her in the same situation that Colleen was in. Confused, unable or unwilling to persevere, she too then left the Company.

The misfortune of Colleen and Chris reminded me that talent and hard work didn't guarantee success. Both these dancers had shown early promise, and accomplished a great deal. What stopped them, and many others, from going further? The simple answer is that further progress became too difficult. In some cases, a kind of inner exhaustion set in and the spirit failed. In other cases, the will to fight on was there, but the dancer needed to progress in ways so subtle that hard work and perspiration didn't necessarily bring about the desired results. It's very sad when careers end prematurely in this way, and the history of the NYCB is strewn with dancers who were as talented as Colleen and Chris were, but who eventually gave up.

I derived no satisfaction from their defeat. Competition with them had been a powerful stimulus, and now I hoped that constructive criticism from others would be a substitute. Instead, I received only compliments. How could I be certain that my efforts to improve were on the right track? How well would I withstand the pressure of "carrying" ballets every evening? Despite such questions, I remained confident and thought I knew what delicate changes still had to be made in my dancing. But knowing and doing were two different things.

Early in 1978, about a year after *Ballo* had premiered, Balanchine planned a new ballet, *Tricolore,* as a homage to France. Together with *Stars and Stripes* and *Union Jack,* it was to form part of an evening-length program titled *Entente Cordiale.* Sean Lavery and I were to dance the lead roles in the middle section, "Pas Degas." It was thrilling to think that I would be in another new Balanchine ballet so soon.

But a few months later, in March 1978, Balanchine was hospitalized with a heart ailment, and it was clear he would not recover in time to choreograph this ballet. The music, a commissioned score that proved disappointing, was divided among Peter Martins, Jerome Robbins, and Jean-Pierre Bonnefous, who choreographed my section. Balanchine's illness naturally cast a pall over the proceedings and, given the circumstances, the ballet seemed doomed from the start.

Our disappointment in this ballet was insignificant compared to the anxiety we all felt over Balanchine's state of health. His illness proved serious and required by-pass surgery. It was many months before he was back in the theater working again.

Balanchine's absence had left its mark on all of us. Suddenly, for the first time since Tanaquil LeClercq had been stricken with polio in 1956 and Balanchine had left the Company for a year to take care of her, we had to experience life in the theater without him. We not only missed working with him, but each of us in his or her own way missed him as a person. He was always approachable and we had grown accustomed to his presence in the theater from morning until night. Balanchine attended to every imaginable detail. When the energy crisis was in the news, he even went around turning out lights in the rehearsal rooms after performance. He would tell us to conserve energy, too—except when we were dancing!

When he was there watching us, or when we thought he might appear, there was indeed no energy shortage. We wanted to do our very best for him as well as for ourselves. He was proud of us, and we didn't want to let him down. Because of his pride and belief in us, we believed we were the best. During his absence, we realized how much we needed him to inspire us. I particularly missed the daily diet of challenge and inspiration in his classes. It was too awful to think that he would be away from us for very long, or that he might not return at all. So I continued working as before, trying to keep his words and ideas perpetually in mind.

After Balanchine recovered, he taught only two or three times a week. Fearing that he might soon stop giving class regularly, I began to write down all the combinations that he gave in the center. I didn't have to write down anything about the way he ordinarily gave the barre, for that was so well ingrained in my mind and body that I could never forget it. But if he gave a particularly noteworthy barre, I wrote that down as well. I only wish I had started years earlier. But these notes are enough to help me give a Balanchine class on my own. On the rare occasions when I teach class now, I use them for inspiration. Fortunately, I find that my descriptions of Balanchine's steps bring back the point of the combinations and the corrections he gave us.

Of course, giving a Balanchine class is one thing, and getting results is another. To say that those in such a class would have to be highly motivated is an understatement; they would have to be willing to subject themselves to unimaginable extremes of tempos and physical effort. A few idealists or perfectionists would always respond, but for the most part, the incentive to improve would have to be better roles or promotions. A successful Balanchine teacher would then have to have both expertise and influence in matters of casting and promotion.

As Balanchine taught less and less frequently, his whole attitude seemed to change. He began to lose his endless patience as he contemplated the growing number of dancers who had never had class with him and who didn't know the basics as he taught them. He saw, too, that while he had been away some of the older dancers who knew what he wanted had gotten lazy and had fallen back into their old, comfortable habits. "Dancers are like racehorses," Balanchine often said; "they need a jockey on their backs." We needed Balanchine on ours. Even when he had been teaching regularly, he felt continually obliged to go back over the basics with every new group of dancers, although mere reminders often elicited the desired results. Now he seemed overwhelmed, even though there were not yet very many new people. "I should have been a dentist," he often said. "It's like pulling teeth to get you to do what I want." But, he no longer had the strength or the energy to undertake the Herculean task of making nearly one hundred dancers do what he wished.

In previous years, when individual dancers had approached him after class to ask for more detailed explanations of corrections they had received, he had spent as much time with them as they needed. But now he felt too tired or frustrated, and either gave a very brief explanation or merely said: "Watch Merrill; that's how you should do."

I heard this from many of the corps people who not only watched me as Balanchine advised but also came to me with their questions. I welcomed them, although I waited to be asked before offering any suggestions. Once I knew who was genuinely interested in learning, I began to take the initiative. Only then did I realize the amount of effort it required to make people first understand and then do what was asked of them.

My heart went out to Balanchine. I knew that, barring a dramatic improvement in his health, things would never be the same again. What frustration he must have felt! Balanchine often repeated: *"Après moi, le déluge!"* I was beginning to see what he meant.

Balanchine's curtailed schedule coincided with the period when Mikhail Baryshnikov was a member of the Company. Some of us had seen Misha during the Company's 1972 tour of the Soviet Union and had felt he was the most extraordinary dancer we had ever seen. After his defection, when we all had a chance to see him, we felt he lived up to his reputation. Still, Balanchine's decision was remarkable, for very few internationally known dancers had found their way into our Company, although some, including Nureyev, had tried.

There were questions in all our minds: How would Baryshnikov adjust to Balanchine's choreography? Would he develop into a Balanchine dancer or would his stay with us be just another milestone in his career? How would he adapt to our repertory without Balanchine's helping hand?

Unfortunately, Balanchine's weakened condition made it impossible for the two of them to be together more than rarely. Misha needed that personal guidance from Balanchine and, without it, he was unable to become sufficiently assimilated into the Company to understand the style of the ballets fully in only a year and a half. Had the two spent more time together, Balanchine would surely have found a way to develop his full potential.

Balanchine had a unique ability to take a dancer's special way of moving and adapt it to the style of a particular ballet. He could always alter steps or modify them in a way that would not violate his choreography, and this helps explain why he often said completely different things to different dancers performing the same role. All the secondhand information available to Baryshnikov was no substitute for a few rehearsals with Balanchine, who would have seen Misha's unique qualities and understood how to use them. If a step had not worked, Balanchine would have changed it without disrupting the ballet.

I gained greater understanding of Misha's situation as I suddenly found myself having to prepare *Swan Lake* on very short notice. I had always loved the music but had had very little desire to dance the Swan Queen; I was still not drawn to the acting side of ballet. I had not watched many performances of *Swan Lake* either by our Company or by others, and so I had few ideas regarding my approach to the role.

So, when Rosemary told me one Sunday afternoon that Balanchine wanted me to learn and dance *Swan Lake* in both performances the following Sunday, I stared at her in disbelief. I couldn't imagine preparing something like *Swan Lake* in such a short period of time. The role may not have had special importance to Balanchine or the Company, but I felt the weight of tradition and significance attached to the ballet. I needed background, ideas, someone to talk to about the role, and time to think. I did not feel optimistic about what a week of hard work would produce. All I could do was wait until rehearsals started on the following Tuesday.

As it turned out I had only three full days to prepare myself, because my full stage rehearsal was on Friday. Rosemary taught me the steps, but she was not really able to help with all my detailed questions about the role. When I learn a role that quickly—especially a role like the one in *Swan Lake*—I prefer to be taught specific arm gestures as well as other details, because I don't have enough time to work out my own solutions.

For *Swan Lake,* however, I had to decide for myself what positions I wanted for my arms and how to make those positions comfortable. Not everything I wanted to do worked naturally. Often the transition from one position to another took more time than the music allowed, and other times the transition was awkward even though I had enough time. I also feared excessive repetition of the same gestures, but I had no one to turn to for help. Whereas Balanchine helped with the pantomime and steps, he specified how I should use my arms in only one or two instances. He corrected my arms only if I made some inappropriate movement. The rest was up to me.

I wanted to discover how to make my arms look fluid and winglike, and I used every free moment for experimentation. I started by looking in the mirror to see what looked good, trying out all sorts of things in class, between combinations. Wanting to memorize the feeling of movements I liked, I found myself practicing them almost unconsciously at odd times during the day—waiting for the elevator, walking down the street, waiting for the water to boil. Mr. B used to suggest that we do tendus in the kitchen while preparing dinner. He wasn't joking. Finally I was doing what he had suggested!

I looked at a film of Kay Mazzo performing the role, but when I tried to reproduce the way she used her arms, which I found very attractive, it felt awkward. The same gestures seemed to produce totally different results. Later I saw a film of Natalia Makarova dancing the *Swan Lake* pas de deux, but even though the choreography was similar the tempos were so excruciatingly slow that all I could get was inspiration, not practical help.

Just after I had learned the role, Balanchine came to the rehearsals and showed a renewed interest in the ballet. I had always had the impression that he kept *Swan Lake* in the repertory primarily because it was so popular with audiences. Now I felt I had rekindled his interest. He made a number of changes; he wanted to make the pas de deux faster; and, in order to be sure it would be played that way, he called the conductor and the violin soloist to the rehearsal. At the same time he changed some of the steps so they would better suit the fast tempos.

Balanchine's most frequent corrections to me during this rehearsal were, "Don't act, don't do anything. Don't look at your partner." Everybody who had ever done the role had acted too much for Balanchine's taste, and he wanted to stop the trend before it got out of hand. He wanted dancers, not actors, in his ballets.

In the souvenir book of the Stravinsky Festival, Balanchine is quoted as saying: "A ballerina is a personality, and a personality means improvisation. The personality feels she owes something special to the public, and what the choreographer has given her is not quite enough, so she adds things; thus, the choreography becomes merely atmosphere for the ballerina. I like best young, well-trained dancers, eternal students always learning."

I think he saw me as a young dancer not yet set in her ways. He knew I was open to his influence, and he probably wanted to make sure I continued to "just dance," hoping to delay my developing into a "personality" as long as possible, although I imagine he thought this would inevitably happen. He felt he had to be particularly vigilant with *Swan Lake* because its story line is so full of emotion. I saw his point but I didn't see how I could convey the story without acting at all, particularly at the end of the ballet. The Prince and I, realizing that our time with each other is running out, are about to be forced to part. I embrace him, then pull him with me to the center of the stage as the corps starts running in big, sweeping patterns around us. At this point in most productions, the Prince and the Swan Queen are locked in an embrace, staring passionately into one another's eyes. Balanchine didn't want us to embrace at all; he showed us a pose in which I was to stand quietly near the Prince, who had his arm around my waist. Balanchine didn't want us looking at each other or doing anything; he just wanted us to stand quietly.

I could see that the couple standing absolutely still in the midst of the swirling corps made a vivid parting image. But I felt that at this moment our anguish had to be conveyed to the audience. Yet, if I inclined my head even slightly toward the Prince or leaned a little in his direction, Balanchine objected.

"Don't lean," he said. "He's not supposed to crush your tutu. In the old days they were never close. They weren't allowed to be. Even when you have to embrace, you shouldn't be on top of each other."

In addition to his interest in the dancing, Balanchine always wanted his women to look as beautiful as possible. The day before my first performance in *Swan Lake,* he said: "You know, dear, I think rhinestone headpiece is not right for you. Feathers would be better, don't you think?"

So off we went to the wardrobe department to see what kind of feathers they had. Knowing that there was no time to make a brand-new headpiece, he asked if an old feathered one was available or if he could put one together from whatever was on hand. We found Maria Tallchief's old headpiece. Mr. B was unhappy that the feathers on it had yellowed with age so I suggested we put white makeup on them and that seemed to

Swan Lake. (© *Steven Caras*)

work. He also didn't want any kind of crown worn with the feathers, so he asked that jewels be sewn on in the center of the headpiece. But later, after he had seen the way it looked in performance, he said: "Awful, dear, looks like hat!"

He then had the costume shop make another feathered headpiece for the next time I danced the role. He didn't see the results until I was actually on stage, warming up with about two minutes to go before the curtain went up. He didn't like the way it looked in general, but he thought it would look better if it were farther forward on my head.

"But, Mr. B," I protested. "The curtain is about to go up."

"Don't worry," he said. "I'll tell them to hold it."

"But I'll ruin my hair when I take all the pins out," I said. "It'll take me ten minutes." It had taken me nearly twenty minutes to pin the headpiece on just right the first time.

"Doesn't matter, dear. I'll help you."

We rushed to my dressing room, which was now on the stage level. Sally Leland, who shared my dressing room, was there and she helped me unpin it. Mr. B showed me where he wanted it and Sally and I pinned it back on.

"Go—you're fine," he beamed.

Racing back out onto the stage, I could hear through the curtain that the audience was restless, but I was more worried about my muscles, which had become cold. The first entrance is one of the hardest moments in the ballet and I find it practically impossible to do smoothly if my muscles are not thoroughly warmed up. Suddenly the curtain went up and there I was feeling rattled and cold and generally worried about the ballet. But at least I knew that Balanchine was pleased with my headpiece that night. In the end, in fact, Mr. B changed his mind one more time, and now I am back in the rhinestone headpiece everyone else wears.

Balanchine never wavered, however, on another key point. No matter how little "acting" I did, it was still too much for him. It is difficult for me to suppress my natural impulse to express the passion and turmoil built into the story and the music. Even in rehearsal, I find the music very moving. Under the influence of the live orchestra, sets, and lighting, I become even more involved. The emotions I display are absolutely genuine. Yet I keep Balanchine's words in the back of my mind and express my emotions only in the few places where it is entirely appropriate. In the variation, for instance, I "just dance."

I have done *Swan Lake* regularly since my first appearance, but, as with so many ballets I dance, I am still working on my approach. I'm constantly experimenting, finding solutions for one performance, only to change them in the next. The more familiar I become with the role, however, the more I sense how easy it would be to become overly dramatic, and that makes me determined not to stray too far from what Balanchine would have wanted.

CHAPTER

6

AFTER Balanchine had recovered from heart surgery, I invited him to my apartment for dinner. He seemed in good spirits, making jokes about his health, saying he was like an old Rolls-Royce with a new engine. It was a pleasant evening, and the conversation flowed smoothly, thanks in part to Kibbe's presence. Balanchine looked so vigorous that I asked him if he was ready to return to work.

He looked at me intently and said, "Well, dear, there's music I have been listening to for a long time. I want to do something to it. I never knew just what to do. Now I know. I thought I'd do a ballet for you. Beautiful ballet."

I was embarrassed, for I felt I had forced him to state his intentions prematurely. But it soon became clear from the way he talked about the music, which was by Fauré (the *Ballade for Piano and Orchestra*), and the costumes and scenery, which would be from *Tricolore* (although slightly modified), that he had been thinking about this for a long time. It meant a great deal to me that, after being away from choreography for two years, he would choose to work with me first.

I listened to the music right away and was puzzled. It was indeed beautiful, very melodic and dreamy and perhaps a little sad, too, like some of Chopin's nocturnes, but I couldn't imagine doing anything but sitting back and letting it wash over me. What steps could Balanchine possibly find for music like that? What would the ballet look like? Beautiful? You could say that about almost every ballet that he did. The word conjured up so many different images.

Balanchine set to work immediately. I was called, along with Sean Lavery as my partner, to the first rehearsal. Many of the questions that I had had before *Ballo* came back to mind. Obviously this wouldn't be exactly like *Ballo,* but would it be another virtuoso ballet? Would I be able to do what he wanted?

Mr. B casually walked into the studio and came over to the piano where Gordon and I were talking. He joined our conversation, remarking on Fauré and the music. Then he asked Gordon to play some of the piano cadenzas in which the pianist sets the tempo. Once the tempos were agreed upon, we started to work.

Balanchine doing a new ballet was always an historic moment. I was well aware of that and yet was so involved in learning the new steps and trying to find a way to do them smoothly that I tended to block out everything that wasn't directly helpful. Later there were interviews: What was it like working with Balanchine on the new ballet? What were your impressions? What did he say? How did he act? What was he dressed like? Most of that had escaped my attention. After *Ballo* I found I couldn't re-create those sessions with Balanchine in all the rich detail that they deserved. I resolved it would be different with *Ballade,* but I was immediately involved in the concrete difficulties at hand, with all my senses attuned to Balanchine's every wish.

This time Balanchine started from the beginning. He walked toward the upstage left corner, with me following. Looking back and forth between his feet and mine as he usually did when he was thinking up combinations of steps, he said softly, "Well, maybe you come in from this corner. Just bourrée in."

As he walked on a diagonal line, he showed me how he wanted my arms to move and how I was to change the position of my body while I continued to bourrée. He hardly commented, except to say, "Well, what foot are you on?" and then he'd put himself in that position to see how to go on from there. I do remember at one point he said that I should move as quickly and lightly as a skater skimming over the ice.

Again I had the distinct feeling that Balanchine hadn't planned specific steps, but that he knew the music and its structure, the tone and shape of the work he was about to create, and the style of movements suitable for it. He knew when and where he wanted the dancers to enter and exit, and when to bring on someone else. He also knew where he wanted the high points to be. Just as when he was choreographing *Ballo,* I was struck by the speed and spontaneity with which he worked. He always seemed to be improvising.

Balanchine was not nearly so hardy as he had been when he had done *Ballo.* This time he didn't partner me unless things were really going wrong or he couldn't verbally explain what he wanted. When he did partner me, I tried not to make him support my full weight, but that always made him a little angry. "No, it's all right; it's okay," he would say. But I was always fearful both of the strain on his heart and also of the possible harm to his vulnerable back and knees. When he gave us steps in our variations, he would explain them with words and hand gestures, or by marking the steps with his feet. Rarely did he do steps full out, the way he had done in the past.

One sequence that Balanchine choreographed very quickly but that subsequently required constant work occurred in the pas de deux in the second section of the ballet. He asked me to step onto pointe with my back to the audience while holding my partner's hand, and then do a side développé with my left leg. Once I had reached the full extension of the développé, he wanted me to lean backward, still holding my leg up, which caused me to turn backward off balance. It looked as if I were out of control and about to fall. He wanted me to control this fall so that it did not happen too quickly, but he also wanted the fall to look spontaneous. The minute he thought the fall was becoming too controlled, he said, "No, you're not falling enough."

While choreographing *Ballo,* Balanchine had asked me which leg was easier to lift to the side, and then he had adapted the choreography to that leg. But, in doing *Ballade* he never asked me this question, and so I had to do the side développé with my "bad" left leg. It is just not as "educated" as the right, not as turned out, and not as comfortable to work with, which made the step even harder to perform. This is one of the few recurring steps in the ballet; it is the only one that is repeated at different points, and I worked on it constantly. At the very end of the ballet, Mr. B wanted the sequence repeated very slowly, saying to me, "Fall in slow motion." I tried doing it as slowly as I could, but I could not find a way to conquer gravity!

In my second variation in *Ballade,* there is a combination related to my unusual turning step in *Ballo*'s second variation. In *Ballade,* Balanchine gave me this tricky combination very simply, saying only, "You *chaîné* [fast traveling turns on pointe] and when you're ready, without coming off pointe [that's the hard part!], do an en dedans pirouette opening into arabesque on pointe, and then repeat it until the music changes." (In this case the en dedans pirouette was a turn to the right on my right leg, with my left leg shooting out from passé into arabesque.)

We were using a rehearsal studio at SAB that day, and the room was crowded with students, teachers, and Company members. Everyone was there to watch Balanchine work on his first new ballet in two years. When we heard what he had asked for, we all burst out laughing because it sounded utterly impossible. I thought he was going to see that I was not as strong as he believed. But I was prepared to give it everything I had to make it work.

I went into a corner, started the turns, and did the series of steps exactly the way he had asked. There were gasps of awe as I finished my first attempt at these turns. I was more stupefied than anyone. I asked to do it again, and once more it went perfectly. Balanchine's eyes twinkled as if to say, "You see, I told you so!" Despite my elation, I had some misgivings. I knew this difficult sequence was in the ballet to stay. Was this just an "on" day or was the step easier than I thought?

The next day, I couldn't do the sequence at all. I had already spoiled it by thinking too much. I kept losing my balance in the middle of the turn as I began to open into arabesque. It took me three weeks before I was able to recapture what I had done that first day. Whenever the step went off, it was really off, like the turning variation in *Who Cares?* There was no covering up. Unlike my experience in *Who Cares?,* however, I found that rehearsing this step made it go better. Here, as was so often the case with difficult steps, the right use of the arms made all the difference.

There was a break in the creation of *Ballade* between the winter and spring seasons. When we resumed work on the ballet, Ib Andersen replaced Sean, who was still recovering from knee surgery. For a while Sean took part in the rehearsals as best he could, hoping to be ready in time for the premiere, but finally, with a week to go, he realized he wouldn't make it.

As we began work on the second part of the ballet, we found that we had forgotten little bits of choreography that had been set a month or so earlier. Balanchine had little difficulty rechoreographing these steps, but he had other more serious problems. He could not get the corps girls to do what he wanted. At one point he stopped and said: "You know, I can't do what I want to do, because I have to stop and teach you how to dance."

Each time he gave them a new step, he would spend several minutes trying to get the girls to place their feet properly, move on the exact count he had given them, start and stop each movement with energy and clarity, or move in the exact pattern he had shown. One time, in particular, when his patience was at an end, he threw up his hands, letting them fall with a slap against his thighs.

"I had good, interesting idea, but you can't do it," he said. "I'm not sure if you'll ever be able to do it. Now I have to think of something else."

Balanchine was using apprentices who had been called to the rehearsal as understudies. The regular corps girls had missed the first hour of rehearsal because of a conflict in their schedules. Balanchine decided that, since he had started using the apprentices in rehearsals, he might as well put them in the ballet. (Apprentices may dance any number of times in two ballets per season.) Balanchine was not inclined to show the apprentices any special lenience, although he did try to be more patient with them. If anything, he was more strict with them because he knew they were not familiar with the way he wanted things done. He could not just give them a brief reminder, as he could the Company members; he constantly had to correct them.

There was nothing unusual about Balanchine's having to use corps girls who were not of his choice; this was especially true during festivals. He would generously allow other choreographers to use the dancers they preferred, and then he would work with

| 1 | 2 | 3 | 4 |

JETÉ

This sequence shows me doing a series of jetés. At the height of the jump (1 and 11), the front leg is straight and the back leg is slightly bent with the foot in coupé back.

2–6 As I land on the front foot (2), the back foot remains in coupé but begins to flex (3) in order to enable the toes to brush along the floor (4) before the back leg is thrust energetically to the side (5 and 6) as the supporting, or front, leg continues to plié.

7 and 8 The extended leg continues to lift as the supporting foot pushes off the floor, propelling the body into the air.

9–11 The moment the supporting leg leaves the floor (9), it bends and begins to move to the coupé

| 9 | 10 | 11 |

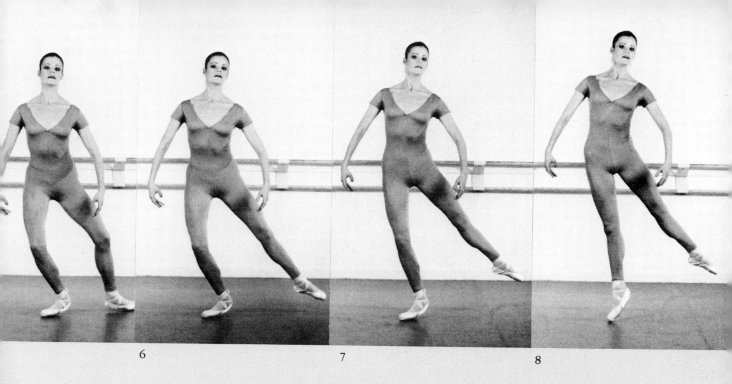

6   7   8

back position, which is finally reached in 11. While the supporting foot is moving toward coupé back, the other foot is moving back toward the center of the body. This not only increases the speed with which the dancer arrives in the coupé position in the air but also ensures that the dancer will land in the same place she took off from, rather than traveling sideways on the jump. Balanchine insisted on seeing this coupé position in the air. In a more conventional version of jeté, the coupé position is not reached until the dancer is back on the ground, and the position seen in the air is similar to the position seen in 8 (except both feet would be off the floor).

12 15 I am once again landing from the jeté, but this time I do not continue into another jeté. Thus, the coupé foot remains pointed and in the same position it was in when in the air, while the front foot moves toward the center of the body during the descent. Balanchine liked to see this "overcrossed" coupé back position in a dancer's landing from a single jeté (15).

13   14   15

Ballade, Merrill in the original costume, 1980. This is a unique variation on the traditional jeté. Balanchine used to say that Merrill was the only one who could do it properly and often asked her to demonstrate it in class. (© *Steven Caras*)

whoever was still available. Although he often had to do so in a small practice room without the pianist of his choice and at hours he did not like, he still produced great choreography.

Balanchine also had to help teach Ib what was for him a new type of partnering. But Ib was eager to learn and adjusted quickly. For a long time, Ib didn't know the first part of the ballet, so I rehearsed half the ballet with Sean and the other half with Ib. Little by little, as each learned the sections he didn't know, I found myself rehearsing *Ballade* with two very different partners. Everything from the phrasing to the mechanics of the steps, not to mention the mood, differed with each. Although this disparity gave me more ideas about possible approaches to the ballet, it also meant I couldn't become really familiar with one way of dancing it, which left me in a state of confusion until a week before the premiere, when it was decided Ib would do the first performance.

Both Sean and Ib were experienced partners, which was a great luxury. Early in my career I had danced with inexperienced partners, some of whom were not tall enough for me and most of whom seemed less interested in partnering than in their own variations. I rarely saw any of them, or the other men, watching from the wings when Peter Martins, Adam Lüders, or Sean were doing their fine partnering, but the wings were suddenly full during their spectacular solo variations.

Dancing with these inexperienced partners had had both good and bad effects on me. It had made me more aware of the technique of partnering (I often had to tell them what to do), but it had also made me want to do too much by myself. It took me a long time to unlearn some of the "survival" techniques I developed during this period.

As Ib and I rehearsed *Ballade,* Balanchine never talked about the mood of the ballet, who we were supposed to be, or what we meant to each other; he simply stressed the steps and patterns. The rest was up to us.

Interesting clues about the ballet as a whole could be found in Balanchine's gestures and in his demeanor as he showed us what he wanted. There were clues, too, about Balanchine's attitude toward women in general, and perhaps toward me in particular. After all, there were many moments in his ballets that seemed to be enactments of his most ardent thoughts and feelings, and an expression of his special kind of love for women. I felt this at one point early in the ballet. As I leaned back slightly with my arms wide apart, Balanchine, showing Sean what to do, placed his head tenderly on my chest, almost as if he were listening to my heart. It is only a fleeting moment in the ballet, one that a spectator could easily miss, but it spoke eloquently to me of Balanchine's emotions during the period he was choreographing *Ballade.* That moment is followed by a series of steps that suggest we are being pulled part, then drawn together, and then torn apart again. Finally, I do a series of chaînés that end with my falling forward toward my partner, who catches me under the arms. With my back arched, I look up at him in supplication. Again, it is only a brief moment before we are pulled apart by forces greater than ourselves. Time and again this theme repeats itself in *Ballade,* and, as I practiced these steps in rehearsal with Balanchine watching, I often saw in them a reflection of forces that had acted on the two of us. I wondered if he saw that, too.

The first comments from Balanchine that gave me any hint of how to interpret the ballet came while he was choreographing the final moments of the ballet. Ib and I were very close to each other, face to face, clasping each other's hands, about to be separated by that unknown force.

"Don't look at him. You're not in love with him."

Balanchine, once again, had made it clear what he did not want. But, what, exactly, was he after? If he did not want me to look at Ib, where *did* he want me to look, and with what kind of expression? If I wasn't in love with my partner, how did I feel about him? The answers to these questions were left up to me, as usual. I felt I couldn't ask for help on such matters; he didn't want us concocting fantasies to help us through ballets. If I had asked him, I am sure he would have replied: "Don't think, dear, just dance!"

Fortunately, I wasn't in the habit of creating specific fantasies to guide me through ballets. But I did at times want to understand my relationship with my partner—for ex-

Ballade, Merrill, in the new costume, and Sean Lavery just before he "listens to my heart." (© *Steven Caras*)

ample, during the closing moments of *Ballade.* To me, that final parting was sweet but sorrowful. Perhaps Balanchine had felt I was being "too sweet" again. I decided a little more distance, a certain elusiveness, was needed.

In many of Balanchine's ballets there is a woman who is distant and elusive. Her partner, whom Balanchine might have seen as an image of himself, is never allowed too close, although he is an ardent lover. That kind of woman is not in my nature, which is warm and more direct, but she is a type I understand, and I am certainly able to play that role. Such a woman, if only because of the ambiguity in the ballet between what is real and what is imagined, has a place in *Ballade.*

In a further effort to understand my role in *Ballade,* I tried to imagine the impact of the ballet as a whole. It would have helped if I could have seen the ballet performed, no matter how well or badly it was done. Then I could have decided more objectively what worked and what did not. In *Ballo* I had instinctively felt my approach was right, but here I sensed something was amiss. I felt I had not yet reached the heart of the ballet, and I was sure I would have to perform it many times before arriving at a clear idea of what I wanted to do with it.

Ballade's gently changing moods appealed to the romantic side of my nature. Balanchine's comment that I wasn't in love didn't change that. The opening of the ballet was wistful, suggesting neither dream nor reality but something in between. My partner appears, disappears, and reappears, our fleeting encounters seeming to suggest both strong desires and vague yearnings. I then have a brief solo that sustains this feeling of ambiguity. Later I dance with the corps girls and am clearly in a more positive mood, letting my spirit and energy dictate the steps and my sweeping gestures.

My partner then reenters and we come together but are once again drawn apart, over and over. At the end, we face each other, clasping hands, and then withdraw in an exact reversal of our first entrance, each returning to his own private world.

Throughout the ballet I seem to be in perpetual motion, an elusive, unattainable figure. My presence is strongly asserted by the uninterrupted succession of difficult steps, flowing arm gestures, and expressive movements of the torso. Yet the music, steps, and gestures tell me that it is a romantic presence. The ballet is not about steps, but it is a virtuoso ballet in every sense—not the bright happy virtuosity of *Ballo* but something that could be called romantic virtuosity, if that is not a contradiction in terms.

When Balanchine had finished choreographing my solo with the corps girls, a little more than halfway through the ballet, I realized that in performance I would reach that point having had only a few moments of rest offstage. What a phenomenal endurance test! Balanchine was not only challenging me to use my upper body in a new and more expressive way; he was testing my endurance, unwittingly, I am sure. He did not seem to realize the cumulative effect of all these steps and sweeping gestures. Even a respite of a half minute would have made all the difference. I was determined, however, not to complain. If he felt there was something I could not do, if he found me losing my fluidity and ease due to fatigue, perhaps he would make a change.

As we worked on the last part of the ballet, my left hip began to hurt. At first, it felt like a bruise I might have gotten from bumping into a doorknob, and I didn't pay much attention to it. Besides, it hurt only when I was in fifth position, not when I lifted my leg. I was sure that, like so many other aches and pains, it would disappear as mysteriously as it had come.

There were constant rehearsals of *Ballade,* and in addition I was dancing even more than before: every morning, I took class; every afternoon, I rehearsed for four or five hours; and, every evening, I performed, sometimes in two ballets. On a number of occasions, I did two of my most demanding ballets—either *Ballo* and *Piano Concerto* or *Square Dance* and *Theme*—on the same program. Although I savored every moment on stage, it was simply too heavy a workload to carry safely week after week.

I underestimated the toll all this was taking. Somehow I hadn't yet realized that I had reached the point of diminishing returns. Balanchine had always said, "More, more!" and I had perhaps taken those words too literally. In my eagerness to overcome all obstacles, I had always found the energy that Balanchine asked for; but now as I worked increasingly on more subtle aspects of my dancing, it became clear that I had not entirely rid myself of the tendency to dance every performance as if it were my last. It was much more exciting for me to dance that way, and I was reluctant to give up a single moment of pleasure. My dancing had finally reached a level that allowed me to revel in the mastery of my body and the steps. It was enormously satisfying and enjoyable to be on stage, feeling confident and at ease and able to bring something of my true self to my performances. But *Ballade* and my hip were soon to teach me a few new lessons.

Ballade was proving to be the greatest physical challenge in my repertory, to speak only of one aspect of the ballet, and I would soon learn that I had to temper my effort if I was to survive. As yet, I had no feeling for where the high points in the ballet were and where I could "rest" a little, but I did sense I was making it harder than necessary.

The pain in my hip began to bother me more and more, and I realized it was no mere bruise. On the day of the premiere, May 8, 1980, it was worse than ever before. For the first time, the hip hurt too much to allow me to walk normally. As I walked the few blocks downtown from my apartment to the theater that morning, I wondered how much I would aggravate my hip during orchestra and dress rehearsals that afternoon. There was no question of my not dancing the world premiere of a ballet Balanchine had done for me, but I didn't want to be distracted by intense pain.

Despite my handicap, the performance went surprisingly well. All the usual trouble spots turned out to be trouble-free. It's impossible to explain why such things happen, but I'm inclined to think that pure chance plays a certain role. The most memorable part of the evening was the struggle I had to get Balanchine to take a bow. I had anticipated the problem and was prepared. Balanchine never wanted to take credit just for himself; in general he went in front of the curtain to acknowledge applause only when it was intended as a tribute to the Company as a whole, as at the end of the season. Both the stage manager and I tried to coax him into going in front of the curtain, but he refused. Finally I took him by the arm and said: "Mr. B, please, do it for me."

"Only if you go with me, dear."

"Don't worry. Ib and I will both go with you."

And with that I took his hand and led him in front of the curtain, where he was cheered by an adoring audience.

People's reactions and the reviews about the ballet fascinated me, giving me the first objective impression of what I had just done. Everyone seemed to have a slightly different interpretation of the ballet, but the word most frequently heard to describe it was *beautiful.* I had thought—if only because the word could be used to describe almost any Balanchine ballet—that it would be the least likely word to be heard on everyone's lips. But, after watching the ballet, everyone invested the word with such meaning and pronounced it with such conviction, that no other adjective seemed to describe the ballet quite so accurately. I was even reminded of the way Balanchine had spoken that word when he first mentioned the ballet to me. It was uncanny. He had found a way to merge nonstop dancing and difficult steps with the music so as to project a single overpowering impression of beauty—beauty that transcended the subject, beauty that made differing interpretations of the ballet equally valid.

The reviews that appeared about *Ballade* were even more interesting than those dealing with new ballets usually are. Apparently, *Ballade* and I had been thought-provoking. One long magazine article contained a number of flattering comments but also said that I was not glamorous or seductive and that my not looking at Ib had left him in a vacuum. Regardless of my initial reaction to such comments, I always assumed the criticism, accurate or not, was pointing to a shortcoming or at least to something that needed reexamination. In this case, I was genuinely perplexed. Balanchine wasn't. He had read the article and brought it up with me in conversation: he said it was "ridiculous." He wasn't trying to teach me anything in *Ballade,* as the article had said. (I nevertheless thought he was.) He said he liked the fact that I didn't look at my partner, for we weren't supposed to be specific characters in the ballet. He was happy with my dancing and it was silly to say I wasn't "glamorous" or "seductive."

"Ridiculous," he laughed. "You're sexiest in Company."

I blushed with embarrassment. It was uncharacteristic of Balanchine to be so blunt about such matters. Not knowing how to respond, I found myself edging away from him.

"But," he went on, "not on the stage."

There was approval in his voice, but I was too embarrassed to pursue the subject. If he had wanted me to be any different on stage, he had certainly missed an easy opportunity to tell me. He clearly knew the other side of my personality. But he didn't like provocative displays in most of his ballets. When they were called for—as with the Siren in *Prodigal Son*—it was obvious. I was sure that in such a role I would have no trouble showing the other side of my personality, and I hoped it would not be too long before Balanchine gave me a chance to dance one of these roles.

This most unusual exchange with Balanchine continued to reverberate in my mind long afterward, but despite my self-questioning I could always derive satisfaction from his compliments regarding my dancing in general and my performance in *Ballade* in particular.

After a couple of performances, Balanchine even said *Ballade* was "like marzipan." Knowing how much he adored marzipan, I was delighted. Later, Peter Martins told me Balanchine had said to him: "The ballet is beautiful, and she does it so well. She hasn't added anything to it. She just does it."

The morning after the premiere of *Ballade,* I awakened to find, much to my surprise, that my hip hurt less than it had the day before. After the long stage rehearsals for *Ballade* and the stress of the premiere, I had expected it to be worse. It was still alarmingly painful, however, and I would not have been tempted to take class if Balanchine had not been teaching. It was, in fact, the first time in many months that he was giving class, and that was an event I could not miss. Even if I had to change or omit a few steps, I wanted to be there to listen and to see what he was emphasizing. As class progressed, many steps were given that I did not dare attempt, but I was greatly relieved that the steps I did try did not make the pain worse. Also, just being in Balanchine's class again did wonders for my morale.

In the weeks that followed, no matter what I did to or for my hip, I found that I couldn't predict the results. It was as if it had a will of its own. A day or two of rest might make it better—or worse. Hard work produced the same unpredictable results. Since no one could tell me what was causing the pain, it was very difficult to judge which movements were safe in class, rehearsal, or performance, and which had to be avoided under any circumstances. The degree of pain was my only guide.

I tried to be cautious, particularly in class. Standing flat-footed in fifth position with the left foot front hurt most of all, and unfortunately most steps started and ended with that position. If I avoided fifth position, I couldn't do many of the combinations that were being given. In order to stay in condition, I finally started giving myself the equivalent of class, a desperate move on my part, since I had never before been able to find the discipline to work by myself regularly.

In performance I still tended to throw caution to the winds, and most of the time I got away with it. Oddly enough, performing seemed less of a strain on my hip than class did. Very rarely in performance did I have to stand flat-footed in fifth position, and when I did it was almost always with the right foot front, which did not hurt. So I decided to continue dancing unless the pain started to hamper me seriously in performance.

I did four more performances of *Ballade* that spring. As I became more familiar with the ballet and with the music as played by the orchestra, I was able to make the steps flow more smoothly and to give the whole ballet more coherence. At the same time, I had increasing difficulty with the technically demanding passages. How liberated one would feel, I thought in moments of frustration, if there were no technical difficulties at all in dancing! I sympathized with dancers whose interest in the technique of ballet was secondary to their desire to be beautiful, serene presences on the stage. At times I even envied those "instinctive" dancers who relied on the inspiration of the moment, rather than the careful preparation of all the "pieces," to get through a performance satisfactorily. But I wanted to have both: the finest possible technique and the serene, alluring presence that would make my technique seem like the most natural thing in the world.

I sought to understand these instinctive dancers, who appear to find their greatest rewards in the spontaneous expression of their personalities and impulses. An aura of improvisation surrounds their dancing. They are quite willing, in the interest of creativity, to accept the possibility of some very awkward moments. They believe the valuable discoveries they make outnumber their sometimes less than graceful movements. If they have to violate the principles of good technique in the process, they find that a small price to pay. In fact, they may at times feel hampered by the demands of technique and even by the choreography.

In the minds of these dancers, opportunities for creativity abound every time they set foot on the stage. Erratic tempos offer a chance to experiment with phrasing or even to add or drop steps. A desire to hold a balance or to add a third or fourth pirouette even beyond what the music allows is often too strong to resist. Facial expressions and arm and hand movements obey spontaneous impulses. When these dancers find a pirouette going off, they are willing to continue turning, secure in the knowledge that they will manage to land and finish in a graceful or at least appropriate position.

I think this facility to create on the spur of the moment often derives more from personality than from physical ability. People who are good at repartee and have quick reactions to the unexpected often engage in this experimentation and risk-taking. Among the men, the same type also seems to make a good partner.

Although I am capable of this kind of improvisation when the circumstances are just right, I thrive on careful preparation and diligent rehearsing. In fact, my pleasure lies in seeking mastery over the demands of technique rather than in freedom from those demands. The very restrictions of ballet are what make it so beautiful and special to me, and the sheer difficulty is an exciting challenge to me. When I work in class or in rehearsal, or when I dance in performance, I want to understand the framework I must work in, the standards of excellence, and the precise components of each step. I can then decide which phrasing to use, how to coordinate my arms with my legs, and which steps should be emphasized over others. I like trying to get each tiny detail right; that is when I am happiest. Translated into painting terminology, it's analogous to the difference between realism and impressionism. I'm the realist. It's ironic, however, that I prefer impressionist art.

I attain a sense of freedom of expression and movement when all the steps and movements are going as planned. Once I sense this mastery over my body, then and only then do I feel free to be creative. Falling off a pirouette is disruptive; erratic tempos are as unwelcome as a lump on the stage, and both can literally knock me off my feet. It is not exciting for me to hear the music racing ahead of me and to have to decide on the spur of the moment which steps to drop or how to catch up. I don't want to *have* to be creative because something has gone wrong; I want everything to go right first, so that I then have the freedom to be creative.

I am the way I am not only by temperament. When I was very young, I was so weak that I couldn't automatically make steps look presentable. What felt natural to me was not always attractive, and I had to learn the right way. Some young dancers have the natural strength and ability to make nearly any step look good. They can incorporate corrections and add something of their own and the result often works out well. Later, such dancers may find that when something goes wrong it is more an opportunity than a source of anxiety.

These are, of course, generalities. Like all dancers, I change from day to day and from ballet to ballet. Facial expressions, arm movements, phrasing of the music, and much more are always amenable to an imaginative approach; on the other hand, much of ballet demands strict adherence to rules and principles, even by those most anxious to break them.

My enjoyment in dancing has increased as the years have passed, and recently I have found great satisfaction in being able to rely more and more on my instincts. But the mirror will always be there to tell me when I have gone astray, and I want my excesses to be confined to the rehearsal hall. Nevertheless, I feel I've tapped a new source of inspiration that will guide me in the future.

During the spring of 1980 Ghislaine Thesmar, a principal dancer with the Paris Opéra Ballet, performed as a guest artist with us. She was the only ballerina, at least since I had been with the Company, whom Balanchine had ever invited to appear with us. She watched some of my performances, offering many compliments, but one evening she told Kibbe she thought I was not "narcissistic" enough and that both Kibbe and I should stop considering me a student. It was true: I did consider myself a student—it would have been difficult to think otherwise with Balanchine as my teacher—but her criticism about my lack of narcissism made me ask myself whether my dancing was not based too much on self-confidence and too little on self-love. Whatever the truth, I could not be sure that I knew exactly what Balanchine wanted. Perhaps I could perform his steps to his satisfaction, and listen attentively to his every word, but did I always know when or how much he was exaggerating to make a point? For example, he couldn't possibly have wanted absolutely no acting in *Swan Lake,* yet that had been his literal message to me. Furthermore, what Balanchine seemed to like on the stage did not always correspond to what he advocated in class and in rehearsals. Ghislaine herself was a case in point, an NYCB paradox. She would have been out of place in much of the Company's repertory; yet, clearly, Balanchine liked her glamorous presence very much. It was a glamour that did not leave her when she left the stage, springing perhaps from her supreme confidence about herself and who she was rather than about what she could do. In contrast, the beauty and elegance that my dancing projected flowed, I thought, from my love of dancing and my belief in myself as a dancer. Did I need to be a little more like Ghislaine; and, if so, how could I go about making the change? A seed had been planted in my mind.

As the season drew to a close and the pain in my hip lingered, I decided the free week between the end of the season and the beginning of our traditional three weeks in Saratoga in July would be a perfect opportunity to take some time off. Perhaps a week of minimal exercise would rid me of most of the pain. My hard ballets had given me a number of other little injuries that were also crying out for relief. For an entire week I did only a few easy barres and tried to keep flexible in order to be ready for the first week of Saratoga. When I went back to work, after the week "off," everything flared up again under the sudden stress. My back went into spasm, my knee started to hurt, and my foot became strained.

As usual, I had only hard ballets ahead. I remember talking with Balanchine about my predicament: we agreed that I shouldn't even try to dance the first week; the second week, I should aim for the only Saratoga performance of *Ballade,* which was part of a gala evening. Days passed and nothing improved. A day of rest would bring momentary relief, and then a day of work would bring back all the pain. In the meantime, I was getting weaker and weaker.

Finally, Balanchine told me he would take *Ballade* out of the gala evening program and that I should rest a little more in order to be well for the European tour, later that summer, to Berlin, Copenhagen, and Paris, when he needed me to do *Ballo, Ballade,* and *Duo Concertant. Duo* had been acclaimed as one of the masterpieces of the 1972 Stravinsky Festival, and no one but Kay Mazzo, who had just retired, had danced the role since then. I had always found it very moving and dreamed of doing it. With this now on my horizon, I found it was easier to give up the Saratoga season.

All the doctors and therapists seemed to feel that my hip problem was muscular, but basically we were all mystified. At least it was clear that the problem was not in the hip socket or deep inside the hip. No matter what therapies I tried, there was no improvement; even Dr. Hsu's acupuncture needles failed to help. This time there was to be no miracle. After Saratoga, I reluctantly accepted the fact that if my hip was ever going to get better, I would have to face a long period of inactivity. If I had known I wouldn't do any permanent damage to my hip, I would have kept dancing, but no one could give me that assurance. So, the European tour and *Duo* were lost. My only consolation was that Balanchine canceled performances of *Duo,* apparently not wanting anyone else to do it.

That summer Kibbe and I took a long vacation in Hawaii, hoping that rest, a change of atmosphere, and the therapeutic powers of saltwater would effect a cure for my hip. We visited the different islands and discovered Hana, a tiny village on Maui, that ended our search for a place to be married. On September 6, 1980, a native Hawaiian minister performed the ceremony under a huge stone cross on the summit of a hill overlooking Hana with the seemingly endless Pacific stretching out to the horizon.

In mid-September we returned to New York. I had no idea what to expect from my hip, which little by little had begun to feel better, but I was optimistic. As soon as I started to work, however, I knew that the road back would be very long. It wasn't just the two months that I had taken off. My technique had begun to deteriorate in the early spring, when I had stopped taking class and started working incorrectly in order to spare my hip. I had to teach myself to work correctly all over again. It was then that I truly appreciated the advantage of understanding technique through and through. If I had been a dancer who worked largely on instinct, it would have been far more difficult, time-consuming, and anguishing trying to return to my former level. As I did my various exercises and looked at myself in the mirror, it was demoralizing to see how weak I had become and how far I had to go. I tried to cheer myself with the thought that at least I knew the path to my former condition. My greatest problem was the daily battle to curb my desire to work harder, to do more. An easy barre, an hour at Judy's, a trip to the chiropractor, and a massage seemed such a frustrating and inadequate way to spend my days, especially since the hardest ballets in our repertory lay ahead. I wanted to be

Kibbe and Merrill moments after they were married.

ready by the opening of the season in mid-November and was continually tormented by the need to work harder and the knowledge that harder work might reinjure my hip.

At first, happily, my hip accommodated my gentle efforts to put some tone back into my muscles and to realign my body. With the season looming and no strong pain to hold me back, and with all the doctors encouraging me to go ahead, I began to work harder. Immediately, the pain increased and I had to back off again. That meant I would miss the two-week pre–*Nutcracker* repertory part of the season.

My thoughts turned to the Sugar Plum Fairy and Dew Drop in *The Nutcracker*. I knew I would be terribly nervous my first time back on stage, since I had never been away from dancing for such a long time. If I started back with Sugar Plum it would be easier on my body, but more difficult to hide my nervousness in the variation in the midst of such dainty steps. I decided the wiser course was to try the role of Dew Drop, even though it was more strenuous. I reasoned that I could expend my excess energy, or at least hide my nervousness better, in all that fast-moving dancing. When I said this to Mr. B, he was perfectly willing to go along: "Just tell me when you want to dance and what you want to do."

Thus, right before the end of the year, I made my return in Dew Drop. Balanchine came to the theater that evening especially to see me, and I still remember him standing in the wings, watching. In fact, most of the Company seemed to be there, wishing me well. I'll never forget the applause, the cheers really, that greeted me when I ran out onto the stage for the first time. In Dew Drop's first entrance I simply run on, bow to the Sugar Plum Fairy, and run off, so I didn't expect any sort of reaction from the audience. The cheers startled me and made me even more nervous than I already was.

I remember my delight and amazement at just finding myself on the stage after such a long time. For the first time I had had a taste of how awful it would be to be "grounded" forever by an injury. I was so grateful to be back, so excited to be dancing. Never before had I felt that degree of elation on- or offstage, and it did not leave me, even as my feet began to cramp near the end of the ballet—I couldn't stay on pointe in a simple piqué arabesque. My feet were numb with fatigue and I had no energy left. Without Tchaikovsky's music urging me on, I would never have made it to the end. I had had no trouble with endurance in rehearsals, but in performance my acute nervous tension and my desperate desire to dance well had done me in. Instead of being boosted by my adrenalin, I was nearly paralyzed by my anxiety.

It took me a couple of days to recover from the effort and excitement of dancing Dew Drop. I was sore all over, but my hip had survived! Three days later, on New Year's Eve, when I did Dew Drop again, I was another person, relaxed and confident, and I sailed through it.

Sunday morning, January 4, a long article on me and my hip injury appeared on the front page of the Arts and Leisure section of the Sunday *New York Times.* An editor at the *Times* had seen me on the opening night of the 1980/81 winter season—cutting, I'm sure, a rather forlorn figure in the audience—and wanted to do a story on how I felt watching the other dancers. The article brought me a great deal of attention and sympathy but didn't please Balanchine, who thought the pain and hard work of ballet should be a private matter. He believed that emphasis on the stress and strain of ballet would spoil the magic and the illusion of effortlessness that we worked so hard to create. He never spoke to me about it directly, but he told our press department that he didn't like articles that focused on injuries.

That same evening I danced Sugar Plum with Sean Lavery, and I felt wonderful. I was calm throughout the harrowing variation and pas de deux, which contain such basic steps that when anything goes wrong it is immediately apparent. It is surprising how difficult it can be to make simple steps look beautiful and effortless. I noted with gratitude that my hip was still behaving itself. Was the ordeal over? Was I finally free to concentrate on bringing my dancing back to its former level?

My euphoria was short-lived. Two days later, while rehearsing *Symphony in Three Movements,* my hip began to hurt again. The classical roles were clearly much safer for me and for my hip than were the modern ones. It was largely a matter of familiarity. In classical movements my hips almost always remained in a square position, not having to be tilted or thrust in any direction. In addition, I knew what I was doing and where my limits were, and my body was accustomed to the stresses and strains of this style of dancing. In modern roles, I often had to get into difficult and unfamiliar positions without being able to predict the effects on my body. Only after I had done a step did I know whether it was safe, and by then the damage had sometimes been done.

Perhaps all that rest and all those weeks of careful work had been for naught. I couldn't face any more rest (and I didn't believe rest would help, anyway). I reminded myself that some dancers in my position had resorted to surgery, exploratory and otherwise, and then regretted it later. Others, in desperation, had danced when they shouldn't have and destroyed their still young bodies. Then at forty, still handsome or beautiful, they found themselves bereft of the means to perform well. I was determined not to go to either extreme. I would set aside my short-term desires and think of my long-term interests, which were also those of the Company.

Although doctors advised me to keep working, to keep dancing, I wondered whether I wasn't doing myself permanent damage. Would I dance with pain in my hip for the rest of my career? Or was I perhaps overreacting to my gloomy thoughts?

Kibbe tried to keep me on an even keel and, as usual, he talked in practical and optimistic terms of trying new forms of healing or therapy, provided they appeared safe. In the process I could learn a great deal that would stand me in good stead if I ever had to deal with another, more serious injury.

I worked almost every day at the theater with Marika Molnar, the Company's physical therapist. Marika, a godsend to all of us, had been hired in 1980 when our first therapist, hired only as recently as the late 1970s, left. Whenever we had an ache or pain, we would seek her out in her tiny cubicle of an office, where she would tell us how serious our problem was and what kind of treatment to try first. She gave us exercises to do either with her or on our own, not only to aid healing but to prevent future injury. If the problem was serious, she would send us to the Company's orthopedic surgeon, Dr. William Hamilton, who has many years of experience treating athletes and dancers.

In my unrelenting search for a cure, I tried Dr. Hsu's needles, chiropractic treatment, Marika's therapies, Judy's exercises, careful barres, and light rehearsing. Now that my hip problem had been publicized, strangers came to me with advice, and I pondered all of it. In the meantime, my hip continued to torment me by giving me days of relief and hope. I even performed a few times late in January and in February. I did two performances of *Swan Lake* that had many people saying I was better than ever. I felt that if only my body would cooperate I really would dance better than ever before.

Several days before the end of the season, as I was preparing for two performances of *La Source,* I suffered a major setback. *La Source* was a ballet I had done for the first time a few years before and, feeling well suited to it and knowing it was not technically difficult, I had not anticipated any problems. But suddenly my hip became worse than ever. This had happened so many times before, alarming me each time, that I decided just to keep rehearsing.

The first performance tested my stamina, but I made it through without making my hip worse. Then came closing night. I was in my dressing room putting the final touches on my makeup, when I received a visit from Balanchine: "Dear, you've changed. You've been listening to other people too much. Too much acting."

The way Balanchine coldly said the words "you've changed" cut me to the quick, but I managed to keep my composure as he continued talking. When he finished, I told him I was grateful he had told me as soon as he had seen signs of things he didn't like. I wasn't trying to act, I said, but if my dancing looked that way I would try to change, and that would be easier to accomplish now than in a few months. Balanchine seemed relieved to find me open to his criticism. It was obvious to me that he had been uncomfortable saying such things, but it was too important to him to let it slide. He gave me a warm hug and left the dressing room.

My mind and my emotions were in a turmoil as curtain time approached. I truly believed that I hadn't been acting, but it was true that I had been listening to other people. What little criticism I had received suggested that my presence on the stage was too modest, too self-effacing. I had begun to want to be freer and more spontaneous. As I tried to sort out my feelings, I remembered something Barbara Horgan, Balanchine's personal assistant, had told me. She had related how much Balanchine abhorred ballerinas who tried to camouflage their declining technique with a big show of personality, diverting the audience's attention away from the dancing. Was it possible that, because of my hip injury, I had unwittingly slipped in that direction? Was that what Balanchine had detected, or was it something else?

I had no time to think more about it, for *La Source* was about to begin. Balanchine watched from the wings and I was so confused and self-conscious that I had no idea to what extent, if any, I had tempered my "acting." I asked Balanchine if he had noticed any improvement. He answered rather flatly that it was better but that I was still "acting" too much.

That was not a happy note on which to end the season, but I had plenty of time to think and to worry, now that the pleasures and distractions of the performances were over. I pondered what I might specifically have done that Balanchine objected to. I knew he was given to exaggeration in order to produce a desired effect, but I had no idea in this case whether he had meant what he said or whether he had only detected a budding tendency that he wanted to stop before it got out of hand. I had certainly noticed others' efforts to take attention away from their dancing or to put their special stamp on a role. Some might draw attention to certain steps with coy or flirtatious looks. Others might inject drama into roles through looks or gestures, as if to say, "No, I won't look at you," or, "Yes, I want you." I was sure I hadn't done any of these things, but I did look at my partner from time to time. Was that my offense?

I didn't know why Balanchine was so strict with me. Was I such a bad actress that he couldn't restrain comment, or was I such a good dancer that he wanted to make sure nothing detracted from my dancing? Or was there some other motivation behind his criticism? I never was able to decide.

To add to my worries, it became clear that I had seriously reinjured myself rehearsing and dancing in *La Source,* and once again I began to wonder whether I would ever be well again. Kibbe, whose support and sympathy were never more important than at times such as these, encouraged me to try any therapy that held out a glimmer of hope in an attempt to avoid the last resort—exploratory surgery.

I tried various kinds of medicines, including cortisone, Naprosyn, homeopathic remedies, and Chinese herbs; I took large doses of vitamins in conjunction with a special diet; I had various types of massage, ranging from vigorous Swedish massage to "psychic" massage; I consulted anatomy teachers regarding my body alignment as I walked and danced. The weeks dragged on and nothing seemed to help. I prepared myself as best I could for the Company's week in West Palm Beach at the end of March. Dr. Hamilton took a new full set of X rays and found nothing, but he said he could "go in and have a look." He also arranged some consultations with other surgeons. None of them had any definite ideas about what was wrong, but some recommended surgery. Those who didn't were as adamantly opposed to it as I was.

Balanchine had been very patient throughout my ordeal and had continually shown concern over the condition of my hip. Finally I thought I had been inactive long enough and suggested that I perhaps try to dance and live with the pain, but he said: "No, dear, you have to get rid of it."

When he heard that Dr. Hamilton was considering surgery, he encouraged me to allow him to "go in and have a look." Was he running out of patience? Or did he believe that surgery was the only alternative, since all other therapies had failed?

Balanchine had ambivalent attitudes toward injuries. He was genuinely concerned over the welfare of his dancers, but he was impatient with the frailties of dancers' bodies. He never concerned himself with the prevention of injuries, although he was always willing to change a step to help a dancer who was already injured. He would not have been able to teach or choreograph as he did if he had been preoccupied with injury prevention.

We all generally wanted to keep our injuries to ourselves, fearful that we might miss an opportunity to dance. (I had hidden my injury from Balanchine many years earlier, when I had danced my first solo in *Divert.*) When we reached the point where we could no longer dance and had to tell him so, we were never sure what his reaction would be. He had been known to put terrible pressure on dancers even when they felt they risked serious injury by dancing. On the other hand, there were times when he wouldn't cast a dancer with an injury even though the dancer herself felt the problem was not serious. Fortunately, Balanchine's treatment of me fell between the two extremes.

Stanley Williams told me about a great Danish surgeon who, he felt, understood the treatment of dancers better than anyone else. Dr. Eivind Thomasen had acquired a reputation for being able to solve some of the most mysterious problems that dancers had brought to him. Stanley added that Thomasen would never recommend an operation unless he was convinced it would help. Through friends, I also heard about Moshe

Feldenkrais, who taught "awareness through movement" (the title of one of his books) and who had won a worldwide following. My friends strongly encouraged me to seek the help of these two experts.

I decided I would dance in West Palm Beach and then fly to London, where Dr. Thomasen had agreed to meet me, and then to Tel Aviv to see if Feldenkrais could help me in any way.

I took all my X rays from Dr. Hamilton to show Dr. Thomasen. Like Dr. Hamilton, he found them completely normal. The two knew each other well and had discussed my case before I arrived. I gave Dr. Thomasen my layman's description of what was wrong, and he asked me if I had any numbness in the hip area. I hadn't noticed any, and Dr. Hamilton had tested the area for loss of sensation and had found none. Dr. Thomasen took a safety pin, nevertheless, and methodically tested a large area. Finally he found a place about the size of a fifty-cent piece that did seem to be a little less sensitive than the surrounding area. He concluded that a nerve, which branches out and is responsible for feeling in that area, was somehow being pinched or irritated, causing pain and a loss of sensation at the nerve endings. To test the theory, he gave me a shot of Novocaine well above the site of the soreness but where it would affect the twelfth thoracic nerve, to see if that would eliminate the pain. It did . . . 95 percent of it.

With that, he was sure my pain was being caused by that nerve, which was caught or was being pinched as it passed through the fascia, the sheath that surrounds the muscle. He proposed that he "release" the nerve. Did that mean he would have to cut it? He said no. As I understood it, the hole the nerve passed through had to be enlarged a little so that the nerve wouldn't be squeezed or rubbed by the muscle sheath. When I asked him how this had happened, he just said that I had a lot of muscular development in the area, leaving me with the impression that maybe the muscle itself had been squeezing the nerve.

When I had decided to go to London, I had not expected to be confronted with a decision about surgery. I had even brought my toe shoes so that I could do a barre every day in my hotel room. I had been hoping either for a diagnosis that would make sense and give me a clear idea of what an effective treatment would be or for one that would reassure me I could go on dancing without doing real damage. The diagnosis I had just heard made sense, but it forced me to make a decision regarding surgery. At least, it explained why Dr. Hsu's needles hadn't worked and why neither rest nor hard work had made any real difference. Certain hip movements caused pain by pulling the nerve, which was like a long fiber, across the hip bone. That had been going on for nearly a year and a half and it would continue, regardless of the amount of rest or activity I allowed myself, until the nerve was "released." I felt great confidence in Dr. Thomasen from the moment I met him, and his diagnosis was the only clear and definite one I'd heard. But his solution involved the one thing I was set against. I decided to call Kibbe in New

York. So often he had shown a sixth sense for medical problems, and I needed his opinion. His immediate reaction was: "It sounds great; it seems just right; since it is *his* diagnosis, have *him* do it."

I canceled my flight to Tel Aviv and two days later, on April 2, checked into the clinic where Dr. Thomasen performed the operation, under local anesthetic. He considered it a minor matter, and only a two-inch incision was required. As it turned out, however, "releasing" the nerve meant snipping off a couple of nerve endings that had apparently been caught in some scar tissue. Because any damage that might have occurred in the area had long since healed, Dr. Thomasen had no idea how it had happened.

Dr. Thomasen visited me the next day. He had told me he thought I would be able to do fifth position with no pain, but when I tried, it hurt . . . a lot! I was terrified. Dr. Thomasen calmly said this didn't necessarily mean the operation had not worked, but I felt it was a bad sign and worried he was just trying to reassure me. He told me to have Dr. Hamilton take out the stitches in ten days and to do no exercise until then.

The following day, I flew back to New York, wondering whether I had been a fool to agree to the operation. Though Kibbe and I were no longer optimistic, we were somewhat relieved when Dr. Hamilton said that, since no muscles had been cut, there was absolutely no chance any damage had been done.

Two weeks after my operation, Dr. Hamilton took out the stitches. I stood in fifth position, and for the first time my hip hurt a little less than it had before the operation. But neither Dr. Hamilton nor I was much impressed. He told me I could start working, but if the pain in the hip flared up he wanted me to consider having another injection of cortisone.

I started doing easy barres in the apartment and exercises with Marika. It felt as though I had been away for months, not weeks. At first, the pain stayed with me throughout my workouts. Later, it tended to disappear as the hip warmed up, and gradually I was able to work harder. Finally, seven weeks after surgery, I was ready to dance again.

I was not nearly as strong as I had been before my hip injury, but it was reassuring to know that after each of my earlier injuries I had come back a better dancer. My impression of improvement had not been merely subjective; others had commented on it to me and expressed their surprise and delight. No one was more surprised than I the first time it happened, but then I came to expect it.

It's impossible to know why one dancer, after injury and subsequent inactivity, will return an improved dancer and another will not. Innumerable factors are involved and the slightest thing, such as working a little too hard a little too soon, can spoil an otherwise perfect comeback. I believe that my improvement has been due primarily to my knowledge of technique and my interest in watching and learning from dancers who are very different from me.

The habits I acquired while I was building my technique are the very ones I need throughout the long rebuilding process after injury and rest. I become my own strict but patient teacher as I reeducate my muscles. During weeks of inactivity, muscles inevitably lose much of their strength and many of their "good habits." Fortunately, they lose some of their "bad habits" as well. It's a perfect opportunity to start fresh, to get rid of long-standing problems or tendencies picked up while trying to dance through an injury or cope with an exhausting season.

Since not much can be done in the way of steps during the early stages of recovery, it is also a perfect time for me to work on my upper body. I "walk through" certain ballets to practice the ideal positions of my upper body, and to give myself some entertainment. It makes me feel like a dancer again.

Weakness is not the only problem when coming back from injury. If there is scar tissue, or if there have been broken bones and a cast has been on for a long time, the body may experience new sensations because the limbs cannot work in familiar ways. Old feelings and instincts can be seriously misleading. It is here that dancers less inclined to analyze technique and more inclined to rely on what comes naturally are at a serious disadvantage. Sensing that they are poorly equipped to regain their natural talents, these dancers are often daunted by the prospect of re-creating their former selves. Fearing inactivity, they often continue dancing, regardless of how badly they are injured or how disappointing their performances become. Such abuse can prematurely destroy what was once a beautiful style.

When I am injured and have more free time than I am accustomed to, I find myself trying to form a clearer picture in my mind of what I want the overall effect of my dancing to be. I try to capture with my imagination that most elusive image of all, the one that would enlighten me as nothing else could: what I look like to others. I also watch other dancers, and am particularly drawn to those who are most unlike me: the instinctive dancers. I enjoy trying to understand what works and what does not for them, although I often find their technical inadequacies jarring. Through them, I have sometimes gained insight into what is effective on the stage and how I can apply this to my own dancing. I've tried to absorb their attitude, too, wanting to be more creative when the moment seems right. The richness, fullness, even the excesses of their dancing are helpful reminders that technical prowess and efficiency on the stage are not enough. My whole orientation, however, will always remain focused on myself as a dancer, not myself as a personality. That perhaps explains the lack of narcissism that my friend Ghislaine once mentioned.

The improvement after long layoffs is due not only to the benefits I have derived from "starting from scratch" or from observing others. During a period of recovery, all dancers are forced to be sensitive to the condition and the needs of their bodies in order to make important decisions about which therapies to try or which advice to listen to. An inexperienced dancer may be inclined to impose his will on his body without heed-ing its subtle messages, and sooner or later the price of disrespect is paid. After an injury, a dancer learns, at least for a short time, to heed his body if only because pain speaks a language almost anyone can understand. This heightened awareness should not disappear once a dancer returns to form; rather it should help him continue to learn about the ways his body moves and reacts.

When an injury prevents me from dancing, my reactions to everything are magnified. A minor setback in my recovery seems disastrous. Watching others dance overwhelms me with fear that I will never be able to do even simple steps well again. On the other hand, I am reminded how much I love to dance and, even if it ever happens that an injury prevents me from reaching my former level of technical virtuosity, my pleasure will not be spoiled as long as I can still dance well. After I return, I feel more gratified, more elated, and less inclined to take the pleasures of dancing for granted, and I can draw on the experience of these emotional highs and lows in my dancing.

These transformations in my dancing do not occur after a layoff of a week or two; it seems I need to have suffered through a long period of inactivity—a month or more. Although I was reduced to total rest for only two weeks after my operation, I had lost a great deal of strength as a result of intermittent dancing during the period from the premiere of *Ballade* in the spring of 1980 to my operation and brief convalescence in the spring of 1981. That period had really been one long comeback.

On May 23, 1981, I made my "second comeback," in the first movement of *Symphony in C.* While I knew this was not an easy role, I felt it was my best possible choice, given the difficulty of the rest of my repertory. It was a role that would be safe for my hip, would come naturally to me, and would not make me nervous (I had done it so many times before). In performance I felt much stronger and less anxious than I had felt as Dew Drop in December, and all went well. The next day I was exhausted, but my hip had survived.

In June, Moshe Feldenkrais came to New York for a brief time and I was very happy to meet the man behind the reputation. By then, I had only minor pain in my hip, but I felt there was still something seriously wrong; above all, I feared the debilitating pain would return. Feldenkrais made an important discovery while examining me: my hips were seriously out of alignment. No one else had ever noticed that (including many chiropractors). The course of his treatment consisted only in his gently touching certain muscles, but I felt a dramatic improvement right away. That convinced me to arrange to see him later in the summer at Hampshire College in Amherst, Massachusetts, where he would be teaching and treating people. Those visits, too, proved extremely beneficial, and without them I very likely never would have regained all my technique.

The Tchaikovsky Festival began on June 5. I was terribly disappointed I had not been well enough to be in any of the new ballets, and since I wasn't yet strong enough to dance most of my Tchaikovsky roles, such as *Theme and Variations* and *Piano Concerto,* I had very little to dance. My regret at not being truly a part of the Festival was outweighed, however, by my pleasure in dancing again and by my amazement that my hip was behaving and that the rest of my body had not broken down under the sudden strain of trying to get back into shape so quickly.

Before and during the Festival, Balanchine's health worsened and his eyesight grew dimmer due to cataracts. He said to me on more than one occasion that he didn't want to choreograph anymore. Was it truly a loss of desire or had it become too physically taxing for him? Years earlier he had said that, when he could no longer demonstrate the steps as he was choreographing, he would stop. Had that time come? Whatever the truth, his comment meant only one thing to me: he felt his decline was irreversible.

Choreographing always as much with his heart as with his mind, Balanchine ended the Festival, not surprisingly, with a ballet reflecting his attitude toward death. All of us who witnessed that unique performance of his *Adagio Lamentoso* will never forget the weeping mourners, the white angels with gigantic wings, the hooded figures, and the monks in black who paraded slowly through the ballet. At the end, a small boy entered holding a lit candle, riveting our attention. After a few moments, the boy blew out his candle, plunging the stage, and us, into darkness. It was a moment filled with foreboding, for it foreshadowed the day we had all begun to dread.

CHAPTER

7

I HAD FIRST begun to think about life without Balanchine when I joined the Company. Even though I had had only the briefest contact with him, I understood that my dancing, my career, and everything that mattered to me depended entirely on him, and I wouldn't have wanted it any other way. But I wondered how much longer he would be with us. Given his age, sixty-two, which seemed old to me at the time, I remember calculating that I might have about five years with him, and I tried to be satisfied with that.

As the years passed, my view of Balanchine's longevity changed. I saw him in the theater from morning until night—teaching class, taking rehearsals, watching all performances from the wings—and he seemed endowed with boundless energy. As I came to know him better, I understood that his energy was generated not only by his natural enthusiasm but also by the inspiration and stimulation he received from working with all his dancers, whose individual qualities he always appreciated. Even our weaknesses inspired him and set his mind thinking about new ways to get the most out of us. I soon found reason to hope he and I might retire at about the same time. He would be ninety when I was forty-four. For a time, I felt very happy with that estimate.

When the curtain fell on the Tchaikovsky Festival, I had to face the terrible truth that I had years of dancing ahead and only limited time left with Balanchine. Even if he did live to be ninety, his truly active days were already over.

As we looked toward the future, harder questions loomed. Who would take over? Peter Martins seemed the obvious choice, but could we be so sure? If so, would he be a strong leader or merely a figurehead? What would happen to the dancing and to Balanchine's ballets? Even before Balanchine had stopped teaching regularly, he used to say to us, after he had been away for a brief while to work or rest: "When I'm away, you all fall asleep. What's going to happen when I'm gone?"

While Balanchine's health was deteriorating, my injuries were mending, and in the remaining two weeks of the season I felt my dancing reached a crescendo, with four performances of *Ballo* and one of *Square Dance*, the first time I had danced those ballets in more than a year. I was finally beginning to feel like myself again.

A long summer of unemployment, following the impending Saratoga season, lay ahead, and so I was very interested when a producer from Hawaii suggested I put together a group of ten dancers and present in Honolulu a full evening of ballets from the NYCB repertory. I had taken part in innumerable concerts with Jacques and others all over the country, but I had never assumed responsibility for the dancing of others. I had given class at the School a few times and had always helped anyone in the Company who had come to me with questions, but deciding on a program, choosing dancers, assigning roles, providing coaching, attending to myriad organizational details, and at the same time keeping my own dancing intact, seemed at first more than I should dare undertake.

I had long been interested, however, in passing on the knowledge I had been privileged to get firsthand from Balanchine, particularly to young dancers who had the desire to work and learn but who had never had classes with Balanchine. This adventure in Hawaii would be a step in that direction. It was a very big first step, but Kibbe kept encouraging me to try, reminding me that I would learn as much as the people I helped, and assuring me that he would take vacation time from the United Nations so that he could make the trip and help me with all the details. By the time a contract was offered, my mind was made up.

Immediately, I went to Balanchine, seeking permission to use his ballets and the Company's costumes. He listened quietly as I told him about a few of the details of the engagement, but his eyes lit up when I said we would be dancing to a live symphony orchestra instead of taped music. When I finished my explanation he simply said: "Dear, do whatever you want. It's fine."

I talked over other details with Barbara Horgan and learned that Balanchine was not in the habit of demanding a fee for the use of his ballets in such concerts. If there was any money left over at the end, I could give him a check. Otherwise, it did not matter. I also learned that the words *New York City Ballet* could not be used in the name of my group, and so I settled, a little uneasily, on *Merrill Ashley and Dancers.* I feared my name would mean nothing in Hawaii but I hoped the balletgoers there would welcome the opportunity to see Balanchine dancers in Balanchine ballets.

The budget was small, but I was determined to make it the most enjoyable concert that every member of my group had experienced. And what more glorious setting could I have than Hawaii?

I decided to present a varied program that would entertain and challenge the Honolulu audience; to provide each dancer with at least one role that he or she would consider a rare opportunity; and to look after everyone's welfare as best I could. I knew what I wanted to achieve, but I wasn't sure I could do it.

First, I had to decide whom to invite. Each dancer would have to be technically strong, dependable, and able to present himself well on stage. It was also important to me that the group be congenial, for any friction would spoil the adventure for everyone. I particularly wanted to take along a few promising young dancers who had been overlooked or underestimated in the Company. I remembered what Jacques's concerts had meant to me, and I wanted to do the same for others.

Finally, I decided on two principals, Sean and Ib; two soloists, Lourdes Lopez and Judy Fugate; and five corps members, two of whom—Darla Hoover and Lauren Hauser—were very talented but had had limited experience in the Company and in concerts. I had spent my whole life learning. This would be the first time I would have sole responsibility for coaching others in preparation for performances.

Next, I had to decide on a program. Above all, I wanted to avoid the succession of pas de deux that small groups are nearly always forced to present. My choice was limited. Not counting pas de deux, there are very few ballets in the NYCB repertory with small casts. In addition, I wanted the mood to change from ballet to ballet throughout the evening. A number of my problems were solved when Balanchine said I could use *Apollo.* I was thrilled to be able to present as the centerpiece of my program his great masterpiece and one of my favorite ballets. It needed only four dancers, which was ideal. The Stravinsky music and the simple but unusual choreography would take audiences far from familiar terrain, but I wanted to educate as well as entertain them.

Each dancer would have to dance twice on each of the three evenings planned, with no one miscast or mismatched. Who would look good with whom? To keep a last-minute injury from spelling disaster, everyone had to have an understudy. It became an enormous jigsaw puzzle, and I spent days fitting all the pieces together. I knew this project would teach me a great deal about working with others—experience that would prove invaluable in the future—but I never would have done it for the experience alone. I was inspired by the chance to give everyone a uniquely enjoyable time.

We rehearsed in Saratoga on the weekends and during any spare moments the dancers had. Because there was so much to do in so little time, I felt a constant urge to try to instill in a few hours what it had taken me years to learn, and it was thrilling when someone responded right before my eyes. Still, I had never before coached anyone all the way through a ballet, and I was not confident I would be able to see which points of technique truly affected the total impression and which could be allowed to pass. I felt a strong need to step back and gain perspective, especially to get an overall impression of the way each dancer presented himself. For that, I would have to wait until we arrived in Honolulu, where I could watch the dancers rehearsing on stage from the audience's vantage point.

The moment we stepped off the plane in Honolulu, everyone was enchanted. Miraculously, airport fumes were quickly replaced by the strong fragrance of tropical flowers and the smell of the sea air, which made all of us think immediately of pounding surf and deserted beaches. Only Sean Lavery and I had ever been to Hawaii before, but all the others acted as if their dreams of a tropical paradise were about to come true.

The next day we rehearsed all day long. During the rehearsal of *Apollo,* I realized I had failed to anticipate a major problem: the Stravinsky music proved very difficult for the Honolulu Symphony Orchestra. It is, in fact, difficult for most orchestras, and the conductor, who had had little experience conducting for dancers, had endless problems with the tempos. It was too late to bring a conductor from New York, so we had to make the best of a difficult situation.

The three performances, in August, played to sold-out houses and were a fantastic success with audiences and critics alike. Although I was the head of the group, I did not want to be the focus of attention and therefore did not include any bravura role for myself. I had sought a balanced program, one that would hold the audience's interest from beginning to end.

I danced the lead roles in *Afternoon of a Faun, Apollo,* and *Who Cares?*—none of which I had ever done in New York. Some of the most favorable comments were made about me in *Faun. Apollo* too went very well, and dancing in it allowed me to recapture many of the feelings I had had when I joined the Company and saw the ballet for the first time. From that moment on, it has been my favorite ballet, the one I find most movingly beautiful. I have, however, to exclude *Ballo* and *Ballade,* precious gifts that occupy a special place in my heart.

After it was over, the dancers in my group said what I had hoped to hear: that ours had been the most enjoyable and best organized concert they had ever done. I think—and hope—this was true, in part, because they found working with me stimulating.

Almost everyone decided to stay on in Hawaii to explore the outer islands. In the days that followed, critics wrote that we should come back the next year; it was wonderfully satisfying to read such comments as I luxuriated on Maui's gorgeous beaches. Even in my exhausted state, I found myself thinking about another Hawaii appearance. But that would depend on whether the NYCB kept us busy with a summer tour or whether we would again have a long layoff.

As it turned out, the Company did not employ us in the summer of 1982, and Merrill Ashley and Dancers returned to Hawaii to renew our mutual love affair with the place. This time Gordon Boelzner came with us to conduct—I had learned my lesson. With only one exception, my second program contained all new ballets, including a bravura pas de deux, Balanchine's *Tchaikovsky Pas de Deux,* which was exactly what the audience had been hoping for. In fact, the whole program elicited even more praise from the critics and everyone else than we had received the first time.

Two summers of directing a small group was both humbling and confidence-building. It gave me experience in dealing with management problems, which in turn helped me to be a little more assertive. And it forced me to try different approaches to teaching, for once again I tried in a few short weeks to get the most out of the young members of my group.

The greatest lesson I learned was that almost all dancers appreciate attention and good, consistent coaching. Dancers are at their best when they are trying to please, but there are so many who want to learn and so few who teach well. In performance, there is the audience, but, in class and rehearsals, a teacher who cares and can show what a dancer should be striving for may make the difference between tedium and excitement. I know that the younger members of my group appreciated my demonstrations of steps they were trying to perfect, and they doubly appreciated being able to work closely and comfortably with me. It was the kind of mutually beneficial and enjoyable relationship that should exist at all times and at all levels in the Company.

In general, I found that token improvements were easy to bring about and that, with constant rehearsing and correcting, I could impose a given style or way of moving on a dancer for a short while. But, without constant vigilance on my part, that new style tended to vanish, even though the dancers were making every effort to be conscientious. This happened largely because there was not enough time for me to go into all the details about each correction, which would have helped the dancers fully understand the reasons behind them. Unless I could do that, it would be not only difficult for them to remember the corrections but impossible for them to apply intelligently their new knowledge to other ballets. But I knew from experience that if they *could* fully understand and apply what they were learning, they would have one of the greatest assets a dancer can possess, one prized by any teacher or choreographer. Balanchine tried to cultivate this ability in his dancers; he tried, in a sense, to make us independent workers and thinkers—but his efforts were often futile. In his frustration, he would often say: "You know, I can buy food for you, wash it, cut it up, cook it, serve it, even chew it for you, but I can't swallow and digest it for you. Only you can do that."

My brief efforts in Hawaii gave me deeper respect and appreciation for all that Balanchine had accomplished in developing such a cohesive high-energy dancing style for his Company. It was all the more remarkable in that he was a gentle man in a job that lent itself to the methods of a rigid disciplinarian.

* * *

Balanchine taught only very sporadically in 1981. He was beginning to have problems with his sense of balance in addition to his other physical ailments. Many dancers, including myself, continued to ask him: "When are you going to teach again, Mr. B?" But the real question in all our minds was whether he was *ever* going to teach again.

I vividly recall the last three times he taught us. On three consecutive days in November 1981 he came to class obviously determined to snap us out of our torpor. Although hampered by his unsteadiness, he became involved, physically and emotionally, in everything he tried to communicate to us. He threw himself as best he could into demonstrations of steps, and, summoning up all his energy, he tried with his barbs and his humor and sometimes even with a show of annoyance to coax out of us what had long lain dormant. He wanted "more, more": more energy, more speed, more control, and more awareness of what we were doing. He forced us to extremes that came as a shock even to those of us who knew him well. To those hearing his words for the first time, the general message, if nothing else, was clear: back to the basics.

But as he confronted both our ineptitude and his own frailty, a deep frustration came over him. Teaching class now demanded more from Balanchine than he was able to give. His dwindling reserves of energy would now have to be used for less strenuous tasks associated with directing our growing Company, and I could only pray he would find some other way to create the spirit that had been missing in Company class when he did not teach.

For years, Balanchine's classes had provided me with my daily sustenance. They had gradually been replaced by uninspiring classes in which teachers gave only a few desultory corrections and often contradicted what Balanchine taught, but I had always believed that Balanchine would again recover his strength and return to regular teaching.

As his health worsened, I realized this was a vain expectation, but I was confident he would soon take action—perhaps bring in a new teacher or oversee the classes himself. His dismay when he saw what had become of us after he had been away for a while convinced me that he would not want us to depend for long on these and the other classes Company members were beginning to attend: classes that made you, as he put it, "feel good" or that were only "good for your health" but did not prepare you to dance in his ballets.

Time passed but Balanchine showed no interest in handpicking or training someone to replace him as a teacher. As class became less and less the source of basic instruction and inspiration, rehearsals became the only time when real learning took place. It was a problem that would have to be confronted sooner or later, and I felt Balanchine would surely find a way to solve it. I waited patiently, then uncomprehendingly, as everyone's energy and enthusiasm flagged with the passing months and nothing was done to remedy the situation. Did Mr. B not care anymore? Was he not even going to *try* to ensure that our classes were given well? Or did he feel that, since no one could truly replace him, anyone would do? Without his classes, what would happen to the ballets, the dancing, and ultimately the Company? Maybe he felt it would be wisest to leave the Company free to sink or swim, to find its own way without the burden of the past; if this were the case, then there was no need to preserve all that he had taught. Or then again, maybe he was testing us to see how hard we would work to live up to his ideals, now that we had only ourselves to rely on for inspiration. If we went too far astray, would he take drastic action to guide us back? I certainly didn't have any answers, but I realized the future was filled with uncertainty.

As long as Balanchine was strong or felt he could recover his strength, or solve his health problems with surgery (as he had done with his successful by-pass operation), he was interested only in the present, in continuing to teach and to create ballets. He had a maddeningly engaging way of warding off the efforts of his supporters, who were bent on preserving everything he had ever created. When they asked him about the future, he liked to retort, "What's the matter with now?" or he might remind them he was a Georgian and would probably live to be over a hundred.

I am sure, too, he was unable to envision his ballets being danced one day by future NYCB dancers whom he hadn't trained and did not even know. Could it even be said that they would still be his ballets? He always thought of the choreography and the dancers as one and the same. During his lifetime, only dancers whom he had trained had ever truly been able to re-create his choreography. He knew that future dancers would not be able to breathe life into his ballets as easily as an actor can read the lines of a playwright long gone.

Balanchine professed no interest in posterity, yet he had a great interest in and knowledge of the long dance traditions to which he belonged. He may not have been interested in preserving his own ballets, but in the final years of his life he began to show an interest in preserving what had been handed down to him. He asked me to learn from Danilova (for preservation on film) all the Petipa variations she could remember. The project is now under way, although it has been interrupted by constant conflicts in our schedules and by my past injuries. The variations I have already learned have not yet been filmed, but I have written down the steps, and all of Danilova's corrections, in great detail.

When Balanchine agreed to the *Dance in America* series on public television, his motivation was not to preserve his ballets (only a handful were filmed anyway, and not in their stage versions but with changes specifically made by Balanchine for the requirements of the screen). He wanted to bring ballet to a wider public, to interest more people in dance and to give people far from New York a chance to see his ballets. Earlier he had agreed to a few attempts to film his ballets, but usually the directors of the projects had their own ideas, which did not correspond to Balanchine's, and these experiences only reinforced his basic lack of interest in recording his ballets.

In 1980 our musicians, sharing the general concern over what would happen to Balanchine's few remaining ballets, finally agreed to allow performances to be recorded live. Like the dancers and the stagehands who had previously agreed to allow these recordings, they stipulated that the recordings could be used only for the internal use of the Company, not for commercial purposes. Before that, the Company had made a few tapes of rehearsals, but no tapes of actual performances. How much better to have a record of a live performance with the lighting, costumes, and casting that Balanchine had wanted. The audience sees the ballet as it is intended, and there is no extra work involved in the shooting!

Balanchine's lack of interest in the future was mirrored in his lack of desire to preserve or revive his own past. While he did bring back and keep alive a few of his masterpieces, they represent only a tiny sampling of his enormous output, almost all of which is now irretrievably lost. He finally had to face the fact that his ability to teach and choreograph was coming to an end, and he began to yield to pressure to preserve his ballets and prepare someone to take over, although I am sure there remained a conflict within him. He had always wanted to do everything himself, but that was feasible only when the Company was smaller and he still had his vitality.

During his final years, as Balanchine became weaker and the Company grew ever larger, delegating authority to others still went against his grain. He had always made it clear that he wanted to make all the important decisions himself, and those who assisted him had gone along with this—which only reinforced his belief that he had to do everything himself for things to be done properly. Right to the end, he was reluctant to relinquish that privilege. He wanted to remain the person to whom everyone would turn for guidance and inspiration.

I could only conclude that Balanchine had contradictory attitudes toward the future of the Company, just as he had about so many other things. He wanted to help us prepare for the future, yet all the while a small part of him found solace in the thought that it would all fall apart without him. Perhaps he even truly believed what I had often heard him say:

"*Après moi, le déluge!*"

Ballade was scheduled to be performed again in January 1982, and, although I had recently managed to overcome an assortment of minor injuries and perform in my most taxing roles, I wasn't at all sure my current injuries would allow me to perform in it. Nearly two years had passed since the ballet had premiered, but I still recalled the magnitude of the effort for each performance. During those two years, whenever the ballet had been scheduled Balanchine was always willing to cancel it, not wishing to teach my role to anyone else. Finally, he seemed unwilling to cancel the ballet again, not just because such cancelations were unpopular with the audiences but because he was eager to see the ballet again himself.

As Sean and I started to rehearse *Ballade* (Ib was injured), we discovered several gaps in our memories, and since there was no film to which we could refer we realized we would have to ask Balanchine to rechoreograph those parts. I was also worried that a new foot injury might prevent my dancing at all. I went to Balanchine with both problems, and he replied brightly: "Don't worry, dear. I will fix it. Just tell me what steps bother your foot and what parts you don't remember, and I will make new steps."

I hesitantly mentioned that I was also worried about not having enough stamina to get through the ballet, which was the most tiring one I had ever done. "Dear, why didn't you tell me sooner?" he exclaimed. "I would have changed it long ago."

While my pride told me not to let him simplify the ballet to spare my foot or save my energy, my common sense told me to let him change as much as was necessary. I could not be responsible for any more cancelations.

A rehearsal was set up with Balanchine to make the necessary changes, but Sean and I were in for a shock. As the rehearsal started, we were forced to accept the obvious: Balanchine's physical infirmities had sapped his enthusiasm for choreographing. Every time we came to a section that needed reworking, he was devoid of energy, inspiration, or even ideas. He simply said, "Just walk," "Just run," or "Just stand still." Both Sean and I were dismayed by his lack of involvement. We sensed that the few new steps he had given us were uninteresting and that we would have to find ways to embellish them on our own. But it was even more disturbing to see Mr. B so dispirited, so lacking in the enthusiasm necessary for wholehearted work with his dancers. His only desire seemed to be to sit back and watch us dance.

The few changes that were made in *Ballade* did make it possible for me to do the ballet that winter. I was amazed at the difference they made. The ballet, which had been almost impossibly hard, suddenly became manageable. One brief rest in the wings was extended by a mere twenty seconds—and what a difference that made!

After each performance, Balanchine showed me some of his old enthusiasm. His eyes were bright as he repeated how beautiful the ballet looked. It made me very happy to bring him that kind of pleasure, and I loved to hear him say the words "beautiful ballet." But there was no longer any ignoring the depressingly obvious fact that his strength was ebbing.

As we prepared for the second Stravinsky Festival in the spring of 1982, celebrating the centennial of Stravinsky's birth, we all hoped that Balanchine, inspired by Stravinsky's music, would become his old self again. It was not to be. His balance problems had become quite serious, restricting his ability to choreograph, and his most valuable contribution became the supervision of the overall plans for the Festival. As had been true of the Ravel and Tchaikovsky Festivals, this Festival produced the outpouring of creative effort for which the NYCB is famous, but the ballets were not of the same high caliber as those in the first Stravinsky Festival ten years earlier, and little of lasting value was produced. The only new ballet in which I danced was Jerry Robbins's *Chamber Works,* which was one of the successes of the Festival.

The spring season ended on the Fourth of July, and I danced in the last ballet that evening. As had become customary during the final curtain calls at the end of each season, Balanchine appeared on stage and bowed with his dancers. Karin von Aroldingen and I were on either side of him, and as he took my hand he quietly said to me: "I need to hold your hand. Don't let go."

As we all walked forward, bowed, and stepped back, I was barely able to give him the support he needed. Then, he stepped forward once again, found his balance, and let go of our hands, explaining to the audience that he wanted to help celebrate the Fourth of July with a gift from Stravinsky. He signaled to the orchestra to start playing Stravinsky's orchestration of the "Star-Spangled Banner." That festive and happy occasion ended with Balanchine taking a solo bow, discreetly holding the curtain for support, on a stage strewn with flowers. No one imagined that it would be his last public appearance.

The following day Balanchine and the Company went to Saratoga. I'm sure he had every intention of going to the theater, watching us, and possibly even rehearsing some of his ballets, but his growing unsteadiness prevented that. Yet, he remained in touch with the Company several times a day and continued to make the major decisions.

One afternoon he invited me to his house to have ice cream—delicious, rich vanilla ice cream he had made himself. He missed the personal contact with his dancers but, embarrassed by his unsteadiness, he invited only a very few to visit him. I was happy and flattered that he wanted to see me, and although he seemed very tired I think he found pleasure in my company.

Throughout the fall, Balanchine's health and sense of balance continued to deteriorate, defying the expertise of the best doctors. Finally, following a fall in which he broke several ribs and cracked his wrist, he entered Roosevelt Hospital, preferring to convalesce there rather than in his apartment. Even after his bones healed, however, he wished to remain in the hospital, where he could receive the care that would be difficult to provide in his apartment. Further tests were all inconclusive. Most of the dancers and many of his other friends visited him continually, bringing him flowers, food, and most of all expressions of their love and concern. Even those who had only recently joined the Company and had never met him went to see him.

By the end of the year, as Balanchine's body weakened further, his mind also began to fail and communication with him became increasingly difficult. In March, Peter Martins and Jerry Robbins took over the Company, as ballet masters-in-chief, with Balanchine named ballet master emeritus. Although his strong Georgian body continued to cling to life, we all knew by then that he would never leave the hospital.

CHAPTER

8

BALANCHINE died very early in the morning on Saturday, April 30, 1983. The Company management tried to ensure that the dancers would be the first to be notified by calling each of us right away. They said it was important not to cancel any of the performances, and so both the matinee and evening performances would be given that day as usual.

I was not scheduled to perform that day, but, like everyone else, I needed to be with Balanchine's "family," the other Company members. As I entered the theater, I met Jerry Robbins, who embraced me wordlessly, his arms trembling. The backstage area quickly filled with Company members, few of whom were able to put a brave face on their grief. We all needed to share our distress, to comfort each other, and to exchange our most cherished memories of him.

Just before the matinee performance began, Lincoln Kirstein, who founded the Company with Balanchine, stepped in front of the curtain and spoke a few words to the audience. His voice, though hoarse and shaking with emotion, was reassuring. He would continue to give us the strength and guidance he had always provided. Our Mr. B was gone, his voice was saying, but we would go on; and if we went astray, Mr. B, now in the very good company of Mozart, Tchaikovsky, and Stravinsky, would send us a

message.

The memorial service for Balanchine, the day before his funeral. Standing behind Merrill are Peter Martins and Lincoln Kirstein. (© *Lars Luick*)

Three days later, the funeral service was held at the Russian Orthodox Cathedral of Our Lady of the Sign. Special arrangements were made for his dancers to stand in the front of the church to view Balanchine, who lay in an open coffin.

The church was filled to overflowing, and a crowd gathered in the courtyard to hear the ceremony over a loudspeaker. Everyone was given a slender yellow candle to be lit at the beginning of the ceremony by passing a flame from candle to candle. As is customary at Russian Orthodox services, everyone stood.

Outside, it was a cool, wet morning. Inside, the air soon became warm and heavy with the smell of burning incense and the heat from hundreds of candles. I was only a few steps from the coffin and could not take my eyes off Balanchine, whose waxen features seemed so much more drawn than when I had last seen him. In particular, his hands, those beautiful, sensitive hands that had always fascinated me, held me spellbound.

Close by stood his dancers, young and old; his former wives; and many of the elderly Russians who had known him since his arrival in the United States. The liturgical chants and the mysterious Church Slavonic sounds brought home to me how much of his life and work I had never truly known.

The heavy weight of grief and the two hours of standing in the damp heat took their toll. Several mourners near me fainted. As the service neared its end and the candles began to be extinguished, I could only stare down at my own candle, the last flickering light of Balanchine's life. My mind jumped to the little boy in the *Adagio Lamentoso* who blew out the candle that had brought the Tchaikovsky Festival to a close. His time with Balanchine had been so brief. I had been more fortunate, for while I too had met Balanchine at about that age, I had known him for more than half my life. Those memories would sustain me for the rest of my life. Now I could blow out my candle. His flame would burn in me forever.

At the conclusion of the service, the dancers and those associated with the Company left the church by a back entrance and gathered in a courtyard. As I passed by Maria Tallchief, she said, "Oh, Merrill, he was so proud of you."

Those words touched me deeply and brought me a little closer to the certainty that I had fulfilled his expectations, and somehow that made it easier to say good-bye to him.

Later, a luncheon was given for those Company members who could not go to Long Island for the burial because they were dancing in the performance that evening. Due to program changes made to ease the burden on the Company, it had not yet been decided whether or not I would be cast. Some dancers would have preferred not to perform in order to be able to come to terms with their grief alone, but in the past I had always found that dancing was the best way for me to calm inner turmoil, and that day I needed it more than ever before. My heart was set on dancing that evening, and not for sentimental reasons. I felt I needed to dance in order to survive, and I shall never forget my unhappiness when I discovered that I had not been included in the evening's casting.

I danced a few days later and many more times before the season ended two months later. Whenever I danced, doing Balanchine's steps the way he had taught me to do them, to music he had chosen, I felt he was with me. But when I was not dancing, I felt alone. I missed his physical presence in the theater, his guidance and inspiration. For those who had been closer to him than I, the void must have been even greater, but, like me, they had their memories to cling to. What about the dancers who had only felt his influence but never had a chance to work with him or even to get to know him? They had no memories to give them strength and could only imagine what they had missed and what might have been.

Whenever I was in the audience watching Balanchine's ballets, I was overcome with sadness. I saw anew how beautiful they were, and the realization that we would have no more ballets from him gave me a hollow feeling of desolation. I knew, too, that those precious ballets that were his legacy to us could so quickly lose their luster if they were not carefully maintained.

Throughout the fall and winter, I continued to take Company class regularly but found it increasingly difficult to maintain my technique, for exercises were rarely done at the fast tempos I needed. The moderate tempos and relaxed atmosphere brought back to mind Balanchine's frequent exhortation to his dancers: "Don't relax! The time to relax is in the grave."

Difficult though it is for me to maintain my technique, I have not forgotten how infinitely more difficult it was to acquire. And I had the advantage of having Balanchine as my teacher! The dancers in the Company today deserve at least to have the opportunity to learn what Balanchine taught those of us who studied with him. But few people are qualified to pass on this knowledge, for only those who have danced with the Company and, most important, assimilated what Balanchine taught can hope to understand the technique our repertory demands. Even among these experienced people, only a handful can communicate their knowledge and experience to others, and it is these few who I feel should be brought in to teach the Company.

The groundwork of technique and style can be laid only in class, for class determines what can be accomplished in rehearsals, and rehearsals are but a step away from performance. But a successful class—one in which the teacher teaches and the dancers learn—requires cooperation on both sides. When dancers come to class wearing ballet slippers and/or bulky clothes that hide the line of the body (Balanchine always insisted on toe shoes and form-fitting clothing in class), it shows they are expecting only a warm-up and are not prepared for the rigors of a Balanchine-type class. If classes serve their proper function, then a brief reminder or correction in rehearsals should produce results (efficient learning is especially needed in the NYCB because of our enormous repertory). If the ballet mistresses find it is necessary to use rehearsal time to try to remedy serious shortcomings, then their attention will be diverted from the presentation of the dancer, which, as Balanchine always made clear to us, should take precedence over all else. Sometimes in class he would concentrate on one dancer, trying to get her to do a step just right. Success would elicit an enthusiastic "that's right!" but even as she was breathing a sigh of relief, he would add: "But now, dear, make it beautiful."

The tendency to take the high quality of our dancing for granted began many years ago while Balanchine still presided over the fortunes of the Company. While the attention of audiences and critics was inevitably focused on the new works he produced every season, Balanchine was busy behind the scenes teaching the dancers. Partly because of the extraordinary ease and speed with which he choreographed and worked in rehearsals, and partly because of his boundless enthusiasm, he had the mental and physical stamina needed to give class, take rehearsals all day long, watch performance in the evening, and still attend to the myriad other organizational matters that continually crop up in such a large company.

As Balanchine gave class less frequently, even many of the dancers still tended to believe that the dancing would somehow take care of itself, assuming perhaps that merely dancing in Balanchine's ballets would magically produce the skills needed. It is becoming clear, however, that the dancers, even those who are highly motivated, cannot teach themselves on their own.

One need not be Balanchine to give a Balanchine-type class. We must not be blinded by his genius and believe that, because he was unique as a choreographer and teacher, he was uniquely able to teach and inspire us. It is perfectly possible for others to teach the same principles he taught and to duplicate many of the results that he obtained in his classes. It is at least worth trying. Dancers would respond favorably to such efforts, for most of them are pursuing some sort of ideal they need help in achieving. Any good dancer craves stimulation and wants to be spurred on to new efforts and new discoveries.

The paramount challenge and true test of the NYCB's creativity is to provide a class that will enable the entire Company to live up to the standards Balanchine set. If the Company fails to maintain them, it runs the risk of losing its individuality and identity and becoming just another ballet company.

No one can say with certainty that Balanchine wanted his successors, regardless of their own inclinations, to devote themselves solely to the preservation of his ballets and his style of dancing. Whatever our goals, however, he would have wanted us to throw ourselves body and soul into our efforts to attain them. He himself knew no other way. He hated anything that was done halfheartedly or with mediocrity. When he asked a dancer to improve the execution of a step, the dancer's attempt would sometimes be prefaced by a timid "I'll try." Balanchine's reply was usually: "Dear, don't try; just do!"

Those words summed up the man, he "just did" whatever he set his mind on. He instilled that spirit in us, and I'm sure he expected at least *that* part of his teaching to remain alive in the Company.

The need to preserve the quality of the dancing of the New York City Ballet has been overshadowed by another seemingly more urgent matter that dominates the attention of all those who contemplate the future of the Company: What balance should be struck between the Balanchine repertory and new choreography? On one side, there are the advocates of innovation and creativity, who fear that undue interest in the past will divert the Company from what they feel is its proper calling: the production of new works. On the other, there are those who cherish Balanchine's works and think every effort should be made to preserve them. They fear that if any of these works are allowed even briefly to fall from view, they will be lost forever, or at best will return in an unsatisfactory or diluted form.

This debate on the old versus the new seems to have obscured the obvious fact that *everyone* stands to gain when the Company dances well. Without good dancing, there will be no preservation of Balanchine's ballets as we have grown accustomed to seeing them, and choreographers will be handicapped in their future creative efforts.

If the great example of Balanchine's ceaseless efforts to instruct and inspire is not followed, we may awaken one day only to find that although we have resolved satisfactorily the issue of the proper balance of ballets—which for the foreseeable future will inevitably be a middle course between the two extremes—we no longer have the dancers we need to dance in those ballets. Then we may find that Balanchine's masterpieces look dull and stale. Some people will understand that the ballets themselves are not to blame; they will simply not have been danced well enough. But these people may assume that the Company has done all in its power to prevent what they considered was the inevitable decline. Others may even believe that the ballets are dated and no longer stimulating and therefore fresh inspiration is needed.

The Company will then have a choice: either to respond with quick-fix efforts to make the ballets look interesting (and the result will be either visible strain, as dancers who are out of their depth try to do the steps well, or "acting" to cover up a lack of skill) or to add more and more new ballets to the repertory. The latter course of action would be a great temptation. Not only would it appear consistent with the Company's long-standing policy of creativity, but new ballets, being tailor-made to the dancers' ability, would for a time make them look better. The ultimate irony would be if the Company, in the name of some spurious creativity, produced new ballet after ballet, all the while turning its back on its glorious past, the past that still lives today in a few of its dancers.

Many years ago Balanchine said, "Some day I'll be known more for my teaching than for my choreography" (*Ballet Review* [Winter 1984], p. 24).

If it ever comes to pass that his ballets lose their luster and every attempt to restore them to their former glory fails, then it will be understood how tightly his choreography and his teaching were interwoven. Balanchine incorporated in his choreography innumerable points on which he worked tirelessly in class. If these elements are missing, or barely visible, then the choreography loses its focus. His teaching therefore should be the foundation for the further development of our art.

What will happen to the dancing? This should be the paramount concern. The fate of the repertory, and perhaps of the Company, depends on this. If we dance as Balanchine taught us, then regardless of the fortunes of individual ballets, regardless of whether or not each old ballet has been well preserved or each new one well conceived, the Company will remain above passing successes and failures, and errors in programming from season to season can easily be corrected without any waning of audience interest.

Like a dancer's body, our dancing is a fragile thing. What has taken years to build could disintegrate in a few short seasons. If our aim is both to preserve Balanchine's ballets and to rejuvenate ourselves with new works, we must devote years of intelligent and determined effort to the preservation of Balanchine's legacy. But, if we delay, the task of rebuilding will be monumental and we will run the risk of being left with only our memories.

With Balanchine's death, an important period in the life of the Company, and in my life, came to an end. We must find a way to live on, and to flourish without the man who made us what we are. Bereft of our primary source of inspiration and knowledge, but still guided by our founder and mentor, Lincoln Kirstein, we must retain our identity, even as we develop and change, and pursue our ideals with ingenuity and energy. There is no goal to which I would rather devote myself than keeping Balanchine's teaching alive. I have always found great fulfillment in the pursuit of his ideals and the hard work necessary has become second nature to me.

I look forward to maintaining and striving to improve my own dancing in a way that will embody and possibly transcend what Balanchine taught. Perhaps I will be fortunate enough to find someone who will challenge me as he did rather than simply help me polish my present skills. What fun it would be continually to be asked, "What happens if you try this?" or, "Is it possible to do that?" It would be like searching for a buried treasure. You don't know if you're going to find it; you're not even sure what you're searching for; but when you make a discovery, the rewards are boundless.

New roles also offer new pleasures. Having danced throughout my career primarily in virtuoso ballets, I now would like to expand my repertory by learning roles that demand qualities I have not yet had to display. There are a number of ballets in the current repertory that would give me this opportunity. I would also love to watch and dance in the few Balanchine ballets that are unfamiliar to me and may be revived. Because of my injuries over the past few years, I have had only limited opportunities to work with our Company's choreographers on their new ballets, and I am eager to be part of that creative process again.

I am particularly interested in continuing to share my knowledge of Balanchine's teachings with others. As in the past, I will teach, coach, and put together small performing groups for concerts, provided of course that those activities do not interfere with my own dancing. But I also want to find new creative ways to pass on that knowledge.

The loss of Balanchine has left me as well as the Company at a crossroads. The future course of the Company is unknown, but the challenge for me will be to find a way to remain true to Balanchine and still continue to grow without his guidance. I am only a small part of a great tradition, but I shall strive to use my talents to bring his artistic vision to life in my dancing and to pass it on to others. By so doing I shall remain forever one of the guardians of Balanchine's legacy, which is truth and beauty expressed in human movement.